The Stock Options Book

Third Edition, Revised

Edited by Scott S. Rodrick

The National Center for Employee Ownership
Oakland, California

This publication is designed to provide accurate and authoritative information regarding the subject matter covered. It is sold with the understanding that the publisher is not engaged in rendering legal, accounting, or other professional services. If legal advice or other expert assistance is required, the services of a competent professional should be sought.

The Stock Options Book • Third Edition, Revised
Editing, design, and typesetting by Scott S. Rodrick

Copyright © 1997, 1998, 1999 by The National Center for Employee Ownership
1736 Franklin Street, 8th Floor
Oakland, CA 94612
(510) 272-9461
(510) 272-9510 (fax)
E-mail: *nceo@nceo.org*
Web: *http://www.nceo.org/*

First printed May 1997
Reprinted with additions and corrections, January 1998, June 1998
Second edition, February 1999
Third edition, July 1999
Third edition, revised, December 1999

Printed in the United States of America on recycled paper.

ISBN: 0-926902-56-3

Contents

Preface

In recent years, more and more companies have begun to use stock options to attract, retain, and reward employees. Increasingly, companies have used "broad-based" programs in which most or all employees, not just a few, are offered options. There is little practical reference material on the subject, however, and even less material that includes coverage of broad-based plans and how companies are using them instead of emphasizing options solely as a means of compensating key employees. The purpose of this book is to fill that knowledge gap and get you started in the right direction by presenting a straightforward, comprehensive overview of broad-based stock option plans and related programs: what they are; the key technical issues in designing, implementing, and administering them; and the experiences of companies that have established such plans. The Introduction provides an overview of stock options and how they work; the following chapters, written by leading professionals, delve into technical issues and provide practical advice.

What the Chapters Cover

The first four chapters— "Employee Stock Options and Related Equity Incentives," "Administering an Employee Stock Option Plan," "Valuing Stock Options," and "Accounting for Stock-Based Compensation"—explain stock options and their treatment in detail. Chapter 5, "Designing a Broad-Based Stock Option Plan," and chapter 6, "Establishing and Maintaining Employee Stock Benefit Programs," offer practical advice for companies that implement such plans. Chapter 7, "Equity Compensation in Closely Held Companies," reviews the vehicles used for equity compensation and discusses issues that arise in closely held companies. Chapter 8, "Employee Ownership and Initial Public Offerings," is a guide for companies considering an IPO.

These technical and practical chapters are followed by two contributions by NCEO staffers who address what companies are doing with broad-based plans today. Chapter 9, "Creating an Ownership Culture: Tapping into the Real Potential of Broad Stock Options," discusses the elements of participative management and contains four case studies of companies with broad-based stock options that have realized the true potential of employee ownership by creating innovative ways for employees to think and act like owners. Chapter 10, "The 1998 NCEO Broad-Based Stock Option Plan Survey," summarizes the results of a comprehensive survey of 96 U.S. companies with broad-based stock option plans.

Companies that want to reward employees with a benefit tied to their stock value do not always want to use the stock itself. Chapter 11, "The Phantom Stock Alternative," explains how to do this.

Finally, the appendix, "A Primer on Stock Options for Employees," presents questions and answers on options from the recipient's point of view.

Second Edition (February 1999)

The second edition replaced the original chapter 9, which reported on the NCEO's 1997 survey of 34 companies with broad-based stock options, with a new chapter summarizing the results of the NCEO's much more extensive 1998 survey. The second edition also updated references to capital gains taxes to reflect recent legislative changes.

Third Edition (July 1999)

The third edition added chapter 5, "Designing a Broad-Based Stock Option Plan," and also included minor changes and corrections to the Introduction and chapter 1.

Revised Third Edition (December 1999)

The revised third edition includes a number of changes and additions:

- The discussion of accounting in the Introduction has been updated.
- Chapter 1 includes a number of changes and additions (mostly minor ones).
- An addendum to chapter 4 discusses forthcoming changes in accounting treatment for options.
- Chapter 9 replaces two of the old case studies with new ones.
- Chapter 10 adds summaries of recent surveys by the National Association of Stock Plan Professionals (NASPP) and PricewaterhouseCoopers LLP, and by Watson Wyatt Worldwide.
- An appendix to chapter 10 discusses the results of the 1999 Trinet/NCEO survey of stock options in venture capital-backup companies.

Introduction

Ed Carberry
The National Center for Employee Ownership

In the past 10 years, there has been a dramatic increase in the number of companies granting stock options far down their organizational ladders. Traditionally, stock options have been used primarily as a way for companies to reward executives, top management, and other "key" employees. The idea was that these employees had to be provided with an equity stake in the company in order to motivate performance and align their interests more closely to those of the company and its shareholders.

For a number of reasons, more and more companies are realizing the practical advantages of sharing equity ownership more broadly. The need for companies to compete in a global economy within rapidly changing market-places and to use the full potential of new technologies has fundamentally altered the roles employees play within business organizations. A growing number of companies realize that all employees make important contributions to the organization and that it makes sense to offer all employees a way to acquire equity. For a variety of reasons, stock options have become an attractive way to accomplish this, and there has been an dramatic increase in the popularity of broad-based stock option plans, particularly since the late 1980s.

In a 1997 survey of 1,100 public companies conducted by ShareData, Inc., and the American Electronics Association, for example, 53% of respondents provided stock options to all employees. Within companies with 500 to 999 employees, the study found that 51% offered options to all employees, as compared to 30% in a similar 1994 study. Forty-three percent of companies with 2,000 to 4,999 employees offered options to all, as compared to 10% in 1994; and 45% of companies with 5,000 or more employees offered options to all, as compared to 10% in 1994.[1] A 1991 survey by ShareData found these percentages to be 31% for all companies and 68% for companies with fewer than 100 employees.[2] A survey conducted in 1995 by the Association for Quality and Participation found that 13% of Fortune 1000 companies offer stock options to 60% or more of their workforces.[3] More recently, a 1997 survey conducted by William M. Mercer found that 30% of the 350 largest U.S. companies make 50% or more of their employees eligible to receive options and that 11% of the 350 actually granted options to 50% or more of their employees.[4] The National Center for Employee Ownership (NCEO) now estimates that at least eight million nonmanagment employees work for companies that make them eligible to receive stock options.

The practice of granting options broadly was pioneered by high-technology, knowledge-based startup companies in California's Silicon Valley, who have been using them as far back as the 1960s. For these companies, stock options have always been a practical way to attract and retain talented employees while conserving startup cash. By the late 1980s, the widespread use of broad stock options among these companies had sparked serious interest in these plans in other sections of the business community. While broad options are now the norm in high-technology companies, they are also becoming popular in many companies in other industries that are turning to broad stock options as part of an overall equity compensation strategy. A diverse group of larger, publicly traded companies such as Pepsico, Starbucks, Proctor & Gamble, Whole Foods, and Merck now grant stock options to most or all of their employees to accomplish a variety of corporate objectives: to create an ownership culture, link the interests of employees with those of the company and its other shareholders, reward performance, or simply because they believe it is "the right thing to do." Many non-high-technology, closely held companies are joining the ranks as well.

The increase in the popularity of broad-based stock options was the impetus for this book. As with any employee ownership plan, assessing the feasibility of a stock option plan requires knowledge of the relevant legal rules as well as an honest appraisal of the company's goals for setting up a plan. Although the operation of broad-based plans involves many of the same issues encountered with traditional stock option plans that target executives and other "key" employees, broad-based plans present their own unique issues. Addressing these issues will bring you to a more realistic decision in assessing whether broad-based stock options are right for your company and, if they are, what characteristics might define your plan.

What Is a Stock Option?

A stock option gives an employee the right to buy a certain number of shares in the company at a fixed price for a certain number of years. The fixed price is called the "grant" or "strike" price and is typically the market value at the time the options are granted. Employees who have been granted stock options hope that the share price will go up and that they will be able to "cash in" by exercising (purchasing) the stock at the lower grant price and then selling the stock at the higher exercise price. The company can (and usually does) set restrictions on when the options can be exercised. These so-called "vesting" restrictions typically require that the employee continue to work for the company for a minimum number of years (three to five in most cases) before part or all of the options can be exercised. In some cases, the options can be exercised only if certain financial targets are met (these options are sometimes called "performance options").

When an employee exercises the option, the company must make that number of shares available, either by buying them from existing owners or issuing new shares. Employees can hold onto the stock after exercise in the hopes of even higher returns or sell them, assuming there is a market or a willing private buyer. If the stock price falls once the option is exercised, however, employees can lose money. Alternatively, employees can let unexercised options expire if the stock is lower than the grant price, losing nothing.

Types of Stock Options

There are two principal kinds of employee stock options: nonqualified stock options and incentive stock options. Additionally, an employee stock purchase plan is sometimes termed a stock option program.

Nonqualified Stock Options (NSOs) A nonqualified stock option (NSO) is any option that does not satisfy the conditions of the Internal Revenue Code for preferential tax treatment. Generally, companies can design nonqualified options in almost any way they like. Like all options, they can be granted to as many or as few employees as desired, on whatever basis desired, and they can be any number of shares.

An NSO is typically granted with an exercise price equal to the market price of the company's stock on the date of the grant. A lower or higher price can be granted, however. Typically, the options vest over three to five years, either on a "cliff" (all at once) basis or in increments. Options are often granted each year, with each new grant subject to vesting from that year forward (for example, with a five-year vesting period, options granted in 1995 would vest through 2000; those in 1996 would vest through 2001, and so on).

The option usually cannot be exercised more than 10 years after the date of the grant. Many companies even limit this period to 5 to 7 years. Employees can purchase the stock with their own cash or through a number of "cashless" mechanisms: a stock swap exercise (in which an employee exercises the option by giving the company shares of stock the employee already owns), a promissory note, a "sell to cover" transaction (in which an employee exercises and sells only the number of options needed to cover the total grant price of all the options), or a broker-assisted same-day exercise and sale. In a nonqualified plan, the employee pays personal income taxes on the spread between the exercise price and grant price. The company can take a tax deduction for this amount. If the employee holds onto the stock after exercise, he or she pays capital gains tax on any subsequent gain when the stock is sold.

Incentive Stock Options (ISOs) The other type of option plan is an incentive stock option (ISO), which must satisfy the conditions of the Internal Revenue Code for preferential tax treatment. Generally, an ISO enables an employee (1) to defer taxation on the option from the date of exercise until the date of sale of the underlying shares and (2) to pay tax at capital gains rates, rather than ordinary income tax rates, on the spread at the exercise date, provided certain holding requirements are met. To qualify for ISO treatment, several conditions must be met:

- The employee must hold the stock for one year after the exercise date or two years after the grant date, whichever is later.
- Only $100,000 of stock options can become exercisable in any year.
- The exercise price must be equal to at least 100% of the market price of the company's stock on the date of the grant.
- Only employees can be granted an ISO.
- The option must be granted pursuant to a written plan that has been approved by shareholders, specifies how many shares can be issued under the plan, and identifies the class of employees eligible to receive the options. Options must be granted within 10 years of the date of the adoption of the plan.
- The option must be exercised within 10 years of the date of the grant.
- The employee cannot own, at the time of the grant, more than 10% of the voting power of all outstanding stock of the company unless the exercise price is at least 110% of the market value of the stock on the date of the grant and the option is not exercisable more than five years from the date of the grant.

With an ISO, the company does not take a tax deduction on the spread between the grant price and the exercise price. The appeal of an ISO, therefore, lies largely where employees' personal tax rates are significantly higher than the maximum capital gains rates. The current capital gains rate is 20% (except for employees in the 15% tax bracket, for which it is 10%), while the current top income tax rate is 39.6%. If an employee is in the 39.6% tax bracket, it may be well worth it to meet the holding requirements so that his or her entire gain is taxed at the capital gains rate. If the employee exercises and sells before the required holding periods have been met, the spread on exercise is taxable at ordinary income tax rates, and any capital appreciation on the ISO shares above the market price on exercise of an ISO is taxed at capital gains rates. In this instance, the option is treated as a nonqualified option, and the company may then deduct the spread on exercise.

ISOs can be more desirable for employees than NSOs because of the favorable tax treatment for ISOs, although many nonmanagement optionees choose to not meet the holding requirements, instead exercising and selling on the same day. For employers, ISOs are more complex in terms of plan design and administration. ISOs are not as flexible in terms of how they are granted and do not provide the employer with a tax deduction unless employees do not meet the ISO holding requirements, which then creates the administrative burden of tracking the disqualifying dispositions. While traditionally ISOs were used primarily for highly paid people for whom the tax benefits of capital gains can make a substantial difference, there has been an increase in companies offering ISOs further down the ranks, especially in knowledge-based startups that use options as a hiring incentive. Other companies simply want to give employees the opportunity to receive the capital gains treatment.

Employee Stock Purchase Plans   A third type of plan sometimes termed a stock option (including at certain points in this book) is the section 423 employee stock purchase plan (ESPP), which is usually used in public companies due to securities law issues that arise in closely held companies. In a section 423 plan, the company allows employees to buy stock at up to a 15% discount, usually by using cash from payroll deductions. Like ISOs, section 423 plans offer preferential tax treatment for employees if certain rules are satisfied; unlike ISOs, section 423 plans cannot be limited to top employees. Although they are sometimes described as stock option plans, we think section 423 plans are more accurately described simply as stock purchase plans.

Advantages for Companies

Stock option plans can be a flexible way for companies to share ownership with employees, reward performance, and attract and retain staff. They are not, however, a mechanism for existing owners to sell shares and are usually inappropriate for companies whose future growth is uncertain. They can also be less appealing in small, closely held companies that do not want to go public or be sold, because these companies may find it difficult to create a market for the shares. The exercise of an option is also considered a stock purchase and subjects companies to securities law issues they may wish to avoid. Nonetheless, some companies that plan to stay closely held do issue broad options and create mechanisms to purchase shares from employees and find ways to minimize securities law problems.

For growth-oriented smaller companies, options are an excellent way to preserve cash while giving employees a share in future growth. They also make sense for public companies whose benefit plans are well-established, but who want to include employees in ownership. The dilutive effect of options, even when granted to most employees, is typically very small and can be offset by their potential productivity and employee retention benefits. Furthermore, existing shareholders can take comfort from the fact that options are exercised only when share value increases, something that benefits all shareholders.

Stock Options and Employee Ownership

Most companies believe (and hope) that if employees receive stock options, they will be more motivated to think and act like owners in order to boost corporate performance. Can options really provide this ownership incentive or are they more of short-term compensation vehicle? The answer depends on whom you ask. Proponents feel that options are true ownership because employees do not receive them for free, but must put up their own money to purchase shares, which involves direct risk and, therefore, creates true ownership. Others, however, believe that because option plans allow employees to sell their shares a short period after granting (anywhere from immediately to 10 years), options do not create long-term ownership vision and attitudes.

Other ownership plans, employee stock ownership plans (ESOPs) in particular, provide specific mechanisms for employees to collectively acquire large blocks of stock. They also require that employees retain ownership as long as they remain employed. ESOPs also confer specific legal ownership rights, such as voting rights, although these rights are limited in closely held companies. Option holders do not have shareholder rights until they acquire the shares, and many do not hold onto the stock for a long period after exercise. On the other hand, options provide an often-substantial personal equity stake that, unlike an ESOP, can periodically be turned into cash, making ownership a less distant benefit.

Obviously, there is no clear answer to the question of whether options are true ownership. The ultimate impact of any employee ownership plan, including a stock option plan, depends a great deal on the company and its goals for the plan, its commitment to creating an ownership culture, the amount of training and education it puts into explaining the plan, and the goals of individual employees (i.e., whether they want cash sooner rather than later).

What is certain, however, is that in companies that demonstrate a true commitment to creating an ownership culture, stock options can be a significant motivator. Companies like Starbucks, Pepsico, Microsoft, and many others are paving the way, showing how effective a stock option plan can be when combined with a true commitment to treating employees like owners. While most of the empirical research on the connection between employee ownership and corporate performance indicates that ESOP companies that have structured opportunities for employees to have input in job-level decisions do markedly better, no evidence suggests these kinds of structures would not work or provide the same kinds of benefits in companies with broad-based stock options.

Furthermore, previous NCEO research that surveyed 3,700 employees in 45 ESOP companies found that three things were strongly correlated to ownership attitudes: the percentage of pay contributed each year, how participatively managed the company was, and the regularity of communications about the plan and the company. Clearly, a stock option plan can meet all of these tests. Conversely, an option plan that provides an irregular or one-time grant and is not related specifically to opportunities for significant employee input into job-level decisions is not likely to change employee behavior.

Practical Considerations

There is no standard definition of a "broad-based" stock option plan, although the NCEO defines it as a plan that actually grants stock options to over half of a company's employees over a period of time. For some companies, a broad-based plan means everyone receives options; for others, it means all full-time employees receive options; for others, it means options are granted down to a certain level; and for others it is a much more selective process.

In general, companies have a great deal of flexibility when granting stock options to employees. This is simultaneously one of their primary attractions and challenges. Depending on the type of option, there may be no strict rules and regulations regarding who can receive options, how many which employees receive, the price at which the options are granted, how often they receive them, as well as vesting and other plan characteristics. Although this flexibility allows companies to tailor a plan to meet its specific needs, since there is no standard plan design structure, this task can be daunting.

Generally, in designing an option program, companies need to consider carefully how much stock they are willing to make available over what period of time, who will receive options, and how much employment will grow so that the right number of shares is granted each year. A common error is to grant too many options too soon, leaving no room for additional options for future employees.

One of the most important considerations for the specific design of a plan is its purpose: is the plan intended to give all employees stock in the company or to just provide a benefit for some "key" employees? Does the company wish to promote long-term ownership, or is it a one-time benefit? Is the plan intended as a way to create employee ownership or simply a way to create an additional employee benefit? Is the plan being created to match similar ones of competitors? The answers to these questions will be crucial in defining specific plan characteristics such as eligibility, allocation, vesting, valuation, holding periods, and stock price. Some basic guidelines for plan characteristics include the following.

Eligibility and Allocation

Companies have a great deal of flexibility in determining who will be eligible to receive options, and there are no strict regulations or guidelines. Even more important, however, is determining who will actually receive the options. A company may, for example, make all employees eligible, yet may reward options based on performance. Generally, companies determine eligibility and/or allocation in one of four ways: all employees, employees above a certain level, key employees, or through some performance measurement. The company's goals for the plan will be essential in deciding who gets options. If the intention of the plan, for example, is to create an ownership culture, a company will most likely give options to most or all employees. Allocating options to a small percentage of employees in this case would counteract the original intention. If a company wants to use options as a significant motivator, it may create performance criteria for grants.

It is also essential to determine how many options will be distributed. Will every employee receive a fixed number of options? Will each employee in a particular grade level get a fixed number of options? Will employees within grade levels have a range of options from which they may be granted? Will all employees receive options in proportion to their pay or on the basis of merit?

Vesting

The vesting of stock options refers to the method by which granted options become eligible for exercise. Employees can not exercise an option until it is vested. Most vesting schedules are from 3 to 5 years, although there are no strict guidelines, and a number companies use unique schedules. Once again, a company's goals for the stock plan will be important in determining the vesting schedule. For most companies vesting is simply a way to make the ability to exercise an option contingent on continued employment with the organization, and vesting occurs periodically over a certain number of years from the date of grant. If options are intended as a reward for past performance, an immediate vesting schedule might make sense. If the options are performance-based with a grant price above fair market value, a longer vesting schedule probably makes sense.

Another consideration is whether options will "cliff" vest (i.e., have all shares become vested at one date) or "gradually" vest (i.e., have a portion of all options vest within a one-time period, 20% per year for instance). Most companies use some form of gradual vesting, although cliff vesting is commonly used for one-time all-employee grants. Few companies have a vesting period over five years.

The length of the vesting schedule is not the only consideration. Determining when within those years an option should vest is also important. Many companies will provide straightforward annual vesting of shares on the anniversary date of the grant. This design is usually easy to administer and reduces the amount of time needed to track each employee's vesting requirements. Other companies, however, may wish to regularly draw their employees' attention to the stock option plan; consequently such companies create vesting schedules that have options that vest every fiscal quarter, every month, or even every day. This can be particularly useful in creating an ownership culture.

Exercise Period

Stock options not only vest but also expire on a certain date. Most companies use a ten-year exercise period on both nonqualified and incentive stock option grants. An exercise period can also help a plan meet its overall objectives. A long exercise period (e.g., ten years after grant) allows employees the opportunity to be eligible for significant returns over many business cycles. A shorter exercise period (e.g., five years after grant) may motivate employees to work to increase share value in the short term. Some companies also have started to use shorter exercise periods in order to shorten for other investors the potential dilution exposure from options.

Exercise restrictions relating to retirement and termination can also be important. Retirement exercise periods are often for one to three years after the last day of employment and termination exercise periods for one to three months after the last day of employment. Companies that allow retiring employees to keep their options until the end of the exercise period, even after they retire, send the message that retirement is not a punishment. Some companies have termination policies that require all employees who leave for other jobs or are terminated for cause must exercise all their vested shares before they leave. This sends a very clear message that if employees leave, they will benefit financially only for the work they have performed while employed by the organization.

Accounting Issues

One of the most sensitive issues surrounding stock options in recent years has been their accounting treatment. In the past, companies have reported the expense of their stock-based compensation according to APB (Accounting Principles Board) Opinion 25 ("APB 25"), which was adopted in 1972. APB 25 requires that companies measure compensation cost according to the "intrinsic value method." In the case of stock options, this means that companies measure the actual value of the options when they are granted. Since the value of an option is the difference between the grant price and the price of the stock when the option is exercised, if the option is granted at fair market price on that day, the option has no value. Therefore, in most cases, companies record no compensation cost for granting options. There are, however, certain situations that can trigger an accounting charge under APB 25 (see below). If options are granted at a discount, this discount is recorded as a compensation expense.

Arguably, however, companies do incur a cost, albeit a future cost, when they grant options. When an employee exercises an option, for example, the price he or she pays for the stock will be less than the fair market value on the date of purchase. The company will either have to buy shares on the market and sell these to employees at the lower price or issue new shares and dilute the stock value of existing shareholders. Either of these imposes a cost on the company. Many believe this cost should be reflected in a company's income statement.

In 1993, the Financial Accounting Standards Board (FASB) proposed changing the standard accounting method to one that requires companies to show the cost of options as a compensation expense in their income statements. This provoked an outcry from many companies whose income statements and stock price would be adversely effected by having to show the cost of options.

Because of widespread and organized resistance from opponents, the final changes issued by FASB came in the form of Statement 123, issued in October 1995. Statement 123 recommends that companies use a "fair value method" to measure what the estimated cost of the option will be to the company in the future. Although Statement 123 only *recommends* this accounting treatment and allows companies to continue to use the old treatment of Opinion 25, companies that do continue to use Opinion 25 must disclose in a footnote what their earnings and earnings per share would have been had they used the new accounting rules. These issues are discussed more fully in Chapter 4, "Accounting for Stock-Based Compensation."

Statement 123 requires that companies estimate the fair value of their stock options using an option pricing model that takes into consideration several specified factors, such as the exercise price of the option, the fair market value of the underlying stock, the expected life of the option, the risk-free interest rate, the expected volatility of the stock, and the expected dividend yield. Common option pricing models that consider these factors include the Black-Scholes model and the binomial method. Statement 123 allows closely held companies to estimate fair value using the minimum value method in recognition of the absence of a trading history for the stock.

Few companies have used the new accounting method detailed in Statement 123; instead, they continue to use the intrinsic value method of Opinion 25 and disclose the fair value of options in footnotes. Either way, the task of complying with the requirements of Statement 123 has added another layer of complexity to stock option plan design and administration. Even when companies continue to follow APB 25 and disclose the fair value estimates in the footnotes to the financial statement, this still means that companies have to value the options. While closely held companies may find it tempting to ignore these issues, where a company prepares audited financial statements, it is essential that the company spend the time and money to comply with Statement 123. Companies should ensure that their accountants understand these issues and advise the companies when they set up stock option plans.

Moreover, in certain situations, APB 25 requires companies to record a compensation expense for options granted to employees. Under APB 25, the intrinsic value of an option is measured on the first date that the company knows two things: (1) the number of shares the optioned can purchase under the grant, and (2) the grant price of the option. If these two things are known on the date of grant (and in most cases, they are), the option is considered to have been granted under a "fixed plan" arrangement, and the measurement date occurs on the date of grant, resulting in no compensation cost.

If either of these two things are not known on the date of grant, however, this is considered to be a "variable plan" arrangement, and the measurement date will occur on the future date when the these two things are known. Until this date, the company must estimate the intrinsic value of the option and show this as a compensation cost on its financial statements each year until the measurement date occurs.

Most companies will want to avoid plan design features that are considered variable plan arrangements because of this compensation expense. These features can include variable vesting and some performance-based stock options, among others. It is essential to take these issues into consideration in the plan design phase, along with those related to compliance with Statement 123.

Setting the Grant Price of Options

Before a company can determine the value of options for accounting purposes, the grant price of the options must be set. The grant price of NSOs can be at, below, or above fair market value. A company cannot, however, offer ISOs with a grant price that is below fair market value. Furthermore, when ISOs are offered to employees who hold more than 10% of the voting stock of the company, the grant price of these options can not be below 110% of fair market value.

Most companies set the grant price of NSOs and ISOs at the fair market value of the company's stock on the grant date or, occasionally, at the average stock price over the course of a set period. Some companies provide employees with NSOs with a grant price below fair market value in order to provide an instant benefit.

Other companies provide employees with NSOs having a grant price that is above fair market value to create a "premium-priced" option that becomes valuable only if the stock price increases above a certain point (usually some fixed percentage of the stock price on the date of grant, such as 150% of fair market value). Premium-priced options can be useful in motivating employees to hit specific performance targets. If the stock price does not reach the target price, however, employees can become disheartened and frustrated with the program.

Lock-up Periods in Closely Held Companies and Post-IPO Companies

"Lock-up periods" are specific time frames in which employees are limited in or prohibited from exercising and/or selling their stock options. Commonly used in privately held companies and companies that have recently undergone an initial public offering, lock-up periods are used to meet very different purposes.

In an IPO situation, companies often are required by their underwriters to place a lock-up period on employee option activity for some period of time after the IPO, typically six months. In addition, options previously issued in the closely held entity would most commonly be issued under Rule 701, an SEC exemption from registration. Options acquired under Rule 701 are considered "restricted securities" and at a minimum must be held for three months following an IPO.

Closely held companies that have not reached an IPO or other liquidity event (i.e., a merger or acquisition) will often use lock-up periods to put off the exercise and selling of options and option shares until a liquidity event is reached. If employees are allowed to exercise their options, they become shareholders and have the ability to vote on all corporate issues. Similarly, if employees receive stock from an option exercise, they will be able to sell that stock either to other employees, to the company, or to others outside the company. If a fellow employee is willing to purchase the additional shares freed up from the exercise of the options, this may work to the company's benefit; however, more often employees are unable to find a buyer in the company and "put" their shares back to the company, forcing the company to either pay cash that was reserved for growth purposes for the stock or to risk having that stock being sold to someone outside the company.

Public and private companies that reprice their stock options may use a lock-up period after the repricing. Often this is to meet the requirement of "adequate consideration" in repricing, whereby participants are asked to forego some benefit in order to justify the additional corporate expense of the repricing. In this case, the foregone benefit takes the form of a reduced ability to sell shares after the repricing.

Valuation Issues in Closely Held Companies

Most companies use the fair market value of their stock on the date of grant as the grant price of the option. Public companies simply refer to the trading price of their stock to establish the fair market value. Closely held companies, however, do not have a trading market to refer to and therefore must determine the fair market value using other means. It is necessary to do this at the time options are granted, and if the company remains closely held, also when employees exercise their options and when they sell the underlying shares.

Typically, closely held companies set the value of their stock in one of two ways. First, they can perform internal valuations based on book value, multiples of earnings, sales, or some formula approach that approximates the value of the company. Alternatively, a company can have an outside valuation performed by one or more independent appraisers.

There is little formal guidance on how closely held companies should value their stock for purposes of a stock option plan. Most companies perform a valuation internally, using book value and adjusting it for outside circumstances. Rarely do closely held companies come under Internal Revenue Service (IRS) scrutiny in how they set the grant price of stock options as long as the valuation is plausible, uses a consistent formula, and is completed in good faith.

If a closely held company is planning on going public, however, its option plan will face more intense scrutiny from both the IRS and the Securities and Exchange Commission (SEC), particularly in the 12 to 18 months before an initial public offering (IPO). In this "pre-IPO" period, it often makes sense to have an outside appraiser perform periodic valuations. The IRS will look at excessively large gaps between the price at which options were granted to employees while the company was closely held and the price at which shares are sold to the public. If the company offered options with a grant price that was too far below fair market value (often referred to as "cheap stock"), the IRS will make employees pay a tax on the discount they effectively received.

The SEC is also interested in issues relating to "cheap stock." If the grant price is too low (there are general ranges; see chapter 8, "Employee Ownership and Initial Public Offerings"), the SEC may require companies to recognize a deferred compensation liability on the discount employees received. As a company gets closer to an IPO and is unsure about whether its internal valuations are on target, it is wise to obtain periodic valuations from an independent appraiser. Even if a company is confident about its internal valuation, getting an independent appraisal in the pre-IPO period can save a great deal of time, money, and hassle down the road, especially if the IRS or SEC takes a close look at the plan. An independent appraisal can also be a useful planning tool at any stage.

Selling the Shares

When an employee exercises a stock option, the company has to make that number of shares available. Public companies either issue new shares that have been previously reserved for the plan or purchase the shares on the open market and then sell these to employees. Employees then own the shares. Most nonexecutive employees will sell the shares immediately; a small percentage will hold onto the shares after exercise.

In public companies, employees will simply sell their stock through a broker. Companies usually help employees find a broker or establish one "captive broker" through which all employees exercise and sell these options. While some employees will use cash to purchase shares, by far the most common mechanism by which employees purchase shares is what is known as a "cashless exercise," in which a broker purchases the shares for employees and immediately sells at least enough of them to cover the purchase price of all the shares.

For closely held companies, the issues relating to providing the underlying shares for stock options as well as liquidity for these shares are a bit more complicated. Most of these companies will tell employees they can sell when the company is sold or goes public, but that could occur years after the employee has purchased the options and paid tax.

If, however, a closely held company is not planning on a public offering, then the company must develop a way to provide liquidity for these optioned shares, such as buying back the shares or facilitating a transaction with a third party. The most common way in which closely held companies provide liquidity for optioned shares is by buying these shares back.

Playing such a brokerage role, however, could trigger securities law issues for closely held companies. They must consider these issues carefully. When employees exercise an option, it is considered an offer to sell securities. As such, it is regulated by state and federal law. Generally, a company implementing any such offering must prepare an anti-fraud disclosure statement similar to a prospectus. With offerings that do not meet one of several exemptions, including small offerings[5] just to employees, the company may not have to register with state and federal securities agencies, but larger, closely held companies implementing broad-based plans often must register. This is an expensive and time-consuming process, one that public companies have already faced.

Another way in which these shares can be sold is through an employee stock ownership plan (ESOP). An ESOP is a tax-qualified defined contribution plan that is primarily invested in company stock. The shares of an ESOP are held in a trust fund. A company funds the plan either by directly contributing company stock or by making cash contributions that the trust uses to purchase stock from existing owners. A company could also make a contribution to an ESOP trust to fund the trust's purchase of the shares of optionees. While an ESOP can be very useful for this purpose, it is a complex mechanism and is not necessarily right for every company.

Deciding How Much Ownership Is Enough[6]

One of the most important issues in establishing a broad-based option plan is to consider how many options the company wants to make available to employees. While there are no set answers, a useful framework for assessing the issue is to look at it from three perspectives: the maximum amount of dilution other owners are willing to allow, the minimum percentage of compensation provided in stock needed to get employees' attention, and the minimum financial goals owners expect year to year. In all likelihood, the final decision will be a blend of these three.

When a company sells optionees new shares, this will dilute the ownership of existing shareholders. This is a contentious issue. Existing shareholders are usually willing to put up with the dilution that a broad employee ownership creates, for one of two reasons: they think it will help the company make more money and/or they think it is the right thing to do. There are limits, however, to how much dilution most owners will tolerate.

In publicly traded companies with stock options, dilution is often represented by what is known as "overhang," i.e., the dilution that would result if all outstanding options were exercised. Overhang for options is generally under 10% in listed companies, but in high-tech companies is often much higher (15%, according to some surveys). In the past, stock analysts usually furrowed their brows when overhang exceeded 10%. Providing incentives to employees was all well and good, they argued, but it was the shareholders who were putting up the real dollars (this argument, of course, ignores the reality that stock sales provide less than 5% of corporate finance needs).

In recent years, however, there has been a marked softening of this position. Data from American Capital Strategies (an investment bank specializing in employee buyouts) has shown that companies with more than 10% broad employee ownership have actually outperformed the market,[7] while high-tech companies have issued large numbers of options and seen their sector lead the market. In light of this, a recent *Wall Street Journal* cover story showed that most analysts were not concerned about dilution or potential dilution per se, but about whether the company could show it needed that amount of employee ownership in order to attract and retain good people. Also remember that ownership percentages rarely are meaningful in themselves compared to the dollar amount that ownership represents.

The other way to look at the question of how much to offer is to view it from the perspective of compensation. Giving employees ownership amounts they regard as token or symbolic can be worse than not giving them any ownership at all. Giving people options on 10 shares, then making speeches on how "we're all owners now," is likely to create more cynicism than motivation. This is especially true if management is being granted huge option packages. One-time grants are also usually a waste. Subsequent hires are often excluded, while employees who get the shares see it mostly as a gesture, not an ongoing part of the company's culture. While all this may seem obvious, a large number of companies operate their plans in just such symbolic ways.

So how much is needed for employees to see ownership as real? There is no bright line between one level and another. Moreover, smaller grants in companies with rapid share price increases can be more meaningful than larger grants accompanied by slower growth. With broad stock option grants, where grants are made annually, the value is most commonly 10% of pay per year. It is very rare to see companies with levels below 5% of compensation creating much of an ownership culture.

If the goal of spreading ownership is to improve corporate performance, then one way to dole out ownership is to grant options based on whether the company meets certain annual targets.

The compensation and profit models of ownership sharing are open-ended. They could provide any percentage of ownership, and an argument could be made that if this is what is necessary to motivate or reward people, then so be it. In fact, of course, owners may have some practical limit that will put a cap on the total allocations, either altogether or annually (although some will say as long as they are getting a bigger dollar value of ownership, the percentage doesn't matter). For these owners, a sensible strategy is to start with the profit model and figure out how that formula will translate into annual stock awards. This should result in a percentage of compensation adequate to make people feel like owners (probably at least 5% of pay per year). That model then can be analyzed in terms of short and long-term dilution. If the result is over the dilution ceiling, owners probably need to either rethink their ceiling or decide that employee ownership is not for them.

Which Outside Experts Should I Hire?[8]

Some companies understand the above issues sufficiently to effectively design, implement, and administer their stock option plans mostly in-house. In fact, many companies have had stock option plans for executives in place for a long time and are, therefore, familiar with the operation of such plans. Unlike other employee ownership plans, such as ESOPs, that must comply with the complexities of the Employee Retirement Income Security Act of 1974 (ERISA), a stock option plan does not necessarily require a high degree of technical assistance to set up and maintain.

With all of this in mind, it may be tempting for a company to just do the plan in-house and save money by not hiring experienced people to help. One should be careful here. This often leads to difficulties later on, and many experts note that the most common problems (not having enough shares for future grants, overhang, inefficient administration) can be prevented with a good plan design and more long-term planning in the beginning. So, despite this relative simplicity and any past experience with an option plan that a company may have, the advice of experienced, knowledgeable professionals is necessary and desirable in designing and administering a broad-based plan that maximizes benefits and best meets corporate objectives.

Design

A plan document defines the basic characteristics of the plan: who is eligible for options, who will receive options, vesting schedules, the option life, and holding periods. Many companies have staff members who can design the basic plan document in-house. At a minimum, companies will need an experienced in-house or hired attorney to review or help design the plan. Often, an accountant and/or a compensation specialist will also review the plan.

Generally, the bigger the company and more complex the plan, the more people will be involved in its design. Less experienced companies may wish to hire any or all of the above professionals to play a more active role in plan design.

Administration

Many companies administer their options plans in-house, especially smaller companies. In fact, there are software programs on the market specifically designed for this. Administration entails tracking the distribution of options to employees, ensuring that options are allocated to the right accounts, maintaining and updating vesting status, accounting for exercises, dispositions, and forfeitures of stocks, and, depending on the link with the broker, acting as a liaison between the broker and the employee.

Companies can also outsource plan administration. This is becoming more common with larger companies, who often find it more cost-effective to have someone else administer a complex plan. Again, the choice depends on the complexity of the plan, the company's knowledge and experience, and the company's willingness to devote staff time and other resources to this process. At companies with broad-based stock option plans, there can be thousands of employees with options "in the money," and they can exercise those shares at any time. If a company has little experience with administration, this can become difficult, confusing, and time-consuming.

An outside administrator can also be useful for companies with few employees or infrequent transactions. From the perspective of employees, probably the most important consideration is access to their administrator.

Many of the bigger firms that handle stock option plan administration also act as the broker when employees wish to exercise and/or sell their options. Having one established broker for all employees can make administration much easier. Some companies allow employees to choose their own brokers to handle their transactions, but this can make administration more complex. Often, employees are required to conduct their option transactions through one of a list of brokers provided by the company.

Appraisers

Unlike the case with ESOPs, there are no legal requirements for a broad stock option plan to have the stock valued by an independent appraiser. However, there are times when an independent appraiser can be useful, as for calculating the "fair value" of options for financial statements (discussed above), setting the grant price (especially in the period before an IPO), or when closely held companies that are not going public buy back shares from employees.

Other Consultants

Companies may wish to hire various other consultants regarding their broad-based stock option plans. Many companies will want to develop a strategy to communicate how the plan works and how employees can benefit from it. An experienced consultant can be very useful in designing this type of program, providing advice on the nature and content of these communications. For companies that wish to go further in creating an ownership culture, these consultants may play a bigger role in communicating the plan, in conducting business and financial education, and in cultivating participative management practices.

Many companies have operations overseas and wish to include the overseas employees in a global stock option plan. Each country has its own unique laws, regulations, workplace practices, and cultural issues that must be taken into consideration to insure that the plan operates effectively and within each country's laws. This will, obviously, add layers of complexity to a stock option plan. In this situation, experienced consultants are essential and will usually play a much larger role in coordinating the design, administration, and communication of the plan.

Notes

1. ShareData, Inc., *1997 Stock Option Survey* (Santa Clara, CA: Sharedata, 1997). ShareData, Inc., *ShareData/AEA Update* (Sunnyvale, CA: ShareData, 1994).

2. ShareData, Inc., *Equity Compensation Trends in Corporate America* (Sunnyvale, CA: ShareData, 1991).

3. Edward E. Lawler, III, Susan Albers Mohrman, and Gerald E. Ledford, Jr., *Creating High Performance Organizations: Practices and Results of Employee Involvement and Total Quality Management in Fortune 1000 Companies* (San Francisco: Jossey-Bass Publishers, 1995).

4. Edward Hansen, *Stock Options Move Beyond Companies' Executive Suites* (New York: William M. Mercer, 1997).

5. Changes made by the SEC in 1999 classify small offerings as those in which the percentage of stock sold to employees in one year does not exceed the greater of $1 million, 15% of the issuer's total assets, or 15% of the outstanding securities of that class.

6. This section was adapted from an article by NCEO executive director Corey Rosen in the NCEO's newsletter: "Deciding How Much Ownership Is Enough," *Employee Ownership Report* vol. 18, no. 2 (March/April 1998), pp. 1, 3.

7. American Capital Strategies maintains the Employee Ownership Index, which tracks the performance of approximately 350 stocks in companies with 10% or more broad-based employee ownership.

8. Input for this section was provided by Mark Borges, Jane Irwin of Hewitt Associates, and attorney David R. Johanson of Johanson Berenson LLP.

CHAPTER 1

Employee Stock Options and Related Equity Incentives

David R. Johanson
Johanson Berenson LLP

Broad-based employee stock ownership, when combined with an effective communications program that is designed to create an employee ownership culture, can be a very dynamic tool for improving employee productivity and thereby increasing profitability and value. Although the focus of this chapter is not solely on "broad-based" employee stock options and related equity incentives, employers should keep this basic concept in mind when designing equity incentives for any employees.

Using employee stock ownership as an incentive compensation device provides many benefits for both the employer and the employee. Employee stock ownership provides an opportunity for employees to share in the growth potential of a company and thereby creates work incentives for the employees. The success of any employee stock ownership plan depends on the employer choosing the correct plan to achieve the desired objectives. In selecting an equity incentive plan, the employer must decide what group of employees it would like to reward, how closely it wants the reward to be tied to performance goals, what type of performance goals would work for the employees, and how the equity incentive plan could be used with incentives currently in place. An employer implementing an equity incentive plan should recognize the various needs and desires of its employees. Incentive compensation strategies for professional and scientific personnel, for example, may be more effective if performance reviews are tied to a project cycle rather than to an annual administrative cycle.

Implementing equity incentive plans can produce greater commitment from employees, provided they understand how their work affects a company's value. Employee stock ownership generally gives employees more rights and responsibility, as well as risks and rewards, and encourages personal initiative.

A qualified retirement plan commonly known as an employee stock ownership plan (ESOP) is one device used to provide stock ownership to employees. An ESOP is a type of qualified retirement plan governed by the Employee Retirement Income Security Act of 1974, as amended (ERISA), and the Internal Revenue Code of 1986, as amended (the "Code"). There are many tax and other advantages for employees, companies, and existing shareholders when implementing an ESOP. ESOPs, however, have some limitations. For example, because ESOPs are tax-qualified plans, they must meet numerous coverage, nondiscrimination, distribution and other requirements of the Code. Furthermore, it is impossible to tailor ESOPs to benefit only a particular group of highly compensated employees. Finally, the Code's ESOP distribution rules also require the employer to make a market for company stock after employees depart.

A variety of equity incentive plans other than ESOPs are available for entrepreneurial growth companies to create employee incentives through pay-for-performance compensation systems. Stock options, performance shares, stock bonuses and stock purchase plans are increasingly used to provide incentive compensation at all organizational levels to merge the interests of employees, managers, and investors.

This chapter explores employee stock options, employee stock purchase plans (which may be classified as a form of stock options), restricted stock and stock appreciation rights as they relate to stock options, and addresses some of the design issues, the benefits and the tax consequences of implementing such plans. These plans may trigger some issues that are not fully discussed here. For employers implementing stock ownership plans in which the underlying stock is subject to regulation under the Securities Exchange Act of 1934, as amended (the "1934 Act"), additional considerations, including securities registration, proxy disclosure and short-swing profit liability, should be addressed before implementing a plan. In addition, the non-ESOP equity incentive plans presented in this chapter are generally not subject to the requirements of ERISA; however, any equity incentive plan that systematically defers payments to the termination of employment or retirement and that covers more than just highly compensated employees could trigger application of ERISA.

Glossary

- *Exercise:* To elect to purchase stock pursuant to an option.
- *Exercise date:* The date that an individual or an entity purchases stock pursuant to an option.
- *Exercise price:* The price at which stock can be purchased pursuant to a stock option. Synonymous with "strike price."
- *Grant date:* The date on which an option is first offered to an individual or entity.
- *Incentive stock option:* An option, qualifying for favorable tax treatment under section 422 of the Code, granted to an employee of a corporation to purchase company stock at a specified price for a specified period of time. Generally, there are no tax consequences until the stock is sold.

- *Nonqualified (nonstatutory) stock option:* A stock option that does not qualify for favorable tax treatment under Code sections 422 or 423.

- *Qualified stock option:* An option to purchase shares provided to an employee of the corporation under terms that qualify the option for special tax treatment under sections 422 or 423 of the Code. Synonymous with "statutory stock option."

- *Restricted stock option or restricted stock:* An incentive or nonqualified stock option or stock that is subject to certain restrictions imposed by the employer; for example, employees may be required to sell their stock back to the employer upon termination of employment at the price they paid for the stock.

- *Section 423 stock purchase plan* (sometimes called an "employee stock purchase plan" or ESPP): A plan under which a company allows employees to purchase stock at up to a 15% discount; purchasers receive favorable tax treatment if the plan meets certain rules.

- *Statutory stock option:* A stock option (incentive stock option or section 423 stock purchase plan option) that qualifies for favorable tax treatment under sections 422 or 423 of the Code. Synonymous with "qualified stock option."

- *Stock option:* A right issued by a corporation to an individual or an entity to buy a given amount of shares of company stock at a stated price within a specified period of time.

- *Strike or striking price:* Price at which an option (e.g., to purchase stock) is exercised. The price at which named stock can be put or called is ordinarily the fair market value when the option is written and is termed the "striking price." Synonymous with "exercise price."

Statutory Stock Options: Overview

Two types of employee stock options receive special treatment under the Code: incentive stock options and ESPPs, a kind of hybrid between a stock purchase plan and stock option plan. There is no recognition of income on the option grant or on the exercise of the option under either of these programs for employee ownership, provided that certain conditions under sections 422 and 423 of the Code are satisfied, as discussed below. (Note: While ESPPs are described here, they are primarily stock purchase plans, albeit with a price discount feature. The main focus of this book is on true stock options.) Additionally, if the stock is disposed of after completion of the statutory holding period, any appreciation will be taxed as capital gain.

Stock options are the most popular form of long-term compensation incentives for executives in major U.S. companies and are now being offered to most or all employees in many companies. They are very easy to administer, primarily because they do not require that the company establish any financial targets. Over 90% of the Fortune 1000 use stock options, according to a survey conducted by TPF&C, a Towers Perrin Company.

A recent ShareData (now E*Trade Business Solutions)/American Electronics Association Survey (1997) reached the following conclusions about the use of stock options after surveying 1,000 publicly traded companies that use stock options:

- 53% of respondents grant stock options to all employees.

- 88% of information technology companies grant stock options to all employees and, in companies with fewer than 100 employees, 68% grant stock options to all employees.

- 74% of companies with less than $50 million in revenues grant stock options to all employees.

- The prevalence of stock options has increased since 1994 (the year of the previous study), and the smaller the company, the more likely it will have a broad-based stock option plan.

Incentive Stock Options

With an incentive stock option (ISO), a company grants the employee an option to purchase stock at some time in the future at a specified price. With an ISO, there are restrictions on how the option is to be structured and when the option stock can be transferred. The employee will exercise the option at some time when the value of the option stock is greater than the exercise price of the option. As the value of the stock increases relative to the option exercise price, the employee has the potential to benefit from the increase in the option stock's value over the option exercise price. The employee does not recognize ordinary income at option grant or exercise (although the spread between the option price and the option stock's fair market value constitutes an item of adjustment for alternative minimum tax purposes), and the company cannot deduct the related compensation expense. The employee is taxed only upon the *disposition* of the option stock. The gain is all capital gain for a qualifying disposition. For a disqualifying disposition (i.e., one not meeting the rules specified below for a qualifying disposition), the employee will recognize ordinary income as well as capital gain.

A disposition of ISO stock is generally defined as any sale, exchange, gift or transfer of legal title of the stock.[1] Section 424(c) of the Code, however, provides exceptions to this general definition. The exceptions include a transfer from a decedent who held ISO stock to an estate, a transfer of ISO stock by bequest or inheritance, an exchange of ISO stock in a nonrecognition transaction such as a reorganization, a transfer of stock between spouses incident to a divorce, a transfer of ISO stock into joint ownership and a transfer of ISO stock by an insolvent individual to a trustee in bankruptcy.

Requirements for ISOs

For a stock option to qualify as an ISO (and thus receive special tax treatment under Code section 421(a)), it must meet the requirements of section 422 of the Code when granted and at all times beginning from the grant until its exercise.[2] The requirements include:

- The option may be granted only to an employee (grants to non-employee directors or independent contractors are not permitted) who must exercise the option while an employee or no later than three months after termination of employment (unless the optionee is disabled, in which case this three-month period is extended to one year).[3] The stock option must be an option to purchase stock of the employer corporation or the stock of a parent or subsidiary corporation. The stock may be capital stock of any class of the corporation, including voting and non-voting common or preferred stock. In addition, using special classes of stock that are authorized to be exclusively issued and held by employees is permissible.[4]

- The option must be granted under a written plan document specifying the total number of shares that may be issued and the employees who are eligible to receive the options. The plan must be approved by the stockholders within 12 months before or after plan adoption.[5] The stockholders' approval must comply with the charter, bylaws and state laws that regulate the stockholder approval required for the issuance of corporate stock. If there is no applicable authority, the plan must be approved by a majority of all outstanding voting stock (whether such votes are in person or by proxy) at a duly held stockholders' meeting with a quorum present or by a method that would meet the applicable state law requirements for approval of actions requiring shareholder voting.[6]

- Each option must be granted under an ISO agreement, which must be written and must list the restrictions placed on exercising the ISO. Each option must set forth an offer to sell the stock at the option price and the period of time during which the option will remain open.[7]

- The option must be granted within 10 years of the earlier of adoption or shareholder approval, and the option must be exercisable only within 10 years of grant.[8]

- The option exercise price must equal or exceed the fair market value of the underlying stock at the time of grant.[9]

- The employee must not, at the time of the grant, own stock representing more than 10% of the voting power of all stock outstanding (including stock constructively owned through attribution pursuant to Code section 424(d)), unless the option exercise price is at least 110% of the fair market value and the option is not exercisable more than five years from the time of the grant.[10]

- The ISO agreement must specifically state that the ISO cannot be transferred by the option holder other than by will or by the laws of descent and that the option cannot be exercised by anyone other than the option holder.[11]

- The aggregate fair market value (determined as of the grant date) of stock bought by exercising ISOs that are exercisable for the first time cannot exceed $100,000 in a calendar year. To the extent it does, Code section 422(d) provides that such options are treated as nonqualified options.

An ISO plan may include other provisions that are not required as long as such provisions are not inconsistent with these requirements. Employers often include provisions enabling the employee to finance the exercise price. For example, the ISO plan can provide that the employee may pay for the exercise of his or her options with stock of the company. The ISO plan also may provide for tandem stock appreciation rights which will assist an employee in exercising options without cash (please refer to the discussion of stock appreciation rights later in this chapter).

The initial ISO plan document should be drafted to include any desired provisions to be used presently and also in the future so that the ISO plan does not need to be modified to include any newly desired provisions. The ISO plan also should provide for amendments.

Advantages of ISOs

ISOs enable employees to share in the appreciation and the value of the stock and provide the employer with more flexible arrangements than allowed in a qualified retirement plan. They may be designed so that employees may put their capital at risk or so that employees are given assistance in financing the exercise price through the use of stock and option exercise programs and employee loan programs. Employees can realize the compensatory gains on the options while employed rather than having to wait until termination of employment. Options also provide executives with the opportunity to realize almost unlimited gains. In addition, the employer can tailor ISOs to benefit particular employees, which would not be possible in a qualified retirement plan.

From the employer's standpoint, the most important advantage of ISOs is that they enable a company to attract and keep talent without draining cash flow by paying higher salaries. ISOs should be especially helpful for cash-poor companies with good growth prospects. This is not as true anymore, however, as high-tech employees begin to expect high current compensation and substantial growth potential from options.

From the employee's standpoint, an employee receiving an ISO recognizes no taxable income upon the ISO's receipt or exercise. If the ISO is exercised more than three months after the employee has left the employ of the company granting the option, however, this favorable tax treatment is not available.

Upon a qualifying disposition, the employee recognizes capital gain, measured by the difference between the option exercise price and the sale proceeds. After the Tax Reform Act of 1986, which substantially reduced the progressive nature of the individual taxpayer's rate structure and repealed favorable tax rates for capital gains, the tax advantage realized upon disposition of the stock was reduced. As of this writing (October 1999), there is once again a substantial differential between the top marginal rate for ordinary income (39.6%) and the 20% capital gains tax rate for those in the 28% to 39.6% tax brackets (of course, for those with a marginal tax rate of 15% for ordinary income, the capital gains rate is 10%). However, ISOs generally are not useful for broad-based stock option plans because most nonmanagerial employees will have ordinary income and capital gains rates that are very close. In any event, most employees in broad-based stock option plans do not hold onto their stock after exercise long enough to qualify for capital gains treatment.

Tax Implications of ISOs for Employees

An employee receiving an ISO realizes no income upon its receipt or exercise.[12] Instead, the employee is taxed upon disposition of the stock acquired pursuant to the ISO. A disposition of ISO stock generally refers to any sale, exchange, gift or transfer of legal title of stock.[13] The tax treatment of the disposition of option exercise stock depends upon whether the stock was disposed of in a qualifying disposition within the statutory holding period for ISO stock. The ISO statutory holding period is the later of two years from the date of the granting of the ISO to the employee or one year from the date that the shares were transferred to the employee upon exercise.[14]

Disqualifying Disposition If disposition occurs within two years of the employee's receipt of the option or within one year of receipt of the stock, the employee recognizes at the time of the disposition (1) ordinary income measured by the difference between the option exercise price and the fair market value of the stock at the time of option exercise (the "bargain purchase element"), and (2) capital gain measured by the difference between the fair market value of the stock on the date of exercise and the disposition proceeds.[15]

> EXAMPLE: On January 1, 1992, X, an employee of ABC Corp., is granted 100 ISOs to purchase shares of ABC Corp. stock at $10 per share, the fair market value of ABC stock at the time of the grant. On March 20, 1993, X exercises all of her ISOs when the price of ABC Corp. stock is $15 per share. On December 31, 1993, X disposes of (sells) 50 shares of ABC Corp. stock acquired pursuant to the ISO before the end of

the ISO statutory holding period for $17 per share. X must recognize, in 1993, $250 in ordinary income (50 shares multiplied by the bargain purchase element at exercise of $5). In addition, the capital gains portion of the disqualifying disposition is $100 (50 shares multiplied by the difference between the $17 per share sales price and the basis of the ISO stock of $15, which is the sum of the exercise price for each share, $10, plus the additional compensation amount recognized in this year, $5).[16]

Qualifying Disposition When an employee disposes of ISO stock after completion of the holding period (after two years of the employee's receipt of the option or after one year of his receipt of the stock), then all of the gain is capital gain, measured by the difference between the option exercise price and the sale proceeds.[17]

Alternative Minimum Tax Considerations Although the exercise of an ISO does not result in an immediate taxable event, there are implications for calculating the Alternative Minimum Tax (AMT). The spread between the option exercise price and the fair market value of the option stock at exercise is treated as an "item of adjustment" for AMT purposes.[18] If a disqualifying disposition occurs in the year in which the option is exercised, however, the maximum amount that will be included as AMT income is the gain on the disposition of the ISO stock. For a disqualifying disposition in the year other than the year of exercise, the income on the disqualifying disposition will not be considered income for AMT purposes.[19] If an employee's items of adjustment for ISOs and for other AMT purposes is substantial (when reviewed alone or together with other items of adjustment), such employee should consult with a tax advisor prior to exercising an ISO and/or selling option stock.

Tax Implications for Employers

An employer granting an ISO is not entitled to a deduction with respect to the issuance of the option or its exercise.[20] The amount received by the employer as the exercise price will be considered the amount received by the employer for the transfer of the ISO stock.[21] If the employee causes the option to be disqualified (by disposing of his or her stock prematurely prior to the end of the requisite holding period), however, the employer usually may take a deduction for that amount recognized by the employee as ordinary income in the same year as the employee recognizes the income.[22]

In addition, the employer that granted the ISO does not have any withholding obligation with regard to the ordinary income an employee recognizes upon a disqualifying disposition (the Internal Revenue Service [IRS] may change this position).[23] The ordinary income resulting from the disqualifying disposition also is not considered wages for FICA or FUTA purposes.[24]

An ISO generally is not subject to ERISA. Therefore, it is not subject to ERISA's reporting requirements. The employer must furnish a statement to the employee who exercises an ISO, however, on or before January 31 of the year following the year of the ISO exercise stating details about the options granted.[25]

Section 423 Employee Stock Purchase Plans

The second type of employee stock options that receive special treatment under the Code are options granted under an ESPP ("purchase plan option"), also referred to as "section 423 plans." Section 423 of the Code provides a basis for employee stock purchase plans to receive favorable tax treatment under section 421(a) (i.e., no tax consequences on grant and capital gains treatment upon a qualifying disposition). Like ISOs, the purchase plan option gives employees an opportunity to share in the growth potential of the company's stock. Purchase plan options are used by employers as a method for employees to purchase stock, usually using payroll deductions to pay for the shares. What the option exercise price is and when the option is granted are variables. Purchase plan options are primarily intended for rank-and-file employees (unlike ISOs, which are primarily intended for key employees).

Requirements for Employee Stock Purchase Plans

Employees receive Code section 421(a)'s favorable tax treatment only if the employee stock purchase plan meets these requirements:

- Only employees of the employer sponsoring the ESPP and employees of parent or subsidiary companies may participate in the ESSP.[26]
- To receive favorable tax treatment, an employee can own no more than 5% of the voting power of the employer or 5% of the value of all shares of stock of the employer.[27]
- The ESPP must be approved by the shareholders of the granting company within 12 months before or after the ESPP is adopted.[28]
- The stock for which the ESPP offers options must be the capital stock of the employer. This capital stock can be of any class, including voting or nonvoting common or preferred stock. It may be treasury stock or stock of original issue. A special class of stock authorized and issued solely to employees also would qualify as stock for this purpose.[29]
- All employees of the sponsoring employer must be included in the ESPP.[30] Employees who have been employed for less than two years, employees whose customary employment is 20 hours or less per week, employees whose customary employment is for not more than five months in any calendar year, and highly compensated employees as defined in Code section 414(q), however, can be excluded from participation in the ESPP.[31] These eligibility rules are similar (but not the same) as those for qualified retirement plans.

- The determination of the option exercise price, the option payment provisions, and all other provisions must be uniform for all employees, with the following exceptions:

  ‣ The ESPP may limit the maximum amount of options that can be exercised under the ESPP.

  ‣ The ESPP may limit the amount of options that all employees may be granted to a specified relationship to total compensation or the base or regular rate of compensation.[32]

- The ESPP must provide that no employee can accrue the right at any time to purchase stock of his or her employer at a rate that exceeds $25,000 of the fair market value of such stock (determined when the option is granted) for each calendar year for which the option was outstanding.[33] The regulations allow an employee to buy more than $25,000 of stock in a calendar year, so long as the total amount of stock which he or she buys does not exceed $25,000 in fair market value (determined at date of grant) for each calendar year in which the option was outstanding.[34]

- The exercise price of the options granted under an ESPP must be no less than 85% of the stock's fair market value at the time the option is granted, or an amount which under the option's terms cannot be less than 85% of the stock's fair market value at the time the option is exercised.[35] For example, if an employee is granted an option at $85 for stock worth $105 at that time, the option does not qualify even if the stock falls to $100 or less when exercised.

- The maximum allowable option exercise period is five years from the date of the option grant for an option that contains an exercise price at least 85% of the fair market value of the company's stock. If the option exercise price is determined in any other manner, such as a fixed dollar amount that will not be less than 85% of the fair market value of such stock at the time of the exercise of the option, the option must be exercised within 27 months from the date of the grant of the option.[36]

- The options granted in the ESPP must not be transferable other than by will or by the laws of descent and distribution. Only the employee may exercise the option during his or her lifetime.[37]

If the terms of an offering under a purchase plan option do not meet the above requirements, all options granted under that offering will be treated as not having been granted under a section 423 plan.[38] A purchase plan option, like an ISO plan, can contain additional terms as long as such terms do not contravene any of the requirements for a purchase plan option. Additional terms could include when an option will be granted, the method of payment of the option exercise price and limitations on when options can be exercised. Restrictions also can be placed on the underlying option stock.

Advantages

Many of the benefits derived from section 423 purchase plan options are similar to benefits derived from ISOs. Under both types of plans, there is no tax on either the grant or the exercise of an option. The employee is not taxed until he or she sells the underlying stock. The income recognized at that time generally is recognized as a capital gain. In addition, the employer is able to implement work incentives for its employees without draining valuable liquid assets.

The requirements under the Code for ESPPs are, generally, more liberal than those governing ISOs. A key feature of a purchase plan option (that differs from an ISO) is that it can offer options with an option price of between 85% and 100% of the fair market value of the stock, either at grant or exercise. ISOs must be offered at an option price of the fair market value of the stock. Employees will not recognize ordinary income when an option is exercised but will recognize such income at a later disposition of the stock if the ESPP meets the requirements of a purchase plan option.

According to a 1991 survey by then ShareData (now E*Trade Business Solutions), a company that provides software for section 423 purchase plan administration, almost all companies offer a 15% discount on the purchase of the shares under a section 423 plan. The offering period ranges from three months to 12 months; only 16% of the companies have offering periods between more than 12 months and 27 months. None of the companies surveyed extended the offering period beyond 27 months. The offering frequency is typically three to six months. In other words, most companies allow their employees to commit to purchase shares at a 15% discount every three to six months, but allow them an option period of three to 12 months after the purchase to actually exercise the option.[39]

Tax Implications for Employees

Neither the grant of an option under a purchase plan option nor the exercise of an option granted under an ESPP has any tax consequences to employees, provided the option is granted pursuant to a Code section 423 purchase plan.[40] Employees are not taxed until they sell the stock acquired through exercise of the option. Employees generally treat any proceeds received from such a sale as capital gain. There are two situations, however, where employees may be subjected to ordinary income tax. The first situation occurs if the option exercise price is below the full fair market value of stock at the time the option is granted. The second is a "disqualifying" disposition of the stock.

Below Fair Market Value The first situation occurs if the option exercise price is below the full fair market value of the stock when the option is granted. In this situation, the employee must include as ordinary income at the time of sale of the option stock or upon the employee's death while still holding the option stock (the transfer of option stock to the estate or beneficiary of a deceased employee is treated as a disposition of the stock for purposes of this rule) the lesser of: (1) the amount, if any, by which the fair market value of the stock when the option was granted exceeds the option exercise price; or (2) the amount, if any, by which the stock's fair market value at the time of such disposition or death exceeds the exercise price paid.[41] This applies regardless of whether the employee has held the stock for the statutory holding period.

> EXAMPLE: On January 1, 1992, all employees at X Corp. are granted options to purchase X Corp. stock at 85% of the stock's fair market value. A holds 10 options for five years. In 1997, A dies when the fair market value of X Corp. stock is $95 per share. A's estate will recognize $100 of ordinary income in the year of A's death. This amount is the lesser of $150 (the difference between the $100 fair market value on the date of grant and the $85 exercise price on the date of grant, multiplied by 10 options) or $100 (the difference between the option exercise price of $85 and the fair market value of the option stock at the time of disposition, $95, multiplied by 10).[42]

Disqualifying Disposition As with an ISO, any disposition of stock before the expiration of the statutory holding period, the later of two years after the granting of an option or one year from the date of transfer of stock pursuant to the option, is a disqualifying disposition. For any disqualifying disposition, the employee recognizes at the time of disposition first, ordinary income measured by the difference between the option's exercise price and the fair market value of the stock at the time of option exercise (the "bargain purchase element"), and second, capital gain measured by the difference between the fair market value of the stock on the date of exercise and the disposition proceeds.[43]

Qualifying Disposition If the disposition of stock occurs after the statutory holding period has expired, the employee will have capital gain measured by the sale proceeds less the employee's basis in the option stock. The basis in the stock would equal the option exercise price plus any ordinary income recognized due to a below–fair market value option.

> EXAMPLE: On January 1, 1990, all employees of X Corp. are granted options to purchase X Corp. stock at 85% of the stock's fair market value. A exercises 10 options at date of grant when X Corp. stock has a fair market value of $100 per share. A holds the X Corp. stock for five years and sells all her shares for $200 per share. In 1995, A will recognize $150 in compensation income (the difference between the $100 fair market value on the date of exercise and the $85 exercise price on the date of grant multiplied by 10 options). The amount of capital gains on the disposition (sale) of stock is $1,000 (the $200 purchase price minus the adjusted basis of the stock—i.e., the original basis of $85 plus the $15 in ordinary income—multiplied by 10 shares).[44]

Tax Implications for Employers

Generally, the granting employer may not take a tax deduction. The employer may take a deduction for any disqualifying disposition.[45] The compensation deduction will be equal to the amount that the employee includes as ordinary income, and the employer will take the deduction in the year of the disposition.[46] The employer may not deduct the difference between the fair market value of the option stock and the option exercise price.[47]

The employer may be required to withhold income tax on a disqualifying disposition from a purchase plan option. In addition, FICA and FUTA tax also is imposed upon a disqualifying disposition.[48] These rules also differ from those for ISOs.

A purchase plan option generally is not subject to ERISA. Therefore, it is not subject to ERISA's reporting requirements.

Nonqualified (Nonstatutory) Stock Options

The term "nonqualified stock option" or "nonstatutory stock option" refers to a number of types of options to purchase company stock that, for some reason, does not satisfy the legal requirements to qualify as an ISO or a purchase plan option. Many broad-based plans (other than section 423 purchase plans) are nonqualified. A nonqualified option is the simplest of the three types of stock options (incentive stock options, section 423 plans and nonqualified stock options). A nonqualified option plan allows employees to purchase shares at a fixed exercise price for a specified number of years into the future, often subject to vesting rules.

A nonqualified stock option is generally taxed to the employee at grant only if it (the option) has a readily ascertainable fair market value at that time, which nonqualified stock options almost never do. If it does not have such a value at grant, it is taxed at the time of exercise unless it is subject to the two kinds of restrictions that are discussed under the "Tax Treatment" heading in the portion of this chapter devoted to restricted stock (see below). The employer has a corresponding compensation deduction at the time of exercise.

Most nonqualified stock options are structured such that employees receive the right to purchase a certain number of shares of stock at a predetermined price. That option may be exercisable immediately or after the passage of a certain amount of time or upon the occurrence of a certain event.

> EXAMPLE: On July 1, 1995, Corporation S grants to A, in consideration for services rendered, options to purchase 1,000 shares of S common stock. The option price is $10 per share, the stock's fair market value at the date of grant. On July 1, 1999, when the stock's value is $40 per share, A exercises the options in full, acquiring 1,000 shares for $10 per share. On July 1, 2000, when the stock's value is $50 per share, A sells the 1,000 shares. Because the option did not have an ascertainable fair market

value at the date of grant, there is no taxable event as a result of the grant. In 1999, when A exercises the option, he recognizes $30 per share compensation income. Under Code section 83(a), the difference between the fair market value of the stock received pursuant to the option exercise ($40 per share) and the amount paid for the stock ($10 per share) is compensation income.

Advantages

Most employers using nonqualified stock options are trying to attain the same (or similar) benefits as are provided by a statutory option without the necessity of conforming to the same requirements of the Code. Using nonqualified stock options to compensate and provide an incentive for employees, the employer is able to give them a tangible reward for their efforts without using any liquid cash resources. As a result of the option, employees receive an opportunity to share in the future growth of the company.

Tax Implications Generally

The tax implications of a nonqualified stock option are governed by section 83 of the Code. Generally, Code section 83 will apply to the grant of the nonqualified option if the option itself, upon grant, has a readily ascertainable fair market value. An option to acquire nonpublicly traded stock does not have a readily ascertainable fair market value. Section 83 of the Code will apply to the exercise of a nonpublicly traded nonqualified option if the property subject to the option does not, at the time of grant, have a readily ascertainable fair market value.

As a generalization, unless a nonqualified stock option has a fair market value that can be readily determined, it will not result in a taxable transaction upon the employee's receipt of the option.

Readily Ascertainable Fair Market Value

Generally, Code section 83(a) imposes ordinary income taxes on an employee upon the receipt of compensatory property at its fair market value. When property is received in the form of a nonqualified stock option, however, Code section 83(e)(3) requires that the option must have a readily ascertainable fair market value. If an option granted to an employee is actively traded on an established market, the option value has a readily ascertainable fair market value.[49] Such an option would be taxable at its *grant* under Code section 83(a). Note that the option itself must be tradable, not the underlying stock. Few employee options are traded on stock exchanges.

Options that are not actively traded on an established market do not have a readily ascertainable fair market value unless the fair market value "can otherwise be measured with reasonable accuracy."[50] The regulations create an irrebuttable presumption that an untraded option does not have a readily ascertainable fair market value unless four conditions are met, including the following:

- The option is transferable by the optionee.
- The option is exercisable immediately in full by the optionee.
- Neither the option nor the underlying property is subject to any restrictions that have a significant effect on the option's value.
- The purchase fair market value of the option privilege is readily ascertainable.[51] Therefore, almost all options for stock not actively traded will be deemed not to have a readily ascertainable fair market value.

Tax Implications for Employees

Publicly Traded Options A publicly traded option having a readily ascertainable fair market value will be taxed at *grant*. The employee will recognize ordinary income in the amount of the fair market value of the option less any amount paid for the option. Once the option's grant is taxed, the transaction's ordinary income consequences to the employee are closed. Thus, once the employee exercises the option, there will be no further ordinary income tax consequences.

If the stock is held as a capital asset, the employee will receive long-term capital gain treatment for the gain recognized upon its disposition. The amount of the capital gain will be measured by the difference between the selling price less any amount paid for the exercise of the option and any amount included in income upon the option's grant.[52]

Options Not Publicly Traded If, as is almost always the case, the option is a nonqualified stock option without a readily ascertainable fair market value at date of grant, there is no taxable event as a result of the grant.[53] The compensatory aspects of the option remain open until the option is exercised.[54] Once the employee exercises the option, he or she will recognize ordinary income equal to the amount of the fair market value of the stock when it is exercised minus any amount paid for the option. The effect of not having a taxable event at the time of the grant is to treat the appreciation in the value of the property as ordinary income and not as capital gain. However, if the stock is held after exercise, any additional gain is then generally treated as capital gain.

Tax Implications for Employers

The employer has a corresponding deduction (in the same amount and at the same time) as the ordinary income recognized by the employee.[55] In general, compensation paid in the form of stock options normally triggers the receipt of wages for the purpose of employment tax and withholding provisions in the amount of the income generated under Code section 83(a).[56]

Choosing Between Statutory and Nonstatutory (Nonqualified) Stock Options

An employer has the choice of two types of stock options that can be used to compensate employees: statutory (i.e., incentive or section 423) options or nonstatutory (i.e., nonqualified) options. Any statutory stock option plan also may provide for the granting of nonstatutory options, as long as the plan does not provide for tandem options.[57] (In the case of tandem options, two options are issued together and the exercise of one affects the exercise of the other. This is not permitted because it may evade the section 422A qualification requirements.) The differences between statutory and nonstatutory options are as follows:

- If in the year in which gain is recognized there is little or no difference between ordinary income and capital gain marginal tax rates, one of the principal advantages (taxation at a capital gains rate) of the statutory stock option is removed.

- The company obtains a deduction on exercise of a nonstatutory option equal to the income recognized by the employee. The company generally receives no deduction in the statutory stock option context unless there is a premature disposition by the employee.

- The statutory option is still arguably preferable for the key employee because no income is recognized on the exercise of the option (unlike the situation with the typical nonstatutory option); income recognition of a statutory option is deferred until the employee disposes of the stock.

- Nonstatutory options provide the employer with flexibility in plan design (because of lack of qualification rules). As a result, employers can tailor nonstatutory options to meet their particular needs. For example, nonstatutory options may be granted to non-employees, such as valued outside contractors or non-employee directors.

- There is no requirement that the option price of a nonstatutory option be equal to the fair market value of the stock at the time of the option grant. Thus, the grantor of the nonstatutory option has complete freedom in setting the option price and the bargain purchase element.

- Unlike statutory options, nonstatutory options can be granted pursuant to a plan that is effective for longer than 10 years, and the options can be outstanding for periods over 10 years from date of grant.

- Nonstatutory options may be fully transferable, and there need not be any restrictions on the amount of options that can be exercised in a single year nor when the employee can dispose of the option stock after exercise.

Design Issues

Using stock option plans to create employee incentives has not escaped criticism. Some criticisms of employee options for publicly traded stock expressed in an article by Robert C. Greenberg are given below, followed in each case by a solution to the problem:[58]

- *Options do not pay for expected performance.* A company's stock price on the market reflects the investors' collective expectations about the company's future performance. So long as companies perform as expected, options tend to provide the same gain no matter what the company's actual financial results. (Options do, however, create rewards for unexpected performance.)

    Solution: Adjust the size of the option grants based on the company's performance in excess of expectations.

- *Option gains do not parallel shareholder returns.* Shareholders have invested their capital in a risky security and will not benefit until they earn an adequate rate of return on that investment as compared with the rate of the market as a whole. On the other hand, employee shareholders will benefit from any appreciation in stock price.

    Solution: Index the option's exercise price to changes in the general level of stock prices as measured by a market index.

- *Options provide only a weak incentive because employees have limited influence on the stock price.* Empirical research shows that over one-half of the variance in a company's stock price is due to industry factors, stock market trends, and macroeconomic conditions. These conditions cannot be influenced by employee performance.

    Solution: Index the exercise price to changes in industry stock prices, using an appropriate industry index.

- *Options allow executives to select the period over which performance will be measured.*

    Solution: Use options that can only be exercised at the end of their term.

- *Options are not cost-effective.* Employees may discount the value of the options they receive if their portfolios are not diversified and the options are thus a riskier investment for them than for the typical stockholder. Another reason for discounting the value of an option is the risk of involuntary termination that could shorten the option's term or make it unexercisable.

    Solution: Adjust the size of option grants to account for risk.

Restricted Stock

A simple way of providing equity incentives to employees or others is to grant stock or options and impose certain restrictions on such stock or the stock purchased pursuant to the options as a condition of such grant. Such restrictions may serve to make the stock subject to a substantial risk of forfeiture upon certain conditions and establish other restrictions upon an individual's or entity's ability to freely transfer the stock to other parties. If the forfeiture and nontransferability conditions are fully enforced, the grantee or optionee may not receive anything as a result of the restricted stock grant or restricted stock option. Therefore, unlike in other stock option and grant transactions, if the risk of forfeiture is substantial, and the stock is not freely transferable, no tax is generally imposed upon the stock grant or the exercise of the option to purchase stock. It is only when the restrictions lapse at a later date that tax consequences ensue.

Stock received by employees in connection with the performance of services may be subject to certain restrictions imposed by the employer. Such restrictions might include a requirement that upon termination of employment, the employee must sell his or her stock back to the employer at a formula price based on book value. (This type of restriction is typically imposed by closely held corporations.)

Tax Treatment

The tax treatment of restricted property may be different from property that is not subject to any restrictions. The law distinguishes between two kinds of restrictions, (1) those that may lapse during the period of ownership by the employee (e.g., restrictions that lapse in 10 years if the key employee is still employed at that time); and (2) those that by their terms can never lapse. If there is a restriction that never lapses, the recipient is taxed on the date of receipt of the stock, and the restriction goes only to the extent of the value of the bargain element.[59] If the transferred stock is both transferable and subject to a substantial risk of forfeiture, the taxable event is delayed until such restrictions lapse. The regulations define the terms for nontransferability and substantial risks of forfeiture as follows:

Substantial Risk of Forfeiture   Section 83(c)(1) of the Code defines a substantial risk of forfeiture as a restriction that conditions a person's right to full enjoyment of property upon the performance of substantial services by any individual. The regulations further provide that the services required to be performed must be substantial and that the forfeiture conditions must be likely to be enforced against the taxpayer.[60] The regulations provide examples illustrating restrictions that would qualify as a substantial risk of forfeiture.

> EXAMPLE: On November 1, 1992, X Corp. transfers 100 shares of X Corp. stock for $90 per share to E, an employee. Under the terms of the transfer, E will be subject to a binding commitment to resell the stock to X Corp. at $90 per share if he leaves the employment of X Corp. for any reason prior to the expiration of a two-year period from the date of such transfer. Because E must perform substantial services for X Corp. and will not be paid more than $90 for the stock, regardless of its value, if he fails to perform such services during such two-year period, E's rights in the stock are subject to a substantial risk of forfeiture during such period.[61]

> EXAMPLE: On December 1, 1992, X Corp. gives to E, an employee, a bonus of 100 shares of X Corp. stock. Under the terms of the bonus agreement, if E terminates her employment for any reason, she is obligated to return the X Corp. stock to X Corp. For each year after December 1, 1992, however, for which E remains employed with X Corp., E ceases to be obligated to return 10 shares of the stock. E's rights in 10 shares each year for 10 years cease to be subject to a substantial risk of forfeiture for each year she remains so employed.[62]

In addition, any stock that if sold could subject a person to potential liability under 16(b) of the 1934 Act is subject to both forfeiture and nontransferability restrictions. The taxable event upon receipt of such stock would be delayed only so long as a sale of the stock would be the event that would trigger 1934 Act section 16(b) liability.

Nontransferability In addition to substantial risk of forfeiture, nontransferability is necessary to have a delay in the taxable event under Code section 83. If either of these conditions is missing, the property will be taxable at its fair market value upon receipt, regardless of the presence of other restrictions.

A restricted option (one that is subject to a substantial risk of forfeiture and is nontransferable) is taxed when restrictions lapse. Employees will recognize ordinary income in the amount of the fair market value of the stock on the date of lapse less the exercise price. Any increase in value after such taxable event will be taxed as capital gain upon disposition.

Code Section 83(b) Election

An employee receiving restricted stock may elect to have the ordinary income element of the restricted property close at the time the property is transferred. Closing the taxable event under Code section 83 gives the employee the opportunity to limit his or her ordinary income from the transaction to any spread on the date the property is transferred between the fair market value and the amount paid for the property. Any appreciation in property after the date of the transfer is potential capital gain income that will be recognized when the property is disposed of by the employee. The Code section 83(b) election must be made within 30 days after the transfer of the property; and once the election is made, it is irrevocable unless the IRS agrees to the revocation. The election is not without risk. If an employee makes the election and recognizes ordinary income and the property is thereafter forfeited pursuant to the restrictions, no deduction is available to the employee.[63]

Examples of Restricted Property Plans

Transfer of C Corporation Stock to Key Employees with Mandatory Repurchase upon Certain Events Employers often want to encourage employees to contribute to the company and tie a portion of their reward to the continued growth of the company. One method of achieving this is through a performance share plan (discussed elsewhere in this book). A second method is through a qualified defined contribution plan such as an ESOP. A third method is to give nonvoting stock to employees that will be repurchased or redeemed by the remaining stockholders or the granting company at some future time. The third option allows employees to literally share in the company's growth while still not diluting the voting control of the owners.

Implementing this transfer of nonvoting stock to a key employee is quite simple. The company is recapitalized to have voting and nonvoting stock. The company now approaches its key employees and provides that it will distribute a certain number of nonvoting shares to each of them on the condition that those key employees agree that their stock will be redeemed by the company upon the earlier of their death or termination of employment.

The key employees have received an actual piece of the business in the form of nonvoting stock. They, however, are contractually bound by the mandatory buyback provision to sell their shares (or direct their estates to sell their shares) back to the company. This mandatory buyback mechanism protects the company from having its shares transferred to non-employees.

One benefit of this plan from a tax standpoint is its simplicity. Upon the key employee's receipt of the nonvoting shares in the company, he or she recognizes ordinary income (additional compensation) equal to the fair market value of the stock. The employer receives an additional compensation deduction in the same amount. As long as the employee's receipt of the stock does not constitute "unreasonable compensation," there are no further implications from the transaction until the stock is repurchased by the company.

Upon the death or termination of employment of the key employee, the company exercises its contractual right to repurchase its nonvoting stock. A redemption during the employee's lifetime causes the employee to recognize a capital gain on the difference between his or her original purchase price and the income which he or she recognized upon his or her redemption of his or her stock. Any interest the employee receives on a promissory note used to purchase the stock also is income to the employee. From the company's standpoint, the repurchase of its stock does not provide a deduction. If the company pays for the stock over a period of years, however, then presumably any interest paid upon the underlying promissory note will be deductible to the company.

There are several benefits to this type of restricted transfer:

- The company has no initial outlay in order to provide the nonvoting shares to the employee.
- Employees receive incentives that are tied to their contributions to the company's overall growth.
- The employee's family is provided for after the employee's death if repurchase is made after the employee's death.
- The company can fund this type of arrangement by purchasing insurance on its employees' lives. Any insurance proceeds that a company receives as a result of the death of a key employee will be subject to the alternative minimum tax of 15%.

Transfer of S Corporation's Stock to Key Employees with Mandatory Repurchase upon Certain Events The transfer to key employees of nonvoting stock in an S corporation, which will be redeemed by the company or repurchased by the remaining stockholders or the company at some future time, provides the same advantages as the same type of transfer to the key employees of a C corporation. The key employees share in the company's growth without diluting the voting control of the owners of the S corporation.

Implementing this transfer of nonvoting stock in an S corporation to key employees is the same as for a C corporation. The company gives its key employees a certain number of nonvoting shares on the condition that they agree that their stock will be redeemed by the company upon the earlier of their death or termination of employment. The tax implications are the same as with the transfer of nonvoting stock in a C corporation. The benefits of this restricted transfer are the same as with the C corporation, with the additional benefit that the key employee enjoys annual dividend distributions.

The owners of an S corporation using this type of restricted stock transfer must be careful to ensure that the restrictions on the key employee's stock do not cause that stock to be considered a different class from the voting stock.

Time-Accelerated Restricted Stock Award Plan

A time-accelerated restricted stock award plan ("time-accelerated stock plan") is a plan by which a corporation may attach performance criteria to the restricted stock. The performance criteria affect the timing of the lapse of the restriction while not affecting the ultimate employee reward. For example, a traditional restricted stock plan may provide that the substantial forfeiture restrictions on the stock award are removed at a fixed rate for a number of years, but a time-accelerated stock plan would allow the restrictions to be removed earlier, based on performance measurements. The restrictions would never lapse, however, later than the original schedule. Such a close tie between performance measurements and lapsing of the restriction is an excellent mechanism to improve employee incentives. This type of stock plan allows companies to tailor performance measurements specifically to meet their needs.

For restricted stock (stock that is subject to substantial risk of forfeiture and is nontransferable), employees will recognize ordinary income in the amount of the fair market value of the stock on the date of the lapse less the exercise price unless they elect to have the compensation element close when the restricted property is transferred. The employer has a corresponding deduction, in the same amount and at the same time as the income recognized by the employee.[64]

> EXAMPLE: Assume that on January 1, 1993, XYZ Company awarded 100 shares under the restricted stock plan to employee X at no cost, subject to certain restrictions (fair market value of each share of stock equals $10). The shares become freely transferable and nonforfeitable at the end of 10 years. In addition, 10% of the restrictions can be lifted each year if the earnings of X's department increase 20% or more over the previous year. If X meets the performance criteria in 1993, the restrictions will lapse for 10% of the stock and X will recognize $100 in ordinary income (100 × $10 × .10).[65]

Restricted Stock Performance Plan

A second type of stock performance plan that combines the attributes of a typical restricted stock plan with performance criteria is a restricted stock performance plan. For a restricted stock performance plan, failure to meet the performance criteria results in forfeiture of the restricted stock (unlike the time-accelerated stock plan, in which the performance criteria may only accelerate the time when the restrictions lapse).

> EXAMPLE: XYZ Company's restricted stock performance plan is identical to the previous example except that instead of 10% of the restrictions being lifted each year if the earnings increase 20% or more over the previous year, 10% of the stock will be forfeited each year the earnings do not increase 20% or more.
>
> For each year X does not meet the performance standard, she will forfeit 10% of the stock initially granted to her. In year 11, when the remaining stock becomes freely transferable and nonforfeitable, X will recognize ordinary income in the amount equal to the fair market value of the stock granted to her under the restricted stock performance plan.[66]

Securities Laws and Stock Options

Securities laws exist at the state and federal level. Each state has its own rules, although there are broad similarities between states. Securities law is a large and complex subject, but the two key elements are registration and disclosure.

Registration means the filing of documents with the state and/or federal securities agencies concerning the employer whose stock is being sold. There are registration procedures for small offerings of stock (under $1 million or $5 million, depending on the procedure) that can be done for relatively small legal fees (as little as $10,000 in some cases), but larger offerings require a lot of complex paperwork and fees often exceed $100,000. Registration requires the filing of audited financial statements and continuing reporting obligations to the Securities and Exchange Commission (SEC) and appropriate state agencies.

Disclosure refers to providing information to buyers about what they are getting, similar to, but frequently less detailed than, what would be in a prospectus. At times, there are specific state and federal rules about what needs to go in these documents, including objective discussions of risks, the financial condition of the company, officers' and directors' salaries, and other information. In the absence of requirements for the registration of the securities, disclosure is intended to satisfy the anti-fraud requirements of federal and state laws.

Federal Securities Law

Registration and Disclosure Generally, offers to sell securities (stocks, bonds, etc.) require registration of those securities unless there is a specific exemption. Individual stock purchases or choices about using existing benefit plan funds to buy company stock would fall under this definition. In addition, companies with 500 or more shareholders are considered public companies under federal law and must comply with the reporting requirements of the 1934 Act even if they do not have to register under the Securities Act of 1933 (the "1933 Act").

There are a number of exemptions from these rules listed below. These are exemptions from registration; any time stock is offered for sale, it should include appropriate financial disclosure to satisfy anti-fraud rules. The principal exemptions under federal law are:

- Offers to a company's employees, directors, general partners, trustees, officers, or consultants can be made under a written compensation agreement. Under SEC Rule 701 (effective April 7, 1999), the maximum dollar amount of stock that may be sold to these people in a year without registration is the greatest of: (1) $1 million, (2) 15% of the issuer's total assets, or (3) 15% of the issuer's outstanding class of stock being sold. The 15% ceiling would not apply if the offering is under $1 million. The offer itself will no longer count for purposes of the available exempted amount. If more than $5 million of securities are being sold, however, the issuer is required to disclose risk factors to potential buyers and deliver financial statements in accordance with Form 1-A of Regulation A.

- Section 4(2) of the 1993 Act allows for no federal registrations in offerings of stock to a limited number of investors who have access to the same information normally provided in a public offering and who are sophisticated enough both to assess and bear the risks. This exemption has been variously interpreted by the courts. Whether it allows such approaches as offering stock to all of a company's "key employees" is unclear.

- Regulation D, issued by the SEC, provides a number of exemptions for small offerings. The best known of these is Rule 505, which provides an exemption to offerings of up to $5 million to as many as 35 nonaccredited investors. If every investor is sophisticated (Rule 505), however, there is no limit on the amount of the offering (but there can still be no more than 35 investors). Rule 504 allows offerings up to $500,000 (or $1 million if there is a registration for up to $500,000 with a state) to as many people as wanted, with no limits of their being sophisticated or accredited.

- Offerings that are made only to residents of the state in which the offering is made are exempt if the offeror has its principal office in that state, gets 80% of its gross revenue from business conducted in the state, and has 80% of its assets in the state.

Form S-8 Where the issuer of securities is an SEC reporting company, Form S-8 is available to register the offer and sale of securities to its employees (and certain "consultants and advisors") in a compensatory or incentive context. On February 25, 1999, in Release No. 33-7646, the SEC finalized amendments to Form S-8, generally effective as of April 7, 1999. The amendments make Form S-8 available for the exercise of stock options by an employee's family member who has acquired the options through a gift or domestic relations order, and Form S-8 is now also available to former employees for the exercise of options and stock appreciation rights that have been transferred. The new instructions to Form S-8 provide that "consultants and advisors" to an issuer may be treated as employees for purposes of registration under Form S-8 (and for purposes of Rule 701) only if they provide bonafide services to the issuer not in connection with the offer or sale of securities in a capital-raising transaction and they do not directly or indirectly promote or maintain a market for the issuer's securities.

Rule 16b-3 Section 16(a) of the 1934 Act requires reports of stock ownership to be filed by directors and executive officers of companies that are subject to the reporting provisions of section 12 of the 1934 Act. These provisions apply only to companies that are subject to the reporting provisions of section 12. They do not apply to closely held companies. Section 16(b) of the 1934 Act provides for the recapture of "short-swing" profits realized from transactions in the issuer's stock by persons who are subject to the reporting obligations of section 16(a). If any such person realizes a profit on a purchase and subsequent sale, or a sale and subsequent purchase, of an issuer's securities within a six-month period, he may be required to pay such profit over to the issuer. If a recoverable profit exists, suit may be brought by the issuer or, if it fails to do so, by any security holder of the issuer for the issuer's benefit.

The SEC has recognized that equity incentive plans provide an important incentive to an issuer's employees, including officers and directors, and has adopted special rules for transactions under employee equity benefit plans. These provisions are found in SEC Rule 16b-3, which exempts from short-swing profit recovery any acquisitions and dispositions of an issuer's equity securities between an officer or director and the company, including those occurring upon the exercise or conversion of a derivative security, whether in or out of the money, subject to certain conditions. The four categories of exempted transactions are: (1) tax-conditioned plans, (2) discretionary transactions, (3) grants and awards, and (4) dispositions to the issuer.

The exemption for tax-conditioned plans applies only to plans conditioned under various provisions of the Code. Transactions under such tax-conditioned plans are exempt not only from the short-swing profit recovery provisions of section 16(b) but also from the reporting requirements of section 16(a). However, incentive and nonstatutory stock option plans do not qualify as tax-conditioned plans.

Accordingly, transactions involving employee stock options must rely on some other exemption. The discretionary transaction exemption is available for transactions only if they are made pursuant to an election made at least six months following the date of the most recent prior such election. This six-month condition applies only to "opposite-way" transactions; that is, elections that affect acquisitions and dispositions must be at least six months apart, prior "same-way" elections (e.g., two or more purchase transactions or two or more sale transactions) within the preceding six months will not render the exemption unavailable.

An exemption is also available for the grant or award of an issuer's equity securities upon satisfaction of one of three alternative conditions. This exemption covers grants of options as well as awards of bonus stock pursuant to a salary-based formula. In addition, participant-directed transactions may also rely on the exemption. The alternative conditions under which the acquisition of company securities, including grants of options, may be claimed are: (1) advance approval by the board of directors or a committee composed solely of two or more nonemployee directors; (2) advance approval or subsequent ratification by the shareholders (which must come no later than the next annual meeting of shareholders); or (3) if an acquisition does not satisfy an approval condition, the exemption can be claimed if the securities acquired are held by the insider for six months after the acquisition, or, in the case of a derivative security (such as a stock option), at least six months elapse between the date of the acquisition of the derivative security and the date of disposition of the underlying security.

Anti-fraud Provisions To comply with the anti-fraud provisions of federal securities laws, disclosure of certain corporate information to the optionees under a stock option plan is advisable. The disclosure standard for registration statements filed under the Securities Act of 1933 (the "1933 Act") may be used as a guideline for the type of information that needs to be disclosed. The following is a list of information that generally must be disclosed in registration statements:

- Description of business.
- Description of property.
- Description of any legal proceedings.
- Market price of and dividends on the company's shares.
- Recent financial statements.
- Other pertinent financial data.
- Management's discussion and analysis of financial condition and results of operations.
- Changes in and disagreements with accountants on accounting and financial disclosure.
- Names of directors and executive officers.
- Executive compensation.
- Security ownership of certain beneficial owners and management.
- Certain relationships and related transactions.
- General plans for the company's future.

It is important to note that meeting the disclosure standard for registration statements filed under the 1933 Act is not a requirement for closely held companies that implement a stock option plan; rather, the disclosure would be helpful in responding to anti-fraud claims by the optionees against the company and its board of directors for transactions arising under a stock option plan.

State Securities Laws: The California Example

State laws generally require that any offer or sale of securities in the state by an issuer must be either qualified by the department of corporations or secretary of state or be exempt from such qualification requirements. In this respect, the California securities laws will be used as an example. California law requires that any offer or sale of securities in the state by an issuer must either be qualified by the California Department of Corporations or be exempt from the qualification requirements.[67] A stock option is a security and an employer distributing them is considered an issuer.[68] Thus, an employer's stock option plan must comply with California securities laws in addition to any federal requirements that must be met. Given the considerable effort and expense involved in qualifying securities issuable under a stock option plan, finding an exemption to the qualification requirement can be important.

Exemptions to Qualification If an employer offers stock options only to key employees, it may rely on the exemption found in section 25102(f) of the California Corporations Code. The exemption is generally limited to sales to no more than 35 people (excluding certain sophisticated purchasers) who have a preexisting personal or business relationship with the offeror or its directors, officers, and managers.[69] If an employer wants to expand the stock option or stock purchase plan to reach other than key employees, the 35-person limit is unduly restrictive.

Recognizing this, the California legislature enacted a new exemption to the qualification requirements in 1996. Section 25102(o) of the California Corporations Code exempts offers and sales of securities in connection with stock purchase or stock option plans or agreements without limiting the number of persons eligible, where the securities involved are exempt from federal registration requirements under Rule 701 of the 1933 Act. In addition, the transaction must meet several other requirements promulgated by the state Corporations Commissioner. Those include:

- A plan must specify the number of shares available for issuance and the persons eligible to receive options or purchase stock.

- The exercise price of options cannot be less than 85% of the stock's fair value at the time of the grant, unless the recipient already owns more than 10% of the issuer's total voting stock, in which case the exercise price must be 110% of fair value. The conditions for purchase plans are the same except that the price must be 100% of fair value for 10% owners.

- The options or purchase rights are not transferable except by will or the laws of descent.

- The plan must be approved by the company's shareholders and must terminate no later than 10 years after the date of adoption or shareholder approval, whichever is earlier.

- Options must be exercisable at a rate of at least 20% per year over five years from the date of grant. The right to exercise in the event of termination of employment, to the extent the optionee is entitled to exercise on the date of termination, must continue for at least 30 days from the date of termination of employment. The plan may allow for an issuer's repurchase upon termination.[70]

- The number of shares issuable upon exercise of all outstanding options and any stock purchase plan (except for a stock purchase plan that provides that all shares will have a purchase price of 100% of fair value) cannot exceed 30% of the then outstanding shares.[71]

- The employees participating in an option or purchase plan must receive annual financial statements unless the issuance of the security is limited to key employees who have access to such information as a result of their job duties.[72]

Special Tax Provisions and Stock Options

Section 162(m)

Section 162(m) of the Code concerns "Excessive Employee Remuneration." It sets forth the conditions an issuer must satisfy to deduct compensation in excess of $1 million paid to its chief executive officer and four other most highly compensated officers for whom disclosure is required to be reported in 1934 Act filings. The compensation element of both incentive stock options and nonstatutory stock options meets the definition of remuneration[73] and is deductible if such compensation conforms to any one of the following three categories: (1) Commission-based compensation payable solely on account of income generated directly by an individual's performance;[74] (2) remuneration based on a binding contract existing prior to February 17, 1993;[75] or (3) "other performance-based compensation," i.e., remuneration payable solely on account of the attainment of one or more performance goals.[76]

For remuneration to count as "other performance-based compensation," it must meet three conditions before payment is tendered. First, performance goals must be determined by a "compensation committee" of the issuer's board of directors. This committee must be comprised of two or more "outside directors."[77] Second, the material terms of payment must be disclosed to and approved by a majority of shareholders in a separate vote. Third, the compensation committee must determine that the performance goals were met.

Section 162(m) of the Code is also coordinated with the "Golden Parachute" provisions of the Code.[78] Remuneration that would have counted toward the maximum deduction, but for its disqualification under the golden parachute provisions, reduces the deduction limit (up to $1 million). In effect, the same thing is accomplished as if the golden parachute payment was allowed to count as applicable employee remuneration.

"Golden Parachute" Payments

Under limited circumstances, provisions of an option plan that provide for acceleration of the option exercise date notwithstanding existing vesting conditions in the event of certain "change in control transactions" may subject "disqualified individuals" to the "golden parachute payment" rules of the Code. If applicable, these rules would prohibit the company from deducting an excess "parachute payment," impose on the "disqualified individual" a nondeductible 20% excise tax on the excess "parachute payment" (in addition to applicable income taxes), and require the company to withhold funds in the amount of the excise tax from wages payable to the "disqualified individual" (which include shares issuable on exercise of the option).

Stock Appreciation Rights and Stock Options

Stock appreciation rights can be used alone or in tandem with statutory or nonstatutory stock options. A stock appreciation right (SAR) is a contractual right to receive, either in cash or employer stock, the appreciation in the value of the employer's stock over a certain period of time. An SAR gives an employee the right to obtain the future appreciation in the employer's stock without risking any capital. In addition, an SAR used in conjunction with a statutory option or a purchase plan option enables employees to exercise options without a cash outlay.

SARs Used in Tandem with ISOs

An ISO plan may provide for tandem SARs where the exercise of one will affect the right to exercise the other as long as the SARs meet the following requirements:

- The SAR must expire no later than the expiration of the underlying ISO.
- The SAR may be for no more than 100% of the bargain purchase element of the underlying ISO.
- The SAR is transferable only when the underlying ISO is transferable and subject to the same conditions.
- The SAR may be exercised only when the underlying ISO may be exercised.
- The SAR may be exercised only when the market price of the stock exceeds the exercise price of the ISO.[79]

A combination of SARs and an ISO plan enables an employee to exercise an ISO without an initial cash outlay.

EXAMPLE: On December 31, 1992, X Corp. grants to A 100 tandem ISO/SARs to either purchase one share of X Corp. stock at $10 per share (the fair market value of X Corp. stock on December 31, 1992) or receive the difference between the fair market value of a share of X Corp. stock at the time of exercise and $10. When the fair market value of X Corp. stock is $15 per share, A may exercise either his ISOs by paying the exercise price of $10 per share and receiving a share of stock worth $15 or his SARs without any current cash outlay and receive $5 in cash or other property for every SAR exercised. If A exercises 75 SARs on December 31, 1993, he will only have 25 of the original tandem ISO/SARs still available.

EXAMPLE: Assume the same facts as in the above example, but A decides that he wants to exercise enough SARs to give him cash to pay the purchase price for the remaining ISOs. A would have to exercise 66 SARs and receive $330 (66 × $5) to get enough cash to exercise the remaining 33 ISOs (33 shares × $10 exercise price). One tandem ISO/SAR remains.[80]

Using SARs with Nonstatutory Options

SARs are often used to ease the burden created by the illiquidity that may arise upon the exercise of a nonstatutory option. There are two situations in which a nonstatutory option may create a cash-flow problem for the employee. First, options sometimes trigger ordinary income to an employee under Code section 83(a) without transferring any cash to the employee. The employee may need cash to pay the tax liability. Second, an employee may need help in financing the exercise price for nonstatutory options (similar to the situation for ISOs). To gain the benefit inherent in an option, an employee may have to invest personal capital which may not be available. SARs can be used to generate the needed cash.

Two basic patterns of tandem SARs and nonstatutory stock options that are commonly used are as follows:

- A simultaneous grant of nonstatutory options and SARs with no connection between the number of options and the number of SARs.

- A tandem grant of nonstatutory options and SARs in which the exercise of a SAR reduces the number of options available, and vice versa. The amount of compensation that the employer is seeking to convey to the employees will lend guidance to the employer to choose between the different types of programs.

The following examples illustrate the usefulness of SARs:

EXAMPLE: On July 1, 1991, P Corp. grants to J, a key executive, 1,000 nonstatutory options to purchase P Corp. stock and 1,000 SARs with respect to P Corp. stock. On July 1, 1991, the stock's fair market value is $10 per share. The exercise price for the options is $10 per share, and the base value for the SARs, from which the appreciation will be measured, is $10 per share. On July 1, 1994, when the P Corp. stock has a value of $30 per share, J exercises all of her nonstatutory options and all of her SARs for cash.

J will recognize $20,000 of ordinary income under Code section 83(a) from the exercise of the nonstatutory options ($30 per share fair market value less $10 per share exercise price) × 1,000 shares). Assuming J is in the 40% combined federal and state tax bracket (disregarding for this purpose the reduction in federal tax brought about by an increase in deductible state income taxes), that $20,000 of income will produce $8,000 of tax liability with respect to the options. The exercise of the SARs for cash also will produce $20,000 of ordinary income to J under Code section 61(a)(1) (($30 per share value at exercise less $10 per share value at grant) × 1,000 SARs). J will incur an $8,000 tax liability with respect to the SARs. After J pays the tax liability attributable to the SARs, there will be $12,000 left over from the cash exercise of the SARs to pay the tax liability from the exercise of the options. Hence, through the use of SARs, P Corp. has been able to confer a benefit upon J (i.e., the spread in the option transaction, plus the ownership of P Corp. stock) without forcing J to sell some of the transferred stock, or creating a liquidity problem for J vis-à-vis the tax liability from the option transaction.

In the above example, the same net result may be accomplished if P Corp. grants to J 1,500 options to purchase P Corp. stock. If J exercises all of the options, she will incur a $12,000 tax liability. J may satisfy that liability by selling 400 shares of P Corp. stock with a fair market value of $30 per share. This would leave J with 1,100 shares of P Corp. stock, 100 more than the result in the above example.

> EXAMPLE: Assume the same facts as the first part of the above example concerning nonstatutory options and SARs. Assume also that J exercises 500 options and 1,000 SARs.
> The exercise of 500 options produces $10,000 of taxable income and $4,000 of tax liability to J. The exercise of 1,000 SARs produces $20,000 of taxable income, $8,000 of tax liability, and $12,000 of after-tax cash to J. The cash available from the SARs can be used to discharge the $4,000 tax liability from the exercise of the options and can also supply the $5,000 exercise price of the options ($10 per share exercise price of the options for 500 shares of P stock) without investing any personal assets. Although the employee has only received one-half the number of shares that she obtained in the previous example, she has acquired those shares without any investment of personal funds. When all 1,000 shares were acquired under the options, the employee had to finance the entire exercise price. The SARs in this context are a financing device that can greatly enhance the desirability of nonstatutory options to employees.[81]

Tax Implications of SARs for Employees

The taxable event for the employee is upon exercise of the SAR, not upon grant of the SAR. If an employee elects to receive the appreciation inherent in the SARs in cash, the cash is ordinary income. If the employee elects to receive the appreciation in the form of stock, the stock received is taxable to the employee under Code section 83(a) to the extent of the difference between its fair market value and the amount the employee paid for the stock; provided, however, there are no restrictions on the stock.

Tax Implications of SARs for Employers

For an employer that uses the cash method of accounting, the employer will be entitled to a deduction for SARs exercised in employer stock when that stock is transferred to the employee.[82] A deduction for such an employer for payment of cash upon exercise of an SAR arises when the cash is includable in the employee's income.[83]

An employer using the accrual method of accounting may deduct the compensation arising from a cash exercise of SARs only when cash is includable in the employee's income.[84] With the accrual method, an employer may deduct the compensation generated by the exercise of SARs for stock under its regular accrual method.[85]

Conclusion

Several methods exist for combining stock options in structuring and implementing non-ESOP equity incentive plans. Regardless of the combination, however, providing equity incentives to employees, when combined with effective communications and participation programs, is a proven form of compensation that (1) motivates employees (and others) to be more productive and make corporations more profitable and valuable and (2) provides mutually beneficial rewards to corporations and their shareholders and employees.

Notes

1. Code § 424(c)(1).
2. Prop. Regs. §§ 1.422A-2(a)(1)(ii) and (iii).
3. Code § 422(a)(2). See Private Letter Ruling (PLR) 8645069 (options on foreign parent's stock issued under U.S. subsidiary's plan qualify as ISOs).
4. Regs. § 1.421-7(d).
5. Code § 422(b)(1); see also Temp. Regs. § 14a.422A-1; Temp. Regs. § 14a.422A-1(c)(1); Prop. Regs. § 1.422A-2(b)(2).
6. Regs. § 1.422-5.
7. Regs. §§ 1.421-1(a)(1) and 1.421-7(a)(1).
8. Code § 422(b)(3); Temp. Regs. § 14a.422A-1(c)(2) and (5).
9. Code § 422(b)(4); Temp. Regs. § 14a.422A-1(c)(4). To determine the fair market value of the underlying ISO stock, the grantor corporation must make a good-faith attempt to determine the fair market value. For stock that is not publicly traded, any reasonable valuation method may be used. Regs. § 1.421-7(e)(2); Prop. Regs. § 1.422A-2(e)(2)(ii). Restrictions that are placed on stock are not to be considered when determining the fair market value of the stock, except when the restriction is one that will never lapse. Code § 422(c)(7) (incorporating the standard used in determining the value of restricted property under Code § 83).
10. Code § 422(b)(5); Code § 422(c)(5).
11. Code § 422(b)(5); Temp. Regs. § 14a.422A-1(c)(5).
12. See Code § 422(a), incorporating by reference the nonrecognition provisions of Code § 421(a)(1).

13. Code § 424(c)(1).

14. Code § 422(a)(1).

15. Code §§ 421(b) and 422(c)(2).

16. 381 T.M., *Statutory Stock Options*, A-8.

17. See Code § 1001(a).

18. Code § 56(b)(3).

19. H.R. Rep. No. 795, 100th Cong., 2d sess. 90 (1988).

20. Code § 421(a)(2).

21. Code § 421(a)(3).

22. Code § 421(b).

23. Notice 87-49, 1987-2 C.B. 355. The IRS states in this notice that it is reconsidering this position and that any determination that income from a disqualifying disposition would be taxable wages for employment tax purposes would be given prospective effect only.

24. Rev. Rul. 71-52, 1971-1 C.B. 278.

25. Code § 6039(a).

26. Code § 423(b)(1); Regs. § 1.423-(b)(1).

27. Code § 423(b)(3), cross-referencing the stock ownership rules of § 424(d).

28. Code § 423(b)(2); Regs. § 1.423-2(c).

29. Regs. § 1.421-1(c).

30. Code § 423(b)(4); see also Regs. § 1.423-2(e)(1), which does not reflect the 1986 T.R. change.

31. Code § 423(b)(4); Regs. § 1.423-2(e)(1).

32. Code § 423(b)(5); Regs. § 1.423-2(f)(2), but see Rev. Rul. 77-419, 1977-2 C.B. 171, where the IRS ruled that the maximum percentage of compensation that can be used to exercise options cannot be determined based on seniority.

33. Code § 423(b)(8); Regs. § 1.423-2(i)(3).

34. Regs. § 1.423-2(i)(3).

35. Code § 423(b)(6); Regs. § 1.423-2(g)(1).

36. Code § 423(b)(7); Regs. § 1.413-2(h).

37. Code § 423(b)(9); Regs. § 1.423-2(h) and (j).

38. Regs. § 1.413-2(h).

39. *Equity Compensation Trends in Corporate America* (Santa Clara, CA: ShareData, 1991).

40. Code § 421(a)(1).

41. Code § 423(c).

42. 381 T.M., *Statutory Stock Options*, A-18.

43. See § 423(a)(1); Regs. § 1.423-1(a). .

44. 381 T.M., *Statutory Stock Options*, A-17.

45. Code § 421(b).

46. Code § 421(b). See Code § 83(h).

47. Code § 421(a)(2).

48. The IRS in Rev. Rul. 71-52 states that an employer did not have an obligation to with-hold taxes on a disqualifying disposition of a qualified stock option, or to include options granted pursuant to a Code § 423 plan, nor was the income generated or the disqualifying disposition subject to FICA and FUTA tax, 1971-1 C.B. 278. In a series of private letter rulings, however, the IRS has required income tax withholding on a disqualifying disposition from a Code § 423 purchase plan. PLR 8921027; but see PLRs 8225050 and 8351020.

49. Regs. § 1.83-7(b)1.

50. Regs. § 1.83-(b)2.

51. Regs. § 1.83-7(b)2.

52. Regs. §§ 1.61-2(d)(2)(i); 1.83-4(b)(1).

53. Code § 83(e)(3).

54. See *Burnett v. Logan*, 283 U.S. 404, 1931.

55. Code § 83(h).

56. See Rev. Rul. 79-305, 1979-2 C.B. 550; Rev. Rul. 78-185, 1978-1 C.B. 304.

57. Regs. § 14(a).422A-2.

58. Greenberg, "The Truth About Executive Stock Options: Flaws, Fixes, and Facts," *Compensation & Benefits Management* 8 (1991): 40.

59. Code § 83(d)(1).

60. Regs. § 1.83-3(c).

61. Regs. § 1.83(c)(4).

62. Regs. § 1.83(c)(4).

63. Code § 83(b)(2).

64. Code § 83(h).

65. 393-2nd T.M., *Accounting for Pensions and Deferred Compensation*, A-46.

66. 393-2nd T.M., *Accounting for Pensions and Deferred Compensation*, A-47.

67. Cal. Corp. Code § 25110 (West Supp. 1996).

68. Cal. Corp. Code §§ 25019 and 25010.

69. Cal. Corp. Code § 25102(f).

70. 10 Cal. Code of Regulations §§ 260.140.41 and 260.140.42.

71. 10 Cal. Code of Regulations § 260.140.45.

72. 10 Cal. Code of Regulations § 260.140.46.

73. 26 U.S.C.A. § 162(m)(4)(E).

74. 26 U.S.C.A. § 162(m)(4)(B).

75. 26 U.S.C.A. § 162(m)(4)(D).

76. 26 U.S.C.A. § 162(m)(4)(C).

77. According to 26 C.F.R. § 1.162-27(e)(3), an outside director is one who: (a) is not a current employee of the publicly held corporation; (b) is not a former employee of the publicly held corporation who receives compensation for prior services (other than benefits under a tax-qualified retirement plan) during the taxable year; (c) has not

been an officer of the publicly held corporation; and (d) does not receive remuneration from the publicly held corporation, either directly or indirectly, in any capacity other than as a director.

78. 26 U.S.C.A. § 280G.

79. Temp. Regs. § 14(a).422A-1.

80. 381 T.M., *Statutory Stock Options*, A-10.

81. 383 T.M., *Nonstatutory Stock Options*, A-(10-11).

82. See Regs. § 1.461-(a)(1).

83. See Regs. § 1.404(a)-12(b)(1).

84. Code § 404(a)(5); see Regs. § 1.40(a)-12(b)(1).

85. Code § 83(h).

CHAPTER 2

Administering an Employee Stock Option Plan

Mark A. Borges

In recent years, stock options have become the most popular non-cash means for compensating employees. While many corporations have historically granted stock options to their senior management as an integral component of their executive compensation programs, a growing number of companies now grant stock options at various levels within the organization. Moreover, broad-based employee stock option programs that award stock options to all or substantially all employees, long used by smaller businesses, are now being adopted by larger corporations as well.

Befitting their popularity, employee stock options are also one of the most comprehensively regulated forms of equity compensation. A multitude of complex and, at times, confusing tax, corporate, and securities laws affect the adoption, implementation, operation, and administration of employee stock option plans. These laws are supplemented by an array of other provisions, ranging from the detailed requirements of the national securities exchanges to the general common-law principles of contracts. While the terms and conditions of individual employee stock option programs vary from company to company, the characteristics of all employee stock options are heavily influenced by the various rules that govern their use.

The laws, regulations, and other principles governing employee stock options are well-documented elsewhere. Less understood are the administrative considerations that arise in maintaining an employee stock option program. This chapter discusses the more common administrative aspects of employee stock options.

Establishing the Plan

When a company decides to implement an employee stock option program, management will typically arrange for the preparation of an appropriate plan document. Typically, the plan's structure, as well as its specific terms and conditions, will be determined in consultation with the company's legal counsel, accountants, and outside compensation or benefits specialists. Factors taken into consideration in designing the plan will include the cost to the

company and to proposed participants, the potential liquidity for participants, and the income tax and financial accounting consequences arising
from the operation of the plan.

Most plans allow for the grant of both nonqualified stock options and
incentive stock options. This permits flexibility in granting appropriate options to selected employees, while effectively limiting the total number of
shares of stock available for granting under the stock option program. (The
rules governing incentive stock options stipulate that the stock option plan
must state the maximum number of shares of stock available for grant under
the plan.) Generally, the company's legal counsel will prepare the plan documents. Once management has approved the stock option program, it will be
presented to the company's board of directors for consideration and adoption. Because under the corporate laws of most states, the board has the responsibility for all issuances of the company's stock, board approval is generally required before the implementation of an employee stock option plan.

Following adoption by the board of directors, an employee stock option
plan is customarily submitted to the company's shareholders for approval.
Shareholder approval may be a requirement under state corporate law, the
company's charter documents, or the rules of the stock exchange on which
the company's securities are traded (if the company's stock is traded on a
national exchange) or listed (if the company's stock is traded over the counter).
Even where shareholder approval is not required, there may be distinct advantages to obtaining shareholder approval of the stock option plan. The
preferential tax treatment afforded by the Internal Revenue Code (the "Code")
to incentive stock options is available only if the plan has been approved by
the company's shareholders. In addition, the exclusion from the deduction
limit of section 162(m) of the Code for "performance-based" compensation
requires that a compensation plan or arrangement be approved by shareholders. In addition, compliance with certain provisions of the federal securities laws may be made easier if the stock option plan has been approved by
shareholders.

Granting Options

Policies and Procedures

Many companies establish formal policies and procedures to facilitate the
efficient administration of their employee stock option plans. Formal policies enhance the plan administrator's ability to operate the plan consistent
with the company's objectives for the stock option program. They also enable
the plan administrator to resolve problems arising during the administration
of the plan. Formal guidelines for processing stock option grants can serve
as an effective means for ensuring that all company procedures are properly
followed.

A comprehensive stock option plan policy should address:

- How option recipients are to be determined.
- How the size of stock option grants (number of shares) are to be determined.
- Which type of stock options to grant: incentive stock options (ISOs) or nonqualified stock options (NSOs).
- How often stock options are to be granted.
- How the vesting schedule is to be determined.
- How stock option grants are handled in special situations.

A written procedure should address the following:

- The company's internal approval process.
- The grant transaction recordation.
- The grant agreement preparation and completion process.
- Inter-departmental communications.

Plan Participation

Under an employee stock option plan, both the selection of recipients and the timing of grants are typically reserved to the discretion of the board of directors. Companies use a wide variety of different approaches and policies for determining which employees should receive stock options. In some instances, only members of senior management are eligible to receive stock options. Other companies will grant stock options to all managers. Still other companies grant stock options to all employees, regardless of their job descriptions.

Some companies grant stock options to all newly hired employees, while others grant options only to employees who have completed a specified term of service with the company. Stock options are frequently used as a form of merit bonus, in combination with or in lieu of a salary increase or in conjunction with a promotion. It is not uncommon for a company to make periodic (for example, annual) uniform stock option grants to all employees.

Number of Shares Granted

Under an employee stock option plan, the number of shares of stock to be granted under option to each employee is typically determined by the board of directors. Companies use a wide variety of different approaches and/or policies for determining the size of a stock option grant. Typically, a company will establish guidelines for determining the number of shares of stock to be granted in each stock option. The number of shares of stock may be determined on an employee-by-employee basis, by job classification, or based on the company's overall performance over a specified period of time. The number of shares of stock may also be determined as a percentage of the employee's annual salary.

Internal Approval Process

In order to grant stock options, generally a company will find it beneficial to establish internal approval procedures. The exact nature of these procedures will vary from company to company. In any event, the procedures should address such matters as who will be recommended for a stock option grant, what the size of the grant will be, and whether any special terms and conditions will be incorporated into the grant. These decisions are usually made by the human resources department and/or other benefits personnel, possibly with input from various management-level employees. For example, in the case of newly hired employees, the hiring manager may provide the first level of stock option grant approval. For merit grants, an employee's direct supervisor may provide the stock option grant recommendation.

Next, all grants, regardless of origin, will be incorporated into a formal proposal to be submitted to the company's board of directors for review and approval. If the board of directors has delegated responsibility for stock option grants to a subcommittee of the board, such as a stock option committee or the compensation committee, the recommendations will be considered and approved. Alternatively, the committee may make its own recommendations, which will be submitted to the full board for review and final approval. Stock option grants generally become effective as of the date of board action.

Grant Agreement

Most companies document a stock option grant by preparing a grant agreement. The grant agreement for a stock option is a written document that specifies the terms and conditions of the stock option grant. The grant agreement typically contains the following:

- The correct name of the employee (the "optionee").
- The effective date of the stock option grant.
- The type of stock option (ISO or NSO).
- The number of shares of stock covered by the option.
- The option price.
- The vesting schedule for the shares that the option covers.
- The expiration date of the stock option.

In addition, the agreement usually sets out the procedures the optionee must observe to exercise the stock option, the permissible forms of payment of the option price, and other related matters. Since the agreement usually will also set out the obligations of the optionee in connection with the receipt and/or exercise of the stock option as well as any restrictions imposed on the option or the option shares, most companies require that the optionee sign the grant agreement. A company should set a time limit within which an optionee must sign and return the grant agreement; the company should address whether there is to be a penalty for failure to return an executed agreement.

When the grant of the stock option is formally approved, multiple copies (at least two) of the grant agreement usually will be given to the employee for signature. One copy is to be retained by the employee for his or her records. The plan administrator should include a copy in the employee's file, and, if desired, a third copy should be sent to the company's legal counsel.

Other documents may be distributed along with the grant agreement. A copy of the stock option plan, a summary thereof, or a plan "prospectus" is usually provided to the employee. This may be required by federal and/or state securities laws. Additionally, it may be helpful to distribute such items as a form of stock option exercise notice, an escrow agreement (if appropriate), and a question-and-answer memorandum or fact sheet that answers the most frequently asked questions about stock options and contains instructions on exercise procedures.

Vesting

Generally, an employee earns the right to exercise his or her stock option and purchase the option shares over a specified period of time. (Occasionally, a company will permit an employee to exercise his or her stock option at any time after the date of grant, subject to a right of repurchase in favor of the company should the employee leave the company before a specified date.) The process of earning the option shares is commonly referred to as "vesting." The vesting period set forth in the grant agreement is commonly referred to as the "vesting schedule."

Stock options typically are not exercisable immediately upon grant, but become exercisable either in one lump sum after a specified period of time or in cumulative increments. Generally, a vesting schedule will provide that at the completion of designated intervals, a predetermined percentage or ratio of the option shares are earned and become available for purchase by the employee. These interim dates are called "vesting dates." Typically, vesting is measured from the date a stock option is granted; however, some companies measure vesting from the date the employee was hired or commenced providing services to the company.

A company will adopt a vesting schedule that best suits the incentive or other objectives of its stock option plan. Many stock option plans provide for annual vesting schedules; that is, the option shares will vest in equal annual installments over a period of several years (typically, three, four, or five years). In certain parts of the U.S., daily, monthly, or quarterly vesting schedules are used. Occasionally, option shares will vest upon the achievement of specified company performance goals, such as earnings-per-share, revenue, or profitability targets.

Term

When a stock option is granted, the grant agreement will specify the date the right to purchase the option shares will expire. This period of time within which the stock option must be exercised is referred to as the "option term." Typically, stock option terms range between five to ten years from the date the option is granted. Occasionally, the expiration date of a stock option will be measured from the date the option shares vest. Once the stock option term has expired, the employee may no longer purchase the option shares.

In the case of an incentive stock option, the maximum permitted option term is ten years. If the employee owns stock possessing more than 10% of the total combined voting power of all classes of the company's outstanding stock, the maximum permitted option term for an ISO is five years.

Special Situations

From time to time, procedural questions may arise in connection with a stock option grant, such as how fractional shares of stock are to be allocated under the vesting schedule for the option. Most companies do not wish to show fractional shares vesting on a vesting date and will either drop or round the fractional amount. If the fraction is dropped, it is merely allocated to a later vesting period until the aggregate amount equals a whole share. If the fraction is rounded, it is usually rounded to the nearest whole share, and, if rounded down, the fractional amount is allocated to a later period until a whole share can be shown.

Exercising Options

Policies and Procedures

Consistent with the efficient administration of their employee stock option plans, many companies establish formal policies and procedures in connection with the exercise of their employee stock options. Formal guidelines for processing stock option exercises can serve as an effective means for ensuring that all company procedures are properly followed.

A comprehensive stock option plan policy should address:

- When the option shares may be exercised.
- The determination of the exercise date.
- How applicable withholding taxes are to be calculated and collected.
- The different treatment for directors and officers subject to section 16 of the Securities Exchange Act of 1934. (Section 16 regulates the trading of their own companies' securities by key corporate insiders, such as officers and directors, by requiring such insiders to publicly disclose their transactions in their companies' securities and to turn over to their companies any profits realized from "short-swing" trading activities.)
- Permissible exercise methods.
- Exercise limits.

A written procedure should address:

- The required documents for processing the exercise.
- The tasks of the plan administrator.
- Transfer agent communications.
- Broker communications (if applicable).
- Inter-departmental communications.

Exercisability

An employee's right to exercise a stock option will be governed by the terms of the grant agreement. Where the stock option is exercisable only as the option shares vest, the employee will be able to exercise the option only on or after the vesting date. Alternatively, where the stock option is exercisable before vesting, the employee will be able to exercise the option at any time during its term. Generally, the date of exercise will be considered to be the date on which the plan administrator receives both an executed stock option exercise notice and payment of the total option exercise price for the number of option shares being purchased.

Notice of Exercise

To purchase the shares of stock underlying a stock option, the employee must follow the procedures established by the company for exercising the option. Typically, these procedures will be set forth in the employee's grant agreement. At a minimum, these procedures will require that the employee provide written notice to the company stating his or her intentions.

To exercise a stock option, the employee will complete and sign a stock option exercise notice identifying the stock option being exercised and indicating the number of option shares that the employee intends to purchase. The exercise notice may also indicate how the employee intends to pay for the option shares. Most stock option plans require a written exercise notice as a prerequisite to a valid exercise in order to establish the exercise date and document the employee's intent to exercise.

The stock option exercise notice may also contain other information, such as (1) specific representations and/or statements by the employee deemed necessary by the company to ensure compliance with all required federal and/or state securities laws, (2) information relevant to the form of payment that the employee has selected to pay the total required option exercise price for the number of option shares being purchased, (3) specific statements pertaining to the tax withholding obligations of the employee, if any, arising in connection with the exercise, or (4) specific statements regarding any restrictions and/or conditions imposed on the option shares.

Generally, the stock option exercise notice must be submitted to the plan administrator or other designated representative of the company in person, or by registered or certified mail, return receipt requested, before the expiration date of the stock option, accompanied by full payment of the total required option exercise price for the number of option shares being purchased and any other required documents. Where the optionee is not a local employee, alternate procedures may be in place for the delivery of the stock option exercise notice and payment of the option exercise price (such as by facsimile transmission).

Where the stock option is being exercised by means of a broker's "same-day-sale" exercise (see below), additional documents may have to be executed by the employee in order to complete the transaction.

Once the exercise notice is received by the plan administrator, receipt should be acknowledged to the employee. This is usually accomplished by having the plan administrator sign the bottom of the exercise notice and return a copy to the employee.

Methods of Payment

An employee stock option plan may provide for a variety of methods for exercising a stock option—that is, for paying the purchase price for the option shares. These payment methods include cash (usually in the form of a check), stock swaps, brokers' "same-day sales," and use of a promissory note. Some plans also permit the delivery of already-owned shares of stock or the withholding of option shares from the stock option exercise to satisfy the withholding tax obligation arising from the exercise. Company policy should set out the methods available to the employee and the relevant guidelines for each.

Cash Exercises   The most commonly used form of payment for a stock option exercise is cash. At the time of exercise, the employee is required to remit the total required option exercise price for the option shares being purchased plus any withholding taxes due to the company. Generally, payment will be made in the form of a check made payable to the company. The company should decide whether a cashiers' check is required for payment or whether a personal check is acceptable, whether separate checks are required for the total option exercise price and the taxes due, and the permissible time period for remitting payment.

Stock Swaps When an employee elects to exercise a stock option by means of a stock swap, he or she is surrendering already-owned shares of stock to pay the total required option exercise price for the option shares being purchased. The surrendered shares are usually valued at the fair market value of the company's stock on the date of exercise. Typically, the employee will be permitted to engage in a stock swap exercise only if the stock option plan expressly authorizes the delivery of already-owned shares of stock as a permissible payment method. The surrendered shares are either held by the company as treasury shares or retired by the company and revert to the status of authorized but unissued shares.

Directors and officers subject to section 16 of the Securities Exchange Act of 1934 may, if certain requirements have been satisfied, engage in a stock swap without the transaction giving rise to either a "purchase" or "sale" for purposes of the "short-swing profits" recovery provision of section 16(b).

For accounting purposes, the surrender of already-owned shares of stock to pay the total required option exercise price for the exercise of an employee stock option may trigger the recognition of a compensation expense for financial accounting purposes. Under the present accounting standards, where the surrendered shares are not "mature," the stock swap will be considered the functional equivalent of the cash settlement of a stock appreciation right, resulting in variable plan accounting treatment (the compensation expense will be estimated at the time of grant and adjusted in each subsequent accounting period to reflect changes in the fair market value of the company's stock) and ultimately the recognition of an expense equal to the difference between the option exercise price and the fair market value of the company's stock on the date of exercise. For shares of stock to be considered "mature," the shares must have been held by the employee for at least six months before the date of exercise. Because of this accounting position, most companies prohibit employees from engaging in "pyramid" exercises. A "pyramid" exercise is a form of stock swap in which an employee uses the unrealized appreciation in a small number of shares of stock to conduct a series of successive stock swaps to exercise a stock option in full.

Reload Stock Options Some stock option plans provide for the grant of so-called "reload" stock options in connection with stock swap exercises. Essentially, a reload option feature provides that upon a stock swap exercise, the employee will receive an automatic grant of a new stock option at the then-current fair market value of the company's stock for a number of shares of stock equal to the number of already-owned shares surrendered to the company to complete the stock swap exercise.

Brokers' "Same-Day-Sale" Exercises A "same-day-sale" exercise is a means by which an employee can finance the exercise of a stock option by immediately selling through a securities brokerage firm that number of option shares from the stock option being exercised necessary to satisfy the payment of the total required option exercise price for the option shares being purchased plus any withholding taxes due to the company.

Generally to effect a "same-day-sale" transaction, an employee will first contact the plan administrator and indicate his or her decision to exercise a vested stock option. At that time, the employee will be advised of the securities brokerage firm or firms used by the company for these transactions and asked to select a broker (if the employee does not already use one of the brokerage firms included on the company's list). The employee will also complete the required forms for a standard stock option exercise (typically, a stock option exercise notice) and the additional forms necessary for a "same-day-sale" exercise (such as a set of irrevocable instructions to the company, a stock transfer power, a Form W-9, and, if a brokerage account needs to be established, a new account form and/or a margin agreement form).

Once the forms have been completed and the plan administrator has confirmed that the employee does, in fact, have sufficient option shares to cover the proposed transaction, the exercise notice and the irrevocable instructions (which may be integrated into a single document) will be immediately transmitted to the securities brokerage firm. The securities brokerage firm will also be instructed as to how many option shares are to be sold (either just enough to cover the total required option exercise price for the transaction and any associated withholding taxes or some greater number, up to all, of the option shares).

Following the sale, the company is notified of the sale price so that the required withholding taxes, if any, can be calculated. This figure is then transmitted to the securities brokerage firm so that it can divide the sales proceeds between the company and the employee.

Generally, within the settlement period (currently three business days), the securities brokerage firm will remit to the company the portion of the sales proceeds necessary to cover the total required option exercise price for the option shares being purchased and any applicable withholding taxes due to the company. This amount is usually paid by check, by wire transfer, or through a deposit into the company's account at the securities brokerage firm.

Typically, the company will not instruct its transfer agent to deliver a share certificate for the "same-day-sale" to the securities brokerage firm until payment of the option exercise price has been made. Upon receipt of the certificate, the transaction will be completed and the balance of the sale proceeds, less brokerage commissions, is remitted to the employee.

A company may make formal arrangements with one or more securities brokerage firms to facilitate "same-day-sale" exercises. Not only do such arrangements simplify the administration of these programs, they also enable the transactions to be completed more expeditiously. Sometimes referred to as "captive broker" programs, the company will keep the securities brokerage firm or firms updated on outstanding stock options and vested shares, thereby enabling the employee to contact the brokerage firm directly when he or she wants to exercise a stock option. To further simplify the administration of these transactions, some companies will establish an "omnibus" account with one or more securities brokerage firms and transfer a block of shares to the account for the purpose of ensuring that sufficient shares are available to deliver upon the settlement of the sale.

For income tax purposes, it is important for a company to satisfy itself as to when the option exercise is deemed to occur in the context of a "same-day-sale" transaction—either the date that the stock option exercise notice is submitted or the date that payment of the total required option exercise price is received. To the extent that these are different dates, the amount of income realized from the exercise, if any, and the applicable withholding taxes may vary. In addition, the determination may result in a difference between the exercise date and the sale date, thereby resulting in variations between the amount of gain reported by the company and by the securities brokerage firm. Companies employ various techniques to ensure that payment of the option exercise price is received or credited for the employee's benefit on the earliest possible date, such as providing in their stock option plans that delivery of the appropriate paperwork for a "same-day-sale" exercise will be an acceptable payment method or by arranging for immediate payment by, or receipt of a short-term "loan" from, a securities brokerage firm. The resolution of this matter for an individual company generally will be based upon the provisions of the company's stock option plan and/or the grant agreement, as well as by any applicable provisions of state corporate law.

Directors and officers subject to section 16 of the Securities Exchange Act of 1934 may participate in these "same-day-sale" exercise programs. As affiliates of the company, however, they are subject to certain restrictions not imposed on regular employees. For example, such "same-day-sale" exercise transactions may be restricted to the company's trading "window period." In addition, as affiliates, their sales of company stock must be made in compliance with the conditions of Rule 144, the federal securities law resale exemption that imposes certain conditions on any sale of securities by a company's directors and officers.

For accounting purposes, the implementation of a broker's "same-day-sale" exercise program does not result in the recognition of a compensation expense, because the company receives the full option exercise price for the option shares purchased, the company actually issues the shares, and no payment related to the exercise originates with the company.

Use of a Promissory Note   Some companies permit employees to deliver a promissory note to pay the total required option exercise price for the option shares being purchased. Generally, the promissory note will be a full recourse obligation secured by the option shares being purchased or other property acceptable to the company.

If the use of promissory notes is permitted, such arrangements must provide for the payment of at least the minimum amount of interest that is required under the Code. If the interest rate charged is less than the applicable federal rate, the Internal Revenue Service (IRS) will treat a portion of the amount repaid as imputed interest, which may have significant income tax consequences to the employee and the company. The applicable federal rates are published by the IRS monthly.

In addition, if the stock option is intended to be an incentive stock option, failure to provide for adequate interest for the promissory note may jeopardize the tax status of the option. Consequently, the promissory note must meet the interest requirements of section 483 of the Code or interest will be imputed, thereby reducing the principal amount of the promissory note. To the extent that this occurs, the amount deemed paid for the option shares will be less than the fair market value of the company's stock on the date of grant. Because less than fair market value will be deemed paid for the shares, incentive stock option treatment will not be available.

Withholding Taxes

Upon the exercise of a nonqualified stock option, the company is obligated to withhold federal income tax from the optionee (if an employee) and, if the optionee is a resident of a state with an income tax, to withhold state income tax as well. In addition, withholding will be required for purposes of the Medicare insurance portion of the Federal Insurance Contributions Act (FICA) and may be required for purposes of the Social Security portion of FICA to the extent that the employee has not already satisfied his or her annual obligation.

Where the optionee is an employee of the company, arrangements must be made to satisfy any withholding tax obligations that arise in connection with the exercise. If the optionee is a local employee, generally any withholding tax payment due should accompany delivery of the stock option exercise notice. If the optionee is not a local employee, generally the date of exercise will be considered to be the date on which an executed stock option exercise notice is received by the company via facsimile transmission and/or funds representing the total required option exercise price for the number of option shares being purchased are wired to the company. The original exercise notice is then mailed to the company along with the necessary withholding tax payment, if applicable.

Where not addressed in the stock option plan or the grant agreement, the company may adopt a formal policy establishing the date on and price at which any applicable income and withholding taxes will be calculated. In accordance with section 83 of the Code, the applicable taxes will be calculated based on the fair market value of the company's stock on the exercise date. If the amount of withholding taxes due cannot be calculated in advance, the policy usually states the time period within which the withholding tax payment must be received by the company. Frequently, a company will hold the certificate for the option shares purchased until full payment of all amounts due is received.

Trading Shares for Taxes

Some companies allow their employees to pay the withholding taxes due in connection with the exercise of a stock option by electing to have a portion of the option shares withheld from the exercise transaction. The number of option shares withheld is usually calculated based on the fair market value of the company's stock on the date of exercise. The employee receives only the net shares (after taking account of the withholding) from the exercise of the stock option.

Exercise Restrictions

To control administrative costs, the company may adopt a formal policy establishing a minimum number of option shares that must be exercised at any one time. This may be especially important if the company's vesting schedule contemplates frequent vesting dates (such as monthly vesting). For example, company policy may restrict the exercise of fewer than 100 option shares at a time unless the balance of the shares remaining in the grant are fewer than the minimum exercise amount.

Exercise of Unvested Shares

As previously described, some companies permit employees to exercise stock options before the date that the option shares vest. These unvested option shares will be subject to a right of repurchase in favor of the company in the event the employee terminates his or her employment before the vesting date. This right of repurchase expires either all at once or as to incremental portions of the option shares over the vesting period. When an exercise for unvested option shares occurs, typically the shares will be issued in the name of the employee and then held in escrow until they vest. The option shares cannot be sold while they are held in escrow, nor can they be used as collateral for loans. Consequently, the employee will usually execute and deliver to the company a form of joint escrow agreement or escrow instructions when exercising a stock option for unvested shares.

The unvested share repurchase right held by the company will be exercisable only upon the termination of employment of the employee and then only to the extent of any shares of stock previously acquired by the employee that remain unvested on the date of termination. Typically, the grant agreement will specify the rights and obligations of the company and the employee under this repurchase right.

Since a right of repurchase on unvested option shares renders the shares nontransferable and is considered to be a "substantial risk of forfeiture," the employee is normally not subject to taxation in connection with the purchase of the option shares until the shares vest. The employee may elect to close the compensatory element of the purchase and accelerate the time at which gain will be realized (and at which taxes, if any, will be paid) to the date of exercise by filing a section 83(b) election with the IRS.

Confirmation of Exercise

After processing the exercise, generally the plan administrator will confirm the transaction by sending a written notice to the employee. In the case of an exercise of an incentive stock option, this notification is required by section 6039 of the Code. The notification must include the following:

- The name, address, and identification number of the employer company.
- The name, address, and identification number of the employee purchasing the option shares.
- The date of grant.
- The date of exercise.
- The fair market value of the company's stock on the date of exercise.
- The number of option shares exercised.
- The type of stock option exercised.
- The total cost of the shares exercised.

In addition, this notification should be kept on file by the plan administrator, and one copy should be submitted to the accounting department along with the payment received for the total option exercise price. If the exercise of the stock option requires the withholding of income and/or employment taxes, a copy of the notification should also be provided to the payroll department.

Issuance of Shares

The plan administrator must provide instructions to the company's transfer agent for the preparation and issuance of a certificate for the option shares purchased. The instructions should include the number of shares of stock to be issued, the number of certificates to be issued, the correct name under which the shares are to be registered, and appropriate mailing instructions. Generally, the transfer agent's instructions require the signature of an authorized company representative.

In anticipation of the initial exercise of any stock options, the plan administrator should provide the company's transfer agent with a list of the relevant legends to be placed on the certificates for the option shares. Transfer agents or the company's legal counsel are usually able to assist with the drafting of these legends. Legends may be required by applicable federal and/or state securities laws in order to prevent transfers of the option shares that are not in compliance with such laws. In addition, if the option shares are subject to repurchase rights or transferability restrictions set forth in the stock option plan or imposed by the company, the certificates should be appropriately legended to notify potential purchasers of these restrictions. Some companies legend certificates for incentive stock option shares in order to track disqualifying dispositions.

If the exercise is pursuant to a broker's "same-day-sale" program, the plan administrator must also be in communication with the securities brokerage firm handling the transaction. Before the exercise, confirmation must be obtained that the option shares being purchased are vested. Although actual practice will vary between companies, the employee will typically verify exercisability and then either the employee or the plan administrator will contact the securities brokerage firm to arrange for the option shares to be sold. The securities brokerage firm will open an account for the employee if none currently exists. In addition to the stock option exercise notice, the employee must complete the appropriate documents authorizing the securities brokerage firm to sell all or a portion of the option shares.

Collateral Documents

In addition to the grant agreement, the company may provide several other documents to an employee in connection with the grant and/or exercise of a stock option. For purposes of compliance with applicable federal and/or state securities laws, it is customary for the company to provide each employee with a copy of the company's stock option plan or with a document (often referred to as the plan "prospectus") that summarizes the principal terms and conditions of the plan, describes the tax consequences of participation in the plan, and advises the employee where to obtain additional information about the company and the plan.

Other relevant documents may include a form of stock option exercise notice, memoranda describing the company's exercise procedures, investment representation letters or statements (in the event the option shares have not been registered with the Securities and Exchange Commission), escrow instructions (in the event the option may be exercised for unvested shares of stock), a form of promissory note and security agreement, and the appropriate forms for conducting a broker's "same-day-sale" exercise.

Many companies also prepare and distribute fact sheets and/or question and answer memoranda that address many of the common questions asked by employees concerning their stock option grants.

Other Common Situations

Termination of Employment

A stock option plan usually addresses the treatment for stock options when an optionee terminates his or her employment or otherwise severs his or her relationship with the company. Typically, the optionee will have a specified period of time following termination in which to exercise his or her stock options to the extent of the option shares that have vested (and have not already been purchased) as of the date of termination. The optionee is not normally entitled to purchase option shares that vest after the termination date. This post-termination exercise period ranges in length from 30 to 90 days, depending upon the terms of the company's stock option plan. In the event that the termination of employment resulted from the death or disability of the optionee, the post-termination exercise period is typically extended to 6 or 12 months.

Repurchase of Unvested Shares

If the employee has exercised his or her stock option for unvested shares (which would be possible if the company allows its stock options to be exercised before the date that the option shares vest) and then terminates employment before these option shares have vested, the unvested shares will typically be subject to repurchase by the company.

Generally, the terms and conditions of the company's unvested share repurchase right will be set forth in the grant agreement. The company must notify the employee in writing within a specified period of time (usually 60 to 90 days following termination) of its decision to repurchase some or all of the unvested shares. The decision to repurchase the unvested shares is typically made by the board of directors. The repurchase price will be an amount equal to the original option price paid by the employee for the option shares. This payment will be made in cash or by cancellation of any outstanding indebtedness of the employee to the company. Typically, the company will hold the unvested shares pending vesting. Alternatively, if the option shares have been issued to the employee, payment of the repurchase amount will not take place unless and until the certificate for the unvested shares is delivered to the company.

Restrictions on Transfer

Occasionally, privately held companies impose restrictions on the ability of employees to transfer or dispose of vested option shares following the exercise of a stock option. Typically, the terms and conditions of these restrictions will be set forth in the grant agreement. The restrictions usually terminate when the company's securities become publicly traded.

Leaves of Absence

From time to time, an employee will be permitted to take a leave of absence from his or her position with the company. If the employee holds a stock option granted by the company, the plan administrator will face various questions concerning the status of the option during the leave of absence. For example, the company's stock option plan or the grant agreement may address how vesting will be calculated during the leave of absence. In the absence of an express provision, the company may want to establish a policy regarding whether the employee will receive vesting credit during all or any portion of the leave. Typically, companies will toll the vesting period (that is, suspend vesting) during an approved leave of absence unless vesting credit has been specifically authorized before the commencement of the leave or is required by law. Similarly, the company may want to establish a policy regarding whether the employee will be permitted to exercise his or her stock option while on leave.

For purposes of the "employment" requirement for incentive stock options, the income tax regulations provide that among other things, an employee must at all times during the period beginning with the date of grant of the stock option and ending on the date of exercise (or on the day three months before the date of such exercise) have been an employee of the company granting the option (or a related company). For these purposes, the employment relationship will be treated as continuing intact while the employee is on military, sick leave, or any other bona fide leave of absence if the period of such leave does not exceed 90 days. A leave of absence in excess of 90 days will not disrupt the employment relationship so long as the employee's right to reemployment with the company is guaranteed either by statute or by contract.

If the employee's leave of absence exceeds 90 days, or his or her right to reemployment is not guaranteed either by statute or by contract, the employment relationship will be deemed to have terminated on the 91st day of the leave. Thus, if the employment relationship is considered to have been terminated, the three-month period for preserving ISO status (and preferential tax treatment) will begin running, regardless of the company's determination of the status of the option for contractual purposes (that is, whether or not the post-termination exercise period will be deemed to have commenced). If the option is exercised within three months of the 91st day of the leave of absence, the option will be treated as an incentive stock option. If the option is exercised more than three months after the 91st day of the leave of absence, the option will be treated as a nonqualified stock option for tax purposes.

Although not relevant for income tax purposes, many companies apply the ISO standards regarding employment status to their nonqualified stock options as well. This enables them to determine when an employee's employment is to be considered terminated for purposes of calculating the commencement of the post-termination exercise period.

Capital Adjustments

From time to time, a company may engage in a transaction that changes or affects its capital structure, including its authorized capitalization and its outstanding securities. These transactions include but are not limited to stock splits, reverse stock splits, stock dividends, corporate combinations, recapitalizations or reclassifications of securities, and other changes that increase or decrease the number of outstanding securities that are effected without the receipt of consideration by the company.

Generally, a company's stock option plan will expressly provide for adjustments to be made in the number and class of shares of stock subject to the plan, and to the number of shares, option exercise price, and class of shares of stock subject to outstanding stock options, to ensure that there is no dilution or enlargement of either the number of shares of stock authorized for issuance under the plan or the individual equity interests of optionees as a result of the transaction. These provisions usually grant the board of directors of the company broad latitude to make the necessary adjustments on an equitable basis.

A stock split occurs on a designated "record date." On that date, all the outstanding shares of record will be adjusted according to the split ratio. Grants and exercises of stock options that occur between the record date and the "payable date" must be adjusted to reflect post-split conditions.

Tax Withholding

Federal and state withholding obligations for income and employment tax purposes will arise at the time of exercise (or at the time of vesting, as the case may be) if the optionee is an employee with regard to the compensation income, or "wages," recognized, if any. Relevant withholding taxes include:

- Federal income.
- Social Security.
- Medicare.
- State income (if applicable).
- State disability or unemployment (if applicable).

For federal income tax purposes, the compensation income recognized upon the exercise (or vesting) of a nonqualified stock option is treated as a supplemental wage payment. This payment is eligible for withholding one of two ways. First, the compensation income may be aggregated with the employee's regular salary payment for the period, with withholding computed on the total amount. Alternatively, the compensation income is eligible for withholding at the flat 28% rate for supplemental wage payments.

In addition, employment taxes under FICA and the Federal Unemployment Tax Act (FUTA) may be due. FICA is made up of two separate taxes: (1) old age, survivor, and disability insurance (Social Security) and (2) hospital insurance (Medicare). The Social Security component of FICA (currently assessed at a rate of 6.2%) is collected up to an annual maximum. The Medicare component (currently assessed at a rate of 1.45%) is collected against the employee's total income. The FICA rates and their applicable ceilings, if any, are subject to change annually. The company's payroll department should be contacted for notification as to when these rate changes occur. FICA taxes are imposed on both the employee and the company, while FUTA taxes are levied against the company.

The withholding taxes collected by the company are only an estimate of the employee's ultimate tax liability. It may be necessary for the employee to make additional quarterly tax deposits depending upon his or her personal tax situation (or to remit additional amounts owed when tax returns are filed). The company must furnish an employee (or former employee) exercising a nonqualified stock option with a Form W-2 for the year of exercise (or vesting) reporting the compensation income recognized as "wages." If the optionee is a non-employee, the compensation income is not subject to withholding but must be reported on a Form 1099-MISC for the year of exercise (or vesting).

Most states follow the federal treatment for income tax purposes and may require the withholding of state disability or unemployment taxes. Generally, state taxes are determined on the basis of the employee's state of residence.

Disposition of Option Stock

Income Tax Issues

Upon a sale or other disposition of nonqualified stock option shares, the optionee generally recognizes a capital gain or loss equal to the difference between the optionee's adjusted tax basis in the option shares and the sale price. However, upon a sale or other disposition of incentive stock option shares, preferential tax treatment is available if certain holding periods are satisfied. These holding periods require that the employee not dispose of the option shares within two years from the date the incentive stock option is granted nor within one year from the date the option shares acquired through the exercise are transferred to the employee. The exact time of transfer may be unclear, but it is generally believed that a transfer takes place no later than when the option shares are recorded in the employee's name in the company's stock records.

If an employee sells or otherwise disposes of the option shares within one year after the date of transfer or within two years after the date of grant, the employee is considered to have made a "disqualifying disposition" of the option shares. Consequently, for the year of the disposition, the employee recognizes compensation income equal to the difference, if any, between the option price and the lesser of the fair market value of the company's stock on the date of exercise and the amount realized from the disposition. Any additional gain recognized as a result of the disposition will be treated as capital gain.

When an employee engages in a disqualifying disposition of ISO shares that were acquired before vesting, the amount of compensation income recognized by the employee will be equal to the difference, if any, between the option price and the fair market value of the company's stock on the date of vesting.

Generally, a "disqualifying disposition" occurs when an employee no longer possesses the legal power to control or further dispose of the option shares. Thus, the transfer of option shares acquired upon the exercise of an incentive stock option into "street name" or into joint tenancy (with a right of survivorship) will not be considered to be a disqualifying disposition. Nor will a pledge of the option shares, a transfer from a decedent to an estate, or a transfer by bequest or inheritance. Finally, transfers of the option shares to certain types of trusts will not be considered disqualifying dispositions. In contrast, a sale or exchange of the option shares, a bona fide inter vivos gift of the option shares, or any other transfer of legal title to the option shares will constitute disqualifying dispositions. Similarly, a foreclosure on pledged option shares in the event of a default will constitute a disqualifying disposition.

Where an employee transfers the option shares to his or her non-employee spouse incident to a dissolution of marriage, the transfer is not considered to be a disqualifying disposition. And, under section 424(c)(4) of the Code, the option shares will retain their ISO status in the hands of the non-employee spouse (including the original holding period). Where the non-employee spouse subsequently disposes of the option shares before the ISO holding periods have been satisfied, the transfer will then constitute a disqualifying disposition. The company should establish a procedure with its transfer agent to track all disqualifying dispositions.

Securities Law Restrictions

Requirements of the federal securities laws may limit the ability of an employee to resell shares of stock acquired upon the exercise of an employee stock option.

In the case of option shares that are acquired under an exemption from the registration requirements of the Securities Act of 1933, such shares are considered to be "restricted securities." Generally, restricted securities must be sold in reliance on the federal securities law resale exemption contained in Rule 144.

In the case of option shares that have been registered for resale with the SEC, the shares may be resold by non-affiliates without regard to Rule 144 and by affiliates in reliance on Rule 144 (but without regard to the holding period condition). The securities brokerage firm handling the sale may request company approval, generally of company legal counsel, before completing the transaction.

Conclusion

Administering an employee stock option plan in today's complex regulatory environment can be a challenging proposition. In addition to the tax, securities, and accounting rules that must be observed, a significant number of procedural matters must also be considered. A company adopting a stock option program for its employees will be well-advised to establish formal policies and procedures in order to ensure that all of the applicable legal requirements are satisfied, as well as the administrative aspects of the program. This includes guidelines for disseminating information and materials about awards granted to employees and for processing exercises when optionees elect to convert their awards to stock and, ultimately, to cash. Additional procedures can be implemented for addressing a variety of other common situations that may arise during the term of the plan. If these policies and procedures are implemented and consistently followed, the company can be assured that its employee stock option program will serve its primary objectives and that a high level of employee satisfaction can be achieved.

CHAPTER 3

Valuing Stock Options

Susan E. Thompson
Hewitt Associates LLC

Under standards established in 1995 by the Financial Accounting Standards Board (FASB), companies must establish the current "fair value" of their options when they are granted. This value must be accounted for as a compensation expense either in the company's financial statements or in a footnote to these statements. FASB requires that companies use an option pricing model that takes into consideration six specific variables. The most common option pricing model used by public companies is the Black-Scholes method. This chapter provides a general overview of Black-Scholes.

The basic definition of an option is the right, but not the obligation, to buy or sell an underlying asset at a specified price at a specified time. The underlying asset is typically stock or a commodity such as grain. Commodity options gave birth to the Chicago Board Options Exchange (CBOE) in the early 1970s. An option is essentially a form of price risk insurance, as it allows the option holder to lock in a specified price at relatively low up front-cost. Basic options are primarily used to protect the option holder from downside price risk. In addition, since options contain no obligation, the option holder does not sacrifice gains from favorable price movements. The lock-in price in the option applies only if the option holder exercises the option; the option holder is not obligated to do so.

A put option is an option to sell the underlying asset, while a call option is an option to buy the underlying asset. Standard options have a stated lock-in price (the exercise price) and a stated expiration date. If the option holder does not exercise the option before the expiration date, the option expires worthless. The option may be exercised at the expiration date only (if it is a "European" option) or at any time up to the expiration date (if it is an "American" option). Most options granted to employees are American options, which allow for exercise any time before the expiration date once vested. The Black-Scholes formula develops an accurate price estimate for standard European options and can be modified for estimates of early exercise for American options. In addition, for a security that pays no dividends, the value of American stock options are mathematically equivalent to European stock options.

All options have value. The value of options traded on the CBOE is determined by the efficient market. Buyers and sellers actively bid on option contracts, with actual trades determining the value of the options. The Black-Scholes formula, described in this chapter, estimates the fair market value of stock options that are not traded on an exchange.

The value of the option can be thought of as having two components; the intrinsic value and the time value. The intrinsic value of an option is the difference between the strike price of the option, and the current value of the underlying asset. The strike price, also known as the exercise price, represents the agreed-upon price that the option holder can pay to purchase one share of stock. An option is "in the money" when the exercise price is below the current market price. In this case, the option holder can make money by exercising the option, paying the exercise price for the share of price, and selling the share in the market at the higher current market price. For example, an option to buy a share of IBM with an exercise price of $100 per share is in the money when a share of IBM is trading at $110. In this example, the option has an intrinsic value of $10 per share, because the option holder could exercise the option, pay $100 for a share of IBM, and sell that share for $110 in the current market, for a profit of $10. A call option is in the money, and has positive intrinsic value, whenever the exercise price is below the current market price. A call option is "at the money" ("out of the money"), and has zero (negative) intrinsic value, when the exercise price is equal to (below) the current market price.

Most options have some positive value even if the intrinsic value is zero, as a result of the time value of the option. The time value of the option is determined by the probability that the underlying asset's price (the stock price) will change before the expiration date of the option. For example, if the option exercise price is $100 per share and the current price of IBM is $90, the option has zero intrinsic value (this option is out of the money). However, if the expiration date of the option is one year away, there is some probability that the stock price of IBM will move above $100 by the end of the year. The time value of the option incorporates the amount of time remaining before expiration and the probability that the share price will move above the strike price by the expiration date. Although the value of the option will effectively approach zero as it moves out-of-the-money, the option still has some small value relating to the time value of the option.

The Black-Scholes Option Pricing Formula

Option pricing methods were originally developed in the early 1970s by Fischer Black and Robert Merton of the Massachusetts Institute of Technology and Myron Scholes of the University of Chicago. Their first use was to price the put and call options traded at the newly formed Chicago Board Options Exchange. The Black-Scholes formula was an immediate success in that it was widely adopted by practitioners and option traders as a practical and useful tool for understanding what the price of an option should be.

The Black-Scholes option formula for a call option is as follows:

$$c = Se^{-q(T-t)} N(d_1) - Xe^{-r(T-t)} N(d_2)$$

where:

c	=	value of the call option
S	=	current stock price
X	=	strike price of the option
q	=	expected dividend yield
T-t	=	time to expiration
r	=	expected risk-free rate
N(dx)	=	probability that a random draw from a standard normal distribution is less than dx

The formula incorporates both the intrinsic value and the time value of the option, and determines the option's total market value.

The Black-Scholes formula is based on an underlying differential equation that must be satisfied by the price of any derivative security (option) dependent on an underlying stock. The Black-Scholes equation is dependent on a number of assumptions that relate to the mathematical properties of stock price movements and the concept of arbitrage. However, this formula is the most practical and most accurate tool available today for valuing stock options. In addition, the formula can be modified to incorporate specific characteristics or variations in security design.

The Black-Scholes formula determines the value based on six critical factors:

- The expiration date of the option.
- The strike price of the option.
- The current value of the underlying security.
- The expected future volatility of the underlying security.
- The expected future dividend yield of the security (if any).
- The risk-free rate (represented by the corresponding length to expiration treasury bond).

In simple terms, each of these factors has a corresponding effect on the value of the option. When structuring employee stock options, the company must consider the value to the employee and the effect on the company of variables such as time to expiration and the strike price. The issuance of stock options dilutes, by the value of the options, the value of the shares held by existing shareholders. The option value is closely linked to the difference between the strike price and the fair market value of the stock, if any, at the time of issuance (the intrinsic value of the option). Table 3-1 shows the effect of changes in the underlying variables on the value of a call option, assuming all other variables are constant.

In table 3-2 the value of IBM in year five, $130 per share, was known for certain, so there was only one final payoff that was possible. Valuing options becomes progressively more difficult as the number of potential payoffs increases above one. In reality, for any given security, one could chart an infinite number of potential final payoffs based on an infinite number of possible ending stock prices. The valuation exercise would then require determining the net present value (NPV) of each of those possible payoffs. Then, the probability of each payoff occurring would also have to be estimated and multiplied by the NPV of the payoff. The difficulty in this example, which Black-Scholes solves, is in estimating probabilities for each of the possible payoffs. However, if one could develop an estimate of the probabilities, the sum of the NPVs of each probable payoff (multiplied by its probability) would be the value of the option. Since each payoff is associated with one ending stock price and expiration, you would in essence need to estimate the future distribution of ending stock prices. This is exactly what the Black-Scholes formula does.

TABLE 3-1. *Effect of Changes in Variables on the Value of a Call Option.*

Underlying Variable	Change in Variable	Change in Option Value
Time to expiration	Increases	Increases
Strike price	Increases	Decreases
Current value of security	Increases	Increases
Volatility	Increases	Increases
Dividend yield	Increases	Decreases
Risk-free rate	Increases	Increases

TABLE 3-2. *Payoffs Based on Differing Stock Values.*

Strike Price	Market Value of IBM at expiration	Final Payoff Value of Option*
$100	$ 80	$ 0
$100	$ 90	$ 0
$100	$100	$ 0
$100	$110	$10
$100	$120	$20
$100	$130	$30

* Final payoffs are never negative, as no one would choose to exercise if the payoff would be negative. In those cases, the options expire worthless.

The company can influence the value of the options by changing the first two characteristics (time to expiration and strike price). The performance of the company, as determined by its employees, will determine the fair market value of the underlying stock. Hence, the employees can increase the payoff of their options by increasing the value of the company over the life of the option. As with any equity security, there are a number of external factors, including volatility and risk-free rates, that affect the value of the options as well. Neither the company nor the employees can control these remaining factors (assuming the company remains in the same line of business).

Understanding Value

The simplest way to understand the value of an option is to think about the final payoff. The final payoff of a call option, which occurs at the expiration date (for a European option), is always the fair market value of the stock minus the exercise price. For different values of the stock, the option would have different payoffs. For example, table 3-2 shows a series of payoffs that could occur at expiration based on different stock values.

If you are valuing the option today and these final payoffs occur at some point in the future, each one would have less value in today's dollars as a result of the time value of money. For example, consider the IBM call option with an expiration date of five years and a strike price of $100. If you knew with certainty that the value of an IBM share would be exactly $130 in five years, you would simply discount the $30 final payoff to determine the net present value of the final payoff in today's dollars. Using a discount rate of 7%, the value of the option on a current basis would be $21.39. For any option for which you knew the final payoff, you could determine the value using a simple net present value approach.

Risk-Free Rates and the Black-Scholes Option Pricing Formula

The question that is key to the Black-Scholes formula is: What discount rate should be used to determine the present value of each of those payoffs? Most people unfamiliar with Black-Scholes assume that the equity discount rate for the stock (typically determined through the use of the Capital Asset Pricing Model) would be the most appropriate discount rate. However, the Black-Scholes formula relies on the theory that the risk-free rate (the government treasury rate for the period remaining on the option) is the appropriate discount rate.

Perhaps the most difficult concept to grasp with respect to the Black-Scholes pricing formula is the use and importance of the risk-free rate. As stated above, the intuitive corporate finance response is that the equity discount rate should be used when determining the net present value of the final payoffs. However, the assumption of the lognormal distribution of stock price changes allows the expected return of the individual stock to drop out of the differential equation that is the Black-Scholes formula. The assumption of the lognormal distribution of stock price changes simply means that the Black-Scholes formula assumes that the log of the changes in stock price in each period follows a standard normal distribution. The assumption that the log of the stock price changes follow a standard normal distribution allows one to assign a probability from the standard normal distribution to each possible future payoff. This is the cornerstone of the Black-Scholes formula and is the most difficult theoretical concept for most people to understand.

The key property of the Black-Scholes differential equation is that it does not involve any variables that are affected by the risk preferences of investors. The variable that is generally interpreted as the rate of return on the stock does not appear at all in the equation. All the variables that do appear (listed above) are independent of individual investor risk preferences. As a result of this factor, the equation relies on the assumption that all investors are risk-neutral. This assumption allows for the use of the risk-free rate for both the expected rate of return in the Black-Scholes formula and the implied discount rate on all future potential payoffs of the derivative security. Although this assumption appears to fly in the face of conventional finance theory and wisdom, it turns out that the Black-Scholes formula generates accurate results even when one moves from the implied "risk-free world" of the differential equation to the real world of risk-return choices by investors.

As John C. Hull remarks, "It is important to realize that the risk-neutrality assumption is merely an artificial device for obtaining solutions to the Black-Scholes differential equation. The solutions that are obtained are valid in all worlds—not just those where investors are risk neutral. When we move from a risk-neutral world to a risk-averse world, two things happen. The expected growth rate in the stock price changes and the discount rate that must be used for any payoffs from the derivative security changes. It happens that these two effects always offset each other exactly."

The Black-Scholes formula determines the value of the option by using certain underlying assumptions with respect to the mathematical properties of the infinite number of final payoffs. The Black-Scholes formula relies on the lognormal distribution of stock prices as a basic assumption to predict the distribution of future stock prices and thus the probabilities associated with each possible final payoff. The probabilities derived from the lognormal distributions approximate the risk of each outcome actually occurring. As a result, the formula incorporates a weighting of all the possible outcomes, which inherently incorporates the risk of each outcome. Therefore, the only element left to discount for is the time value of money for each outcome.

Criticisms of Black-Scholes

One criticism of the Black-Scholes formula is that it is sensitive to the expected future volatility of the asset. The expected future volatility is difficult to estimate if the stock has not been publicly traded for at least three years, and even harder to estimate if the stock is closely held. Volatility is a measure of a stock's price change relative to a prior period; it is typically measured as the standard deviation of a sample of price changes, such as the standard deviation for monthly price returns over a five-year period. The volatility factor is important because it determines the breadth of possible future payoffs, and small changes in it can dramatically change the value of the option. The impact of the volatility assumptions, however, decreases (as a percentage of the option value) as the options become more in-the-money, when more of the option value results from intrinsic value. Although the volatility assumption is important and difficult to estimate, reasonable assumptions based on past stock performance or peer group analysis can be used, and a narrow range of value for the options can be determined.

Another criticism of the Black-Scholes formula is that it determines the value of European options, while many employee stock options are American options, which allow early exercise. A related criticism is that many employee stock option programs incorporate a vesting requirement. However, it is important to realize that the Black-Scholes formula can be modified to incorporate these types of structural differences. In fact, FASB Statement 123 has indicated that modifications must be made to reflect the specific nature of each option. Statement 123 requires companies to use the "expected life" of the option for the time to expiration input, rather than the actual expiration date. A good financial analyst could develop an analysis based on typical date of exercise and probability of forfeiture (lack of vesting) for a company to determine a reasonable estimate for the expected life of the options. The analyst would also take into consideration the past history of option grants at the company, the length of the vesting period, and other characteristics of the company or the option that would reasonably affect the life of the option. It is important to realize that although the Black-Scholes formula has some drawbacks, it can be modified appropriately by a qualified financial analyst. As a result, it is a highly flexible, accurate tool which can be widely used by most companies.

For privately held companies, the most difficult factors to estimate in order to use the Black-Scholes are the underlying stock price and the volatility. Many privately held companies that have employee stock options may rely on other methods to determine the value of those options. One such method is the minimum value method, which, as its name indicates, determines the lowest possible value for the options. Although these alternate methods may be simple, it is critical to realize that they do not represent the fair value of the options. In determining either the true cost of compensation to employees or the level of dilution to existing shareholders, these alternate methods systematically underestimate the value of the stock options. Companies would be wise to consider whether the cost of hiring outside advisors to value the company and the options outweighs the cost of underestimating the value of the stock options.

Conclusion

The Black-Scholes formula provides a widely accepted estimate for the value of stock options. The formula incorporates assumptions about the probabilities of the various final payoffs and determines the value of those final payoffs. The volatility of the underlying security and the exercise price are key inputs that affect how likely and how valuable the final payoffs will be. The use of the risk-free rate (implying risk-neutral valuation) is a critical cornerstone of the Black-Scholes formula.

With appropriate modifications, the Black-Scholes formula is the most powerful, most accurate, and easiest-to-use model that currently exists for standard option valuation. Monte Carlo simulation and more complex binomial models further develop the valuation principles in the Black-Scholes formula and provide a refined option valuation tool for more complex option securities. For extremely unique and complicated situations, Monte Carlo simulation can be used to develop a model that incorporates unique features. These models are extensive, highly complex, and can be more time-consuming and costly to implement than Black-Scholes. For most companies valuing employee stock options, the Black-Scholes formula continues to be the tool of choice.

CHAPTER 4

Accounting for Stock-Based Compensation

Alan A. Nadel
Benjamin S. Neuhausen
Gregory M. Kopp
Arthur Andersen LLP

From the time companies started granting stock options to employees, they typically have not been required to include the cost of these benefits in their income statements. Many economists would argue, however, that options do have a cost. When an employee exercises a stock option, the company must make the shares for those options available to the employee. If the company goes out and buys the shares, their price will, by definition, be higher than what the employee will pay for them, imposing a cash cost on the company. If the company satisfies the option by issuing new shares, shareholders bear the costs through dilution. While these costs will not occur until a future date, they arguably have a present value. The previous chapter in this book explores how this can be calculated.

In 1993, the Financial Accounting Standards Board (FASB) proposed that the fair value of these costs be included in a company's income statement. That raised a considerable outcry from companies relying heavily on options as a compensation strategy, because in many cases it would adversely affect their income statements. After much debate and controversy, FASB agreed to recommend that companies include the costs on their income statements, but not require that they do so. Instead, the costs could simply be disclosed in a footnote. This chapter addresses how companies should deal with accounting for stock-based compensation under these rules.

FASB Statement 123

In October 1995, FASB issued Statement No. 123, "Accounting for Stock-Based Compensation," bringing closure to FASB's 11-year project on stock compensation accounting. Statement 123 *requires* all companies to change what they disclose about their employee stock-based compensation plans, *recommends* that they change how they account for these plans (by recognizing their value in the financial statement), and *requires* those companies who do not change their accounting to disclose (in a footnote to the financial statement) what their earnings and earnings per share would have been if their accounting had changed.

Historically, companies have reported stock-based compensation under APB (Accounting Principles Board) Opinion 25 ("APB 25"), which requires companies to measure compensation cost using the "intrinsic value method." In the case of a typical nonqualified stock option, the compensation cost is measured at the time that both the exercise price and the number of shares are fixed and determinable. Thus, in a typical stock option grant, assuming that at the date of grant the exercise price equals the fair market value, this results in a zero compensation charge to the income statement.

These new rules are in response to criticism of the existing rules under APB 25 for producing anomalous results and for measuring the cost of stock options using only the intrinsic value component of fair value. Statement 123 is based on the precept that a stock option grant has an inherent value, i.e., the "fair value method." Thus, the notion is that a stock option grant with an initial intrinsic value of zero (fair market value on the date of grant – exercise price = $0) has a fair value because of its potential, at some point over the life of the option, to be "in the money" and result in stock appreciation for the option holder.

By only recommending, not requiring, that companies change how they account for their employee stock-based compensation plans, FASB has preserved the existing accounting rules. Companies who do not follow FASB's recommendation will thus continue to follow APB 25. Therefore, for fiscal years beginning after December 15, 1995, companies that elect to continue accounting for stock option grants and other equity awards under APB 25 will be required to disclose pro forma net income and earnings per share as if they had implemented Statement 123. Additionally, all companies, whether they follow APB 25 or Statement 123 accounting, will have expanded disclosure requirements.

We anticipate that few companies will elect the recognition requirements of Statement 123 and that the vast majority will continue to report their results using APB 25, thus being responsible for providing the additional footnote disclosures required by Statement 123. Reasons for not electing Statement 123 include:

- *Philosophy.* Some companies simply disagree with FASB's recommended accounting method, e.g., they believe the unique aspects of employee options are not captured by the new methodology.
- *Flexibility.* If a company selects FASB's recommended accounting method and dislikes its results, the company cannot switch back.
- *"All or nothing."* If a company selects FASB's recommended accounting method, it must apply it to all its employee stock-based compensation

arrangements, not just those for which it thinks APB 25 produces anomalous results.

Overview of Statement 123

This chapter is based on an interpretation of Statement 123. Statement 123 permits a company to choose either a new fair value-based method or the current APB 25 intrinsic value-based methodology of accounting for its stock-based compensation arrangements. Statement 123 requires pro forma disclosures of net income and earnings per share computed as if the fair value-based method had been applied in financial statements of companies that continue to follow current practice in accounting for such arrangements under APB 25.

Statement 123 is a comprehensive document that applies to all stock-based employee compensation plans in which an employer grants shares of its stock or other equity instruments to employees, except for employee stock ownership plans (ESOPs). The statement also applies to plans in which the employer incurs liabilities to employees in amounts based on the price of the employer's stock (e.g., stock appreciation rights). Statement 123 also applies to transactions in which a company issues stock options or other equity instruments for services provided by nonemployees, such as consultants and bankers, or to acquire goods or services from outside suppliers or vendors. Companies are required to adopt Statement 123 for nonemployee transactions entered into after December 15, 1995.

A company must apply either the fair value-based method of accounting described in Statement 123 or the intrinsic value-based method of APB 25 in accounting for all of its employee stock-based compensation arrangements. One objective of FASB's stock compensation accounting project was to level the playing field between fixed awards and performance awards. The irony is that APB 25 encourages companies to grant fixed awards, which do not incorporate a performance measure, as this generally results in zero charge to earnings. By contrast, performance-based awards, which, in theory, should be viewed more favorably by shareholders, usually result in variable accounting under APB 25 and a charge to earnings if the price of the stock increases.

The discussion of the fair value-based accounting methodology throughout this chapter applies equally to measuring compensation cost for those companies that adopt the fair value method for accounting purposes, and for companies that continue to report under APB 25 and are required to provide pro forma net income and earnings per share.

Major Provisions

The most significant provision of Statement 123 is FASB's decision to permit companies to disclose the fair value of equity awards through a footnote disclosure rather than to recognize the value in the financial statement; if it were recognized in the financial statement, the companies' reported net income would be adversely affected. The footnote disclosure requirements of the statement, which apply to all companies regardless of the method used to account for stock compensation arrangements, can become very cumbersome. An example of the new disclosure footnote statement is provided below under "Example of a Footnote Disclosure." Other significant provisions of Statement 123 include the following:

- Compensation cost will be recognized (or calculated for the pro forma information) for most stock-based compensation arrangements.

- Stock options and other equity instruments issued to nonemployees and other suppliers of goods or services should be accounted for based on fair value. As stated earlier, companies are required to apply Statement 123 for stock options and other equity instruments issued to nonemployees regardless of whether a company adopts Statement 123 or continues to report under APB 25 for its employee stock-based accounting.

- Compensation cost for all stock-based compensation awards issued to employees is measured on the date of grant except in instances where it is not possible to estimate fair value at grant date, such as when the exercise price of a stock is indexed to the underlying stock price.

- Compensation cost is measured based on the estimated fair value of the equity instruments awarded. The estimated fair value of stock options is measured using a pricing model that considers specified factors. Under APB 25, compensation cost is determined by the intrinsic value at the measurement date.

- Fluctuations in the underlying stock price after the date of grant do not change compensation cost determined at grant date.

- Most existing broad-based employee stock purchase plans (such as Internal Revenue Code section 423 plans) will be compensatory. Only certain plans with a small purchase discount, generally 5% or less, and no option-like features will be treated as noncompensatory.

Example of a Footnote Disclosure

Exhibit 4-1 (see following pages) is a financial statement footnote prepared pursuant to Statement 123. The hypothetical company is a public company that has elected to continue to account for its employee stock-based compensation plans under APB 25. If the company had elected to implement Statement 123, the pro-forma disclosures would not be required.

With respect to the company's transactions with employees, the footnote assumes there were no options granted with exercise prices either above or below the market price of the company's stock, no performance-based plans, and no modifications of previously granted awards. All of these situations require additional disclosures.

Timing

If Statement 123's recommended accounting for employee awards is not adopted, the related disclosure requirements are effective for financial statements for years beginning after December 15, 1995. These disclosures must show what earnings and earnings per share for years beginning after December 15, 1994, would have been had the recommended accounting been applied. For purposes of calculating these pro forma amounts, however, companies are to apply the recommended accounting only to awards made in fiscal years beginning after December 15, 1994. Prior awards should not be included in the calculation unless they are amended after this date. Statement 123's *required* accounting for nonemployee awards is effective for transactions entered into after December 15, 1995.

Implications

The changes required by Statement 123 could affect employers' financial statements in many ways. Companies that historically have provided fixed stock options to employees or have established broad-based plans, such as section 423 stock purchase plans, generally will experience a charge to earnings (either in the financial statements or in the pro forma net income disclosures). The effect on net income (or pro forma net income), whether positive or negative, will be magnified for companies that incorporate stock-based compensation awards as a key component in their compensation programs. Table 4-1 summarizes the differences between APB 25 and Statement 123.

Measurement of Awards

Statement 123 requires compensation cost for all stock-based compensation awards, including most plans currently considered noncompensatory under APB 25 (i.e., broad-based plans), to be measured by a new fair value-based method of accounting.

Currently, under APB 25, compensation cost for fixed and variable stock-based awards is measured by the excess, if any, of the fair market value of the stock underlying the award over the amount the individual is required to pay. This is the intrinsic value concept. Compensation for fixed awards is measured at the grant date, when both the number of shares and the price the holder is required to pay is fixed and definite. The compensation cost for

Exhibit 4-1: Sample Footnote Disclosure

Footnote 1. Summary of Significant Accounting Policies

The Company has elected to account for stock options and other equity awards issued to employees under APB Opinion No. 25.

Footnote 10. Stock-Based Compensation Plans

The Company has two stock option plans, the 1990 Top Executive Plan (the "1990 Plan") and the 1991 Middle Manager Plan (the "1991 Plan"), plus an employee stock purchase plan (the "1994 Plan"). The Company accounts for these plans under APB Opinion No. 25, under which no compensation cost has been recognized. Had compensation cost for these plans been determined consistent with FASB Statement No. 123, the Company's net income and earnings per share (EPS) would have been reduced to the following pro forma amounts:

		1996	1997	1998
Net income:	As Reported	$10,126,400.00	$14,750,400.00	$13,643,800.00
	Pro Forma	7,265,500.00	12,111,300.00	10,226,100.00
Primary EPS:	As Reported	$ .90	$ 1.30	$ 1.23
	Pro Forma	.65	1.07	.93
Fully diluted EPS:	As Reported	$ .84	$ 1.21	$ 1.13
	Pro Forma	.61	1.00	.86

Because the Statement 123 method of accounting has not been applied to options granted before January 1, 1995, the resulting pro forma compensation cost may not be representative of that to be expected in future years. Additionally, the 1996 pro forma amounts include $1,268,500 related to the purchase discount offered under the 1994 Plan, which was subsequently amended. The pro forma cost of the amended plan is zero.

The Company may sell up to 10,000,000 shares of stock to its full-time employees under the 1994 Plan. The Company has sold or will sell 522,000 shares, 710,000 shares, and 811,000 shares in 1996, 1997, and 1998, respectively, and will sell 2,626,000 shares through December 31, 1998. The Company sells shares at 95% (85% in 1996) of the stock's market price at date of purchase. The weighted average fair value of shares sold in 1996 was $27.

The Company may grant options for up to 2,000,000 shares under the 1990 Plan and 5,000,000 shares under the 1991 Plan. The Company has granted options on 1,660,000 shares and 3,775,000 shares, respectively, through December 31, 1998. Under both Plans the option exercise price equals the stock's market price on date of grant. The 1990 and 1991 Plan options vest after three and four years, respectively, and all expire after eight years.

A summary of the status of the Company's two stock option plans on December 31, 1996, 1997, and 1998, and changes during the years then ended is presented in the table and narrative below:

	1996		1997		1998	
	Shares (000's)	Wtd. Avg. Ex. Price	Shares (000's)	Wtd. Avg. Ex. Price	Shares (000's)	Wtd. Avg. Ex. Price
Outstanding at beg. of year	2,505	$20	2,575	$22	2,613	$25
Grant	700	27	720	30	700	33
Exercised	(470)	17	(432)	19	(453)	20
Forfeited	(160)	22	(235)	26	(450)	26
Expired	–		(15)	31	(50)	32
Outstanding at end of year	2,575	22	2,613	25	2,360	27
Exercisable at end of year	930	18	1,088	19	1,060	21
Weighted average fair value of options granted	$8.25		$8.81		$9.95	

925,000 of the 2,360,000 options outstanding at December 31, 1998, have exercise prices between $17 and $25, with a weighted average exercise price of $20 and a weighted average remaining contractual life of 3.3 years. All of these options are exercisable. The remaining 1,435,000 options have exercise prices between $25 and $33, with a weighted average exercise price of $31 and a weighted average remaining contractual life of 6 years. 135,000 of these options are exercisable; their weighted average exercise price is $27.

The fair value of each option grant is estimated on the date of grant using the Black-Scholes option pricing model with the following weighted-average assumptions used for grants in 1996, 1997, and 1998, respectively: risk-free interest rates of 6, 6.7, and 6.4% for the 1990 Plan options and 6.3, 7.0, and 6.9% for the 1991 Plan options; expected dividend yields of 3.5, 3.5, and 3.65%; expected lives of 5.4, 4.9 and 6.1 years for the 1990 Plan options and 5.7, 5 and 5.2 years for the 1991 Plan options; and expected stock price volatility of 30, 33, and 34%.

TABLE 4-1. *Comparison Between Opinion 25 and Statement 123.*

COMPENSATION VEHICLE	OPINION 25	STATEMENT 123
Fixed Stock Options		
Measurement Date	Grant date	Same
Compensation Amount	Excess of quoted or fair market value over exercise price	Estimated fair value at grant date using an accepted option pricing model
Performance-Based Stock Plans		
Measurement Date	Date both the number of shares and share price are known (generally the exercise or settlement date)	Grant date
Compensation Amount	Intrinsic value at measurement date	Estimated fair value at grant date using an accepted option pricing model
Effect of Changes in Stock Price after Grant Date	Final compensation cost based on the ending quoted or fair market value of the stock at the end of the performance period	No effect—the expense is "locked in" at the date of grant
Restricted Stock Plans (No Performance-Based Conditions)		
Measurement Date	Grant date	Same
Compensation Amount	Quoted or fair market value of nonvested shares less amount employee is required to pay	Same

variable awards is estimated until both the number of shares an individual is entitled to receive and the exercise or purchase price are known (the measurement date).

Fair Value of the Consideration Exchanged

The goal in quantifying employee stock-based compensation transactions is to estimate the fair value of the consideration exchanged at the time the transaction occurs.

Current accounting principles require that a stock-based transaction be accounted for based on the fair value of the consideration received or the fair value of the equity instruments issued, whichever is more reliably measurable. For transactions with employees, Statement 123 presumes that the fair

TABLE 4-1 *(continued)*

COMPENSATION VEHICLE	OPINION 25	STATEMENT 123
Employee Stock Purchase Plans		
Compensation Cost	Noncompensatory if plan is broad-based and discount is 15% or less	Noncompensatory if plan is broad-based, discount is 5% or less, and plan has no option features
Plans with Option Feature	Noncompensatory if plan is broad-based	Cost equals fair value of option component
Cash-Only Plans (e.g., SARs and Phantom Plans)		
Measurement Date	Settlement date	Same
Compensation Amount	Cash paid to employee at settlement date	Same
Cash Settlements of Stock-Based Awards		
Employer May Issue Stock or Cash at Its Discretion	Payment of cash upon settlement considered final measure of compensation	Cash paid to repurchase award (not in excess of fair value) charged to equity
Employer Is Obligated to Pay Cash at Employee's Election	Accounted for as a liability with compensation cost determined at date of settlement	Same
Earnings per Share: Calculation of Weighted Average Shares Outstanding		
Primary Earnings per Share	Include all dilutive common stock equivalents outstanding	Include dilutive common stock equivalents expected to vest
	Include all dilutive common stock equivalents outstanding	Same

value of employee services is not readily determinable and thus requires use of the fair value of the equity instruments issued.

The method of determining the fair value of an equity instrument varies by instrument. Fair values of shares of stock come from trading prices or, in the absence of a trading market, appraisals. Fair values of stock options or their equivalents come from option pricing models (e.g., Black-Scholes or binomial models), which incorporate the following six variables:

- Fair market value of the company stock on the date of grant.

- Exercise price of the option.

- Risk-free interest rate (the rate on a treasury strip security maturing in a period of time equal in length to the expected life of the option).

- Expected life of the option. FASB recognized that most options are exercised before the expiration of the contractual option term (typically 10 years). Therefore, FASB permits companies to use a lesser term that will more accurately reflect the expected life of the option until exercise. Typically, the estimate is based on the company's exercise history.

- Expected volatility of the underlying stock (an estimate of the future stock price variability of the stock over a period equal in length to the expected life of the option). The volatility statistic is not required for private companies.

- Expected dividend yield. This should reflect the company's expectation of future dividend yield as a percentage of stock price over a period of time equal to the expected life of the option.

The first three variables are relatively easy to identify, but the last three variables can create a significant challenge to develop. Statement 123 requires that the use of an option pricing model consider management's expectations concerning the life of the option, future dividend yield, and stock price volatility. Both the volatility and the dividend yield components should reflect reasonable expectations commensurate with the expected life of the option. These estimates permit a company to include a subjective element into determining the appropriate variables. However, a company should have support for any and all of its assumptions.

The option pricing models should not consider restrictions on transferability or risk of forfeiture. These two factors will be reflected in the accounting methodology.

The option pricing models are used only to value stock option instruments. Restricted stock awards will be measured using the fair market value of the stock (assuming the stock is publicly traded), or the estimated market price if it is not traded publicly.

Option Pricing Models

The most commonly used methodologies for valuing publicly traded options include the Black-Scholes model and the Cox-Ross-Rubinstein binomial pricing models. Private companies can use the Minimum Value Method, which does not incorporate a stock volatility element. Basically, the Minimum Value Method is a present value methodology.

The Black-Scholes and binomial pricing models are based on complex mathematical formulas. The Black-Scholes model was originally developed for relatively short-lived traded market options or stocks that bear no dividends. The binomial model was developed to encompass a broader variety of conditions.

Effect of the Six Variables on the Option Pricing Values

The impact of each variable on the stock option value (assuming all other variables remain fixed) is as follows:

- *Exercise price of the stock option:* An increase in the exercise price results in a decrease in the value of the stock option.
- *Fair market value of the company stock:* An increase in the fair market value of the stock results in an increased stock option value.
- *Risk-free rate:* An increase in the risk-free rate results in an increase in the stock option value.
- *Expected dividend yield:* An increase in the dividend yield results in a lower stock option value.
- *Expected stock option term:* An increase in the term results in an increase in the stock option value.
- *Expected stock volatility:* An increase in the volatility results in an increase in the stock option value. This variable typically has the greatest impact on changes in the stock option value.

Expected Volatility Volatility is the measure of the amount that a stock's price (including dividends) has fluctuated (historical volatility) or is expected to fluctuate (expected volatility) during a specified period. Volatility is expressed as a percentage; a stock with a volatility of 25% would be expected to have its annual rate of return fall within a range of plus or minus 25 percentage points of its expected rate two-thirds of the time. Because of their greater risk, stocks with high volatility provide option holders with greater economic upside potential and result in higher option values under the Black-Scholes and binomial option pricing models.

Statement 123 suggests that volatility be calculated over the most recent period equal to the expected life of the options. Thus, if the weighted-average expected life of the options is seven years, historical volatility should be calculated for the seven years immediately preceding the option grant. However, under Statement 123, companies are not expected to calculate stock volatility without considering the extent that historical experience reasonably predicts future experience.

To that extent, companies are permitted to exclude events that caused unusual volatility in the historical period if it is remote that this event will occur in the future; some examples are as follows:

- A company whose common stock has only recently been publicly traded with little, if any, historical data on its stock price volatility.

- A company that significantly changes its line of business (e.g., as the result of merger and acquisition activity).

- A company that has been a takeover target and as a result has seen dramatic spikes in the stock price. To the extent this is not "normal" or expected behavior for the future, a company should make an adjustment for this period of stock history.

Expected Dividends The assumption about expected dividends should be based on publicly available information. While standard option pricing models generally call for expected dividend yield, most models may be modified to use an expected dividend amount rather than a yield. If a company uses expected payments, any history of regular increases in dividends should be considered.

Expected Option Lives The expected life of an employee stock option award should be estimated based on reasonable facts and assumptions on the grant date. The following factors should be considered:

- The average length of time similar grants have remained outstanding.
- The vesting period of the grant.
- Expected volatility of the underlying stock.

The expected life must at least include the vesting periods and, in most circumstances, will be less than the contractual life of the option. Additionally, experience indicates that employees tend to exercise options on highly volatile stocks earlier than on stock with low volatility.

Option value increases at a higher rate during the earlier part of an option term. For example, a two-year option is worth less than twice as much as a one-year option if all other assumptions are equal. Generally, the majority of an option value is recognized in the first seven years of the option term. As a result, calculating estimated option values, based on a single weighted-average life that includes widely differing individual lives, may misstate the value of the entire award. Therefore, companies are encouraged to group optionees into relatively homogeneous groups and calculate the related option values based on appropriate weighted-average expectations for each group. For example, if executives at the senior management level tend to hold their options longer than middle management, and nonmanagement employees tend to exercise their options sooner than other plan participants, Statement 123 indicates that it would be appropriate to segment the employees into different bands for purposes of calculating the weighted-average estimated life of the options.

Minimum Value Method

Statement 123 indicates that a private company may estimate the value of its options without consideration of the expected volatility of its stock. This method of estimating an option's value is referred to as the Minimum Value Method, which is a present value concept. Following is an example of a Minimum Value calculation for a private company, assuming a 10-year expected life, a $50 exercise price, a 2% expected dividend yield, and a 7% risk-free rate:

Current Stock Price	$ 50.00
Present Value of Exercise Price	(24.83)
Present Value of Expected Dividends During Option Term	(7.15)
Option Value	$ 18.02

In this example, the present value of the exercise price, $50, discounted at 7% over the life of the option, would yield a value of $24.83. In theory, if an individual invested $24.83 risk-free (i.e., at 7%) for 10 years, the investor would have the amount required to exercise the option at the end of the term ($50). An investor who owned the stock, however, would have received dividends during the term of the option—a present value of $7.15. Therefore, the net benefit of deferring payment of the $50 exercise for 10 years is $18.02. If no dividends were payable, the dividend component would be removed from the equation.

Recognition of Compensation Cost

As previously mentioned, Statement 123 permits a company to choose either the fair value-based method or the current APB 25 intrinsic value-based methodology of accounting for its stock-based compensation arrangements. Statement 123 requires pro forma disclosures of net income and earnings per share computed as if the fair value-based method had been applied in financial statements of companies that continue to follow current practice in accounting for such arrangements under APB 25. Statement 123 applies the same basic accounting principles to all stock-based plans. At the date of grant, compensation cost is measured as the fair value of the total number of awards expected to vest. Changes in stock price after the date of grant do not affect the measurement of the fair value of awards or the related compensation cost.

Awards for past services would be recognized as a cost in the period the award is granted. Compensation expense related to awards for future services are rendered by a charge to compensation cost and a corresponding credit to equity (paid-in capital). Unless otherwise defined, the service period would be considered equivalent to the vesting period. Vesting occurs when the employee's right to receive the award is not contingent upon the performance of additional services or the achievement of a specified target.

Adjustment of Initial Estimates

Measurement of the value of stock options at grant date requires estimates relative to the outcome of service- and performance-related conditions. Statement 123 adopts a grant date approach for stock-based awards with service requirements or performance conditions and specifies that the estimated option value and resulting compensation cost should be adjusted for subsequent changes in the expected or actual outcome of these factors.

A performance requirement adds another condition that must be met for employees to vest in certain awards, in addition to rendering services over a period of years. Compensation cost for these awards should be recognized each period based on the probability that the performance-related conditions will be met. When the award contains performance conditions that adjust the number of equity instruments to be issued under the award, the entity will make its best estimate of the award that will ultimately be issued. If this estimate changes, then the cumulative effect of the adjustment is recorded in the period the change occurs at the original fair value of the award at the grant date.

For awards where the performance condition adjusts the exercise price (e.g., the exercise price decreases based on the company's market share), the company estimates at grant date the fair value of each award using alternative exercise prices. The initial estimate of compensation expense is based on the company's best estimate of the exercise price when the performance period is completed. Again, as either changes in estimates are made or actual experience is known, adjustments to compensation expense are recorded in the period the change occurs. Note that any changes are based on the estimate of fair value of each alternative calculated at the grant date.

If the performance condition is the achievement of a targeted stock price or specified amount of intrinsic value, compensation expense would not be adjusted subsequently for failure to meet the condition. For awards that incorporate such features, compensation cost is recognized for employees who remain in service over the service period, regardless of whether the target stock price or amount of intrinsic value is reached. Statement 123 does indicate, however, that a target stock price condition generally affects the value of such options. Previously recognized compensation cost should not be reversed if a vested employee stock option expires unexercised.

Modifications to Grants

Statement 123 requires that a modification to the terms of an award that increases the award's fair value at the modification date be treated, in substance, as a new award. Additional compensation cost resulting from a modification of a vested award should be recognized immediately for the difference between the fair value of the new award at the modification date and the fair value of the original award immediately before its terms are modified, based on the shorter of its remaining expected life or the expected life of the modified option. For modifications of nonvested options, compensation cost related to the original award not yet recognized must be added to the incremental compensation cost of the new award and recognized over the remainder of the employee's service period.

Exchanges of options or changes in their terms, in conjunction with business combinations, spinoffs, or other equity restructurings, are considered modifications under Statement 123, except for those changes made to reflect the terms of the exchange of shares in a business combination accounted for as a pooling of interests. This represents a change in practice, as such modifications do not typically result in a new measurement date under APB 25, and therefore additional compensation expense is not recorded.

Specific Types of Plans

Tandem Plans and Combination Plans

Employers may have plans that offer employees a choice of receiving either cash or shares of stock in settlement of their stock-based compensation awards. Such plans are considered tandem plans. For example, an employee may be given an award consisting of a stock option and a stock appreciation right under which the employee may demand settlement in either cash or in shares of stock and the election of one option cancels the other. Because the employee has the option to receive cash, this plan would be accounted for as a liability plan whereby total compensation cost is recognized over the service period. The amount of the liability will be adjusted each period to reflect the current stock price. If employees subsequently choose to receive shares of stock rather than receive cash, the liability is settled by issuing stock.

If an employer, at its discretion, may settle an award with a combination of stock and cash, and expects at grant date that settlement will be made in a combination of stock and cash, the plan would be treated as a combination plan. In a combination plan, an estimate would be made of each settlement component and accounted for separately. The stock-based portion would be accounted for as an equity transaction measured at grant date, and the cash portion would be recorded as a liability and adjusted based on fluctuations in the underlying stock price.

Employee Stock Purchase Plans

Some companies offer employees the opportunity to purchase company stock, typically at a discount from market price. If certain conditions are met, the plan may qualify under section 423 of the Internal Revenue Code, which allows employees to defer taxation on the difference between the market price and the discounted purchase price. APB 25 treats employee stock purchase plans that qualify under section 423 as noncompensatory.

Under Statement 123, broad-based employee stock purchase plans are compensatory unless the discount from market price is relatively small and the plan has no option features. Plans that provide a discount of no more than 5% would be considered noncompensatory; discounts over this amount would be considered compensatory under Statement 123 unless the company could justify a higher discount as (1) a reasonable discount in a recurring offer of stock to stockholders, or (2) a reasonable estimate of the per-share amount of stock issuance costs avoided by not having to raise a significant amount of capital in a public offering. If a company cannot provide adequate support for a discount in excess of 5%, then the entire amount of the discount should be treated as compensation cost.

For example, if an employee stock purchase plan provides that employees can purchase the employer's common stock at a price equal to 85% of its market price as of the date of purchase, compensation cost would be based on the entire discount of 15% unless the 5% can be justified under one of the two approaches described in the preceding paragraph. In the U.S., it is unlikely that either approach would support a 15% discount.

Discount from market price is not considered stock-based compensation if an employee stock purchase plan meets all of the following criteria:

- The discount from the market price does not exceed the greater of (1) the per-share public offering costs avoided or (2) the per-share discount that would be reasonable in a recurring stock offering, with discounts of 5% or less automatically deemed to meet these criteria. By contrast, transactions with discounts of up to 15% automatically fit within this safe harbor under APB 25. Discounts this large are unlikely to qualify under Statement 123.

- The company offers the arrangement to substantially all full-time employees who meet certain employment qualifications, and the terms of the participation are equitable. This condition is essentially unchanged from APB 25.

- The equity instruments sold are shares of stock or partnership units but are not in form or in substance options thereon. By contrast, options that are exercisable for up to five years fit within the safe harbor under APB 25. Most existing employee stock purchase plans have one or both of the following option features: (1) a plan that establishes a purchase price for the stock, gives employees a period of time to accumulate funds from payroll withholdings, and then permits employees to proceed with the purchase or receive the cash withheld, or (2) a plan that gives employees the lower of two purchase prices—for example, 85% of the lesser of the market price at the enrollment date or the market price at the purchase date.

Awards Requiring Settlement in Cash

Typically, an employer settles stock options by issuing stock rather than paying cash. However, under certain stock-based plans, an employer may be required to settle the awards in cash. For example, a cash stock appreciation right derives its value from the appreciation in employer stock but is ultimately settled in cash. Such plans include phantom stock plans, cash stock appreciation rights, and cash performance unit awards.

Under APB 25, cash paid to settle a stock-based award is the final measure of compensation cost. The repurchase of stock shortly after exercise of an option is also considered cash paid to settle an earlier award and ultimately determines compensation cost. Statement 123 indicates that awards calling for settlement in stock are considered equity instruments when issued, and their subsequent repurchase for cash would not require an adjustment to compensation cost if the amount paid does not exceed the fair value of the instrument repurchased. Awards calling for settlement in cash (or other assets of the employer) are considered liabilities when issued, and the liability and compensation cost are adjusted every period until final settlement.

Earnings per Share

The goal of including the shares associated with these transactions in earnings per share is to depict the dilution that will occur if all those who could own the shares exercised their options.

The earnings-per-share calculation typically includes shares under option in earnings per share on less than a one-for-one basis due to the earnings-per-share calculation's use of the "treasury stock method." The treasury stock method assumes that the options are exercised at the beginning of the year (or date of issue if later) and that the proceeds from the exercise of options and warrants are used to purchase common stock for the treasury.

Thus, only the excess of the shares issuable upon exercise over the hypothetical treasury shares that could be purchased is added to shares outstanding. Although this earnings per share methodology has not been changed by Statement 123, the interaction of Statement 123's provisions with this methodology yield, all other things being equal, a different number of incremental shares, for three reasons:

- First, every dollar of compensation cost (a presumably higher amount under Statement 123) that has yet to be expensed is proceeds used to buy hypothetical treasury shares under the treasury stock method. This results in fewer incremental shares.

- Second, the "windfall" tax benefit, which also is treated as proceeds used to buy treasury shares under the treasury stock method, usually will be smaller under Statement 123. With higher compensation amounts, less of the tax benefit is extra or a "windfall." This results in more incremental shares.

- Third, if a company elects to estimate forfeitures from the time the awards are granted, then for primary earnings per share the incremental shares are based on the assumed exercise of only the options expected to be earned. This results in fewer incremental shares for primary earnings per share. Fully diluted earnings per share continue to be computed based on all options outstanding. Under the FASB exposure draft on earnings per share, the primary per-share computation will be eliminated; only basic and diluted earnings per share will be calculated.

Disclosures

Statement 123 supersedes the disclosure requirements under APB 25 and requires disclosure of the following information by employers with one or more stock-based compensation plans, regardless of whether a company has elected the recognition provisions or retained accounting under APB 25:

- A description of the method used to account for all stock-based employee compensation arrangements in the company's summary of significant accounting policies.

- A description of the plans, including the general terms of awards under the plans—such as vesting requirements, the maximum term of options granted, and the number of shares authorized for grants of options or other equity instruments.

- For each year for which an income statement is presented:
  - The number and weighted-average exercise prices of options for each of the following groups of options: those outstanding at the beginning and end of the year; those exercisable at the end of the year; and those options granted, exercised, forfeited, or expired during the year.
  - The weighted-average grant date fair value of options granted during the year. If the exercise prices of some options differ from the market price of the stock on the grant date, weighted-average exercise prices and fair values of options would be disclosed separately for options whose exercise price equals, exceeds, or is less than the market price of the stock on the date of grant.

‣ The number and weighted-average grant-date fair value of equity instruments other than options (e.g., shares of nonvested stock) granted during the year.

‣ A description of the method and significant assumptions used to estimate the fair values of options, including the weighted-average risk-free interest rate, expected life, expected volatility, and expected dividends.

‣ Total compensation cost recognized in income for stock-based compensation awards.

‣ The terms of significant modifications to outstanding awards.

In addition to the disclosures described above, companies that continue to apply the provisions of APB 25 should disclose the following for each year an income statement is presented:

• The pro forma net income and, for public entities, the pro forma earnings per share, as if the fair value-based accounting method prescribed by Statement 123 had been used to account for stock-based compensation cost.

• Those pro forma amounts should reflect the difference between compensation cost, if any, included in net income in accordance with APB 25 and the related cost measured by the fair value-based method, as well as additional tax effects, if any, that would have been recognized in the income statement if the fair value-based method had been used. The required pro forma amounts should reflect no other adjustments to reported net income or earnings per share.

For the latest balance sheet date presented:

• The range of exercise prices, as well as the weighted average exercise price.
• The weighted average contractual life.
• When the range of exercise prices is wide (the highest exceeds the lowest by 150%), segregate the ranges in meaningful categories and disclose for each range:
  ‣ The number, weighted-average exercise price, and weighted-average remaining contractual life of the options outstanding.
  ‣ The number and weighted-average exercise price of options currently exercisable.

Conclusion

Initially, we do not expect that many companies will elect to implement Statement 123. The vast majority of companies will continue to report their stock-based compensation programs under APB 25 and, in the case of stock options (assuming certain criteria are met) will not be required to recognize any compensation cost for the stock options in the financial statements. These companies will be required, however, to provide the "cost" in the footnote statement by indicating what the cost would have been if the company had adopted Statement 123.

Additionally, all companies, regardless of accounting method, will be required to provide additional footnote disclosures on existing programs and awards. Companies should continue to review the impact of Statement 123 on their stock-based compensation programs. There may be planning opportunities, particularly for companies with performance-based incentive stock awards.

Other Issues

In March 1997, FASB announced that it would change accounting standards for the way companies calculate net earnings per share. The new rules are effective December 15, 1997. The rules will have a particular impact on companies with stock options. Under current rules, companies report "primary" earnings per share. In other words, options, warrants, and other convertible securities are counted as outstanding shares. Under the new procedures, companies will instead report "basic" earnings per share, excluding these securities. By reducing the number of shares in the denominator of the earnings per share calculation, the resulting ratio will be larger, all other things being equal.

The FASB rules also change fully diluted earnings reporting procedures. Under current rules, these include the fully diluted effects of options, warrants, and other convertible securities. To determine the value of stock options, companies currently calculate the value of options using the greater of the average price during the quarter or the price on the last day of the quarter being reported. Under the new rules, the average price during the quarter will be used. This would potentially mean a higher price/earnings ratio in a rising market.

Addendum: Anticipated Changes to APB Opinion No. 25

This chapter was originally written in 1996 following the issuance of FASB 123 to discuss its impact on stock-based compensation accounting. The purpose of this addendum is to address the implications of FASB 123 since its issuance in October 1995 and to provide an update on pending changes in APB Opinion No. 25 ("APB 25").

As discussed in the main body of this chapter, FASB 123 was issued in response to conflicting opinions as to whether APB 25 provided a valid methodology for stock option accounting. It was expected that FASB 123 would supersede APB 25. As we know, the resulting conclusion was a compromise. Companies are not required to adopt FASB 123. Companies may continue to report their financial statements using APB 25 (thus preserving the ability to grant stock options which, if structured properly, will result in no compensation expense), but must disclose the impact of FASB 123 in their annual report footnote disclosures. In the alternative, companies may adopt FASB 123 and implement the "fair value" method to determine the compensation expense that will be recognized on a company's financial statement. As we suspected, most companies are unwilling to permanently forego the opportunity of granting stock options with no earnings impact. Therefore, it is not surprising that only a handful of companies have adopted FASB 123.

FASB Issues APB 25 Exposure Draft

Because the vast majority of companies continue to use APB 25 to account for stock-based compensation, FASB was forced to address the diversities in practice that have arisen from the ambiguities of APB 25. In response, on March 31, 1999, FASB issued the APB 25 Exposure Draft (the "Exposure Draft") entitled "Accounting for Certain Transactions Involving Stock Compensation—An Interpretation of APB Opinion No. 25." The Exposure Draft was prepared in a question-and-answer format and addresses the following issues:

- Whether APB 25 applies to stock-based compensation granted to independent contractors or independent members of an entity's board of directors.

- Whether APB 25 applies to stock of an entity other than the employer granted as compensation to an employee (for example, parent-company stock granted to an employee of a subsidiary).

- Whether a plan with a look-back option can qualify as a noncompensatory plan.

- When a new measurement date is required for a modification to the terms of a stock option or award other than those specifically addressed in APB 25.

- How to account for a change to the exercise price or the number of shares of a stock option that was being accounted for as a fixed award (that is, option repricing).

- How to account for an exchange of employee stock options in a business combination.

Comment Period

Following the issuance of the Exposure Draft, FASB provided a 90-day comment period that closed on June 30, 1999. The purpose of the comment

period was to gauge the business community's perceptions of the preliminary positions taken by FASB. Over 150 responses were received. As of October 1999, FASB had addressed two-thirds of the responses. FASB is expected to issue its final interpretation of the Exposure Draft in the first quarter
of 2000.

Based on discussions with FASB, we find it likely that several of their
initial positions will be modified or reversed. In particular, two issues seem
to have drawn the most attention from the business community: (1) awards
to outside directors and (2) repriced stock options.

Awards to Outside Directors

The Exposure Draft proposes that awards to outside directors would not be
accounted for under APB 25. Companies would be required to use the "fair
value" method to determine the compensation expense of awards granted to
outside directors, which would be recognized in a company's financial statements.

The proposed approach is a departure from the current practice, in which
the general practice is to account for awards granted to outside directors using
APB 25, which, in the case of stock options, typically results in no compensation expense. The suggested modification to current practice has generated
significant criticism. Critics argue that although outside directors are not
employees of a company, they do have a fiduciary responsibility to represent
shareholder interests by overseeing general operations of a company. Accordingly, their role is more similar to that of an employee rather than that
of an independent contractor. Therefore, a company should be able to use
the same accounting methods for awards to its employees and outside directors. FASB has deliberated this point, and it appears that FASB will reverse its
position and support the position that companies may account for awards to
outside directors under APB 25.

Stock Option Repricing

Stock option repricing has been a long-debated practice. Stock option repricing occurs when a company reduces the exercise price on an option because
of a precipitous decline in stock price. The perception is that an option that
is significantly underwater loses its ability to retain and motivate employees.
Repricing the stock option is one approach used by companies to mitigate the
perceived reduced benefits of an underwater stock option.

The Exposure Draft requires a company to account for a repriced option
as a variable stock option award. The company will be required to recognize
compensation expense for increases in the stock price above the reduced
exercise price until the option is exercised. Currently, there is not one established practice to account for stock option repricing. Current practices range

from one to three repricings of the same option before variable award accounting is imposed. With respect to the stock option repricing issue, it is unlikely that FASB will modify its position. Accordingly, it appears that companies will be required to use variable accounting for all repriced stock options.

Conclusion

There are a variety of other issues addressed in the Exposure Draft that are still being deliberated. It is likely that the final interpretation will be significantly different from its "draft" predecessor. Therefore, we recommend that readers obtain a copy of the final interpretation and discuss it with their accounting professionals to understand its impact on current practices and policies. The changes are likely to affect compensation strategies in the future.

For more information or to obtain a copy of the Exposure Draft, visit the FASB Web site at <http://raw.rutgers.edu/raw/fasb/>.

CHAPTER 5

Designing a Broad-Based Stock Option Plan

Corey Rosen
The National Center for Employee Ownership

Many companies seeking to provide broad-based equity compensation to employees are attracted to stock options because within the applicable legal limitations, companies still have considerable discretion as to how to operate their plans. This advantage, however, means that designing these plans can be much more complex than, for instance, designing an employee stock ownership plan (ESOP), where decisions about many issues, such as eligibility and vesting, must occur within a narrow band of requirements. While stock option companies can look to surveys and peers for ideas on how similar companies set up their plans (see, e.g., Ryan Weeden, Ed Carberry, and Scott Rodrick, *Current Practices in Stock Option Plan Design* (Oakland, CA: NCEO, rev. ed. 1999), each company needs to devise a plan that is adapted to its own particular circumstances. This chapter lays out the principal areas where decisions need to be made, suggesting some considerations about how to think about making them. Because every situation is so different, however, it does not attempt to provide any universal guidelines, but rather is a checklist of things to consider.

How Much to Share

The first decision is how much ownership to share. This issue will differ for closely held companies and public companies, so considerations for each kind of company are discussed separately.

Closely Held Companies

The most typical way a decision is made about how much ownership to share in a closely held company is for the current owner or owners to set aside an amount of stock that is within the maximum dilution level with which they are comfortable. This approach can create problems, however.

Typically, once this number is set, a large portion of those shares is either optioned immediately to existing employees or allocated to employees over a certain number of years. The problem with this strategy is that if the company grows faster than anticipated, there are no or relatively few shares left to give to new employees. That can be a severe problem in attracting and retaining good people. It can also create two classes of employees, some with large option grants and some without them, within the company. Moreover, this model often does not create an explicit link between employee effort and the rewards of ownership.

A second approach focuses on what percentage of compensation in the form of options is necessary to attract, retain, and motivate people. While there is no "bright line" dividing point, studies of option and other ownership plans indicate that the median point for the value of ownership to employees is about 1.5 times one year's pay (in real dollars) at the end of 10 years of work and 4 times at the end of 20 years (these numbers are in real dollars and reflect the actual data from employee ownership companies). Based on a recent NCEO survey, typical stock option plans are making annual grants with a face value of the option equal to about 10% to 20% of pay. In other words, if an employee makes $40,000, he or she would get options to buy $4,000 to $8,000 of stock annually. These numbers, of course, will vary considerably from company to company, often depending on the company's competitive labor market conditions, its expectations about growth, its corporate culture, and how well it is doing financially.

Rather than thinking about "how much" in terms of a total percentage of company shares or total compensation, it might make sense to use a more dynamic model based on performance. In this approach, the issue for existing owners is not "what percentage of the company do we own," but "how much is what we own worth?" Owners in this model would rather own 10% of a $10 million company than 90% of a $1 million company. Robert Beyster, CEO and founder of Science Applications International Corporation (SAIC), for instance, diluted his ownership to under 10% in the first few years of the company's existence, and to under 2% today, but the company he heads now employs over 30,000 people. Beyster believes that by continually sharing ownership with employees, the company grew much faster than it could have otherwise.

This notion can be made into an explicit plan by telling employees that if the company meets or exceeds certain targets, they will get a percentage of the incremental value created by that performance in the form of options. If the company exceeds its goals, then, by definition, sharing part of the surplus value leaves both the employees and the existing owners better off than they would have been. The targets can be anything—sales, profits, market penetration, and so on—but perhaps the most useful way to create a target is to decide on a "critical number," the particular measurement that most drives the company. In a manufacturing company, it might be output; in an engineering company, it might be billable hours as a percentage of total hours worked. Managers almost always have these critical numbers in their heads.

In the option model proposed here, this number is shared with employees as the goal whose achievement will target an option reward. Deciding how much of the increment to share can then be based on an assessment of what would be motivating to employees, an analysis along the same lines as the percentage of payroll calculations above. For instance, management might set a realistic goal that, if achieved, would provide a level of options consistent with the assumptions used in the percentage of compensation model. Unlike the pure compensation approach, however, what employees actually get could be higher or lower depending on whether performance falls above or below the goal.

Of course, this model is subject to some risk—indeed, every model is. For instance, if things go very well, a company might end up giving out a lot of options; then if things go poorly, very few, meaning new employees will see no ownership. But a fixed approach (x% of outstanding shares per year, up to x% of total shares available overall, or the gradual division of shares up to a maximum percentage, for instance) also has risks associated with unexpected growth or decline. The benefit of the model proposed here is that the risk are at least tied to specific measures of performance and the amount provided adjusts with the success or difficulties of the company.

This model will not work on its own for every company, however. In some labor markets, it may be necessary to *always* provide a certain amount of ownership, at least to some employees. Data on industry practices can be obtained from stock option-specific surveys, such as the NCEO's *Current Practices in Stock Option Plan Design*, as well as a number of general compensation analyses available for a fee (the World Wide Web has a number of these sites that compare compensation). These issues apply mostly to more highly compensated employees, however. For the broader sector of the workforce, options may be a benefit either never expected at all or, if they are, expectations about a specific level of rewards will usually not be so defined.

Publicly Traded Companies

Publicly traded companies face many of the same design issues as their closely held counterparts and may want to use some of the same decision guidelines. There are some significant differences in their investor and regulatory market environments, however, that can affect these decisions.

First, investors may object to "overhang" (the potential dilution of outstanding options) levels they view as excessive. For broad-based plans, the NCEO's 1998 stock options survey discussed in *Current Practices in Stock Option Plan Design* found that the average overhang was about 12%, with higher percentages for the information technology sector and lower for manufacturing. These percentages include options available to management and non-management groups; in general, about half the value of the options goes to management. Investors and stock market analysts seem less concerned about dilution resulting from options for rank-and-file employees than they do for dilution from management employees, but, ultimately, it is the total number that matters most. The tolerance for dilution will vary from industry to industry and company to company, depending on such factors as the investors' perceptions of what is necessary to compete in the labor market, how well the stock has performed, whether the company will issue new shares to satisfy the option exercises or will buy back existing shares (thus offsetting the dilution factor), and what impact the outstanding options will have on the company's financials. In any event, a public company will not have the same flexibility that a closely held company has. A Robert Beyster could dilute his ownership dramatically, but if his company had been public, providing the amount of ownership he did to employees would almost certainly have resulted in shareholder desertion, lawsuits, or both.

A second consideration is the growth prospects of public companies. Because they are usually at a more mature stage of their growth cycle, public companies will have more modest expectations about how large a component of compensation options will play than will, for instance, a high-tech startup. Of course, the risk that the options will have no value is lower as well. Because of this risk/reward factor, public companies can usually afford to provide a smaller percentage of their total equity to employees while, on a risk-adjusted basis, providing comparable value. Of course, these issues will vary from company to company.

Finally, because a public company is public, it does not have to worry about issuing options to so many employees that it becomes a de facto public company, a consideration that might cause it to limit the number of option holders it would want to include.

What Kind of Options?

Most broad-based stock option plans use either incentive stock options (ISOs) or nonqualified options (NSOs). (Note that this chapter does not discuss employee stock purchase plans.) A nonqualified stock option is any option that does not satisfy the conditions of the Internal Revenue Code for preferential tax treatment. When an employee exercises a nonqualified stock option, the "spread" on exercise (the difference, if any, between the exercise price of the option and the market price of the stock on the date of exercise) is taxable to the employee as ordinary income, even if the shares are not sold. A corresponding amount is deductible by the company. There is no legally required holding period for the shares after exercise, although the company may impose one. Any subsequent gain or loss on the shares after exercise is taxed as capital gains or losses.

An incentive stock option (ISO) is a stock option that satisfies the conditions of the Internal Revenue Code for preferential tax treatment. Generally, an ISO enables an employee to (1) defer taxation on the option from the date of exercise until the date of sale of the underlying shares and (2) to pay tax at capital gains rates, rather than ordinary income tax rates, on the spread at exercise, provided certain holding requirements are met. To qualify for ISO treatment, several conditions must be met:

- Only employees can qualify for an ISO.

- The employee must hold the stock for at least one year after the exercise date or two years after the grant date, whichever is later.

- Only $100,000 in value of stock options (determined as of the grant date) can first become exercisable in any year.

- The exercise price must be equal to at least 100% of the market price of the company's stock on the date of the grant.

- The option must be granted under a written plan that has been approved by shareholders, that specifies how many shares can be issued under the plan, and that identifies the class of employees eligible to receive the options. Options must be granted within 10 years of the date of the adoption of the plan.

- The option must be exercised within 10 years of the date of the grant.

- The employee cannot own, at the time of the grant, more than 10% of the voting power of all outstanding stock of the company, unless the exercise price is at least 110% of the fair market value of the stock on the date of the grant and the option is not exercisable more than five years from the date of the grant.

The company does not take a tax deduction when the spread on the exercise of an ISO is taxed at capital gains rates. Their appeal, as a result, lies largely in those cases where employees' personal tax rates are much higher than the maximum capital gains rates. Under current laws, that difference can be as high as 19.6% just for federal taxes. If the employee exercises and sells before the required holding periods have been met, the spread on exercise is taxable at ordinary income tax rates, and any capital appreciation on the ISO shares in excess of the market price on exercise of an ISO is taxed at capital gains rates. In this instance, the company may then deduct the spread on exercise.

Stock option plans may provide for only NSOs, only ISOs, or some of both. Most broad-based option plans provide NSOs for rank-and-file employees because few of these employees will be able or want to meet the buy-and-hold conditions of the ISO (most will want to use a form of cashless exercise, as described below, that allows them just to get the spread on the options without having to come up with cash to buy them). Many of those who do want to hold onto the shares, moreover, will not get a large benefit from being able to pay capital gains taxes rather than ordinary income tax rates. Because the employees will not use the benefits of an ISO anyway, companies reason they might as well get the tax benefit of an NSO.

On the other hand, many plans aimed at highly paid employees are ISOs because these employees can greatly benefit from capital gains treatment, and they may demand such options to come to work for or stay with a company.

Some people have argued that companies should structure their plans as ISOs for all employees regardless. Their argument is that if an employee fails to meet the ISO requirements, the tax treatment for the employee and the company defaults to NSO status. So if employees can use the ISO treatment, they get an advantage. Meanwhile, the company does not have to pay payroll taxes (social security and Medicare) or withhold on the spread, regardless of whether the employee gets NSO or ISO treatment. Instead, the spread becomes an item for employees to add into their annual tax returns.

Those opposed to this approach caution that there is no specific law stating that no payroll taxes or withholding are due; rather, the authority is an IRS ruling many people believe will be changed. The ISO approach also puts an added reporting burden on employers, requires more complex administration by the company ("disqualifying dispositions," i.e., dispositions before the end of the one year/two year holding period required for ISOs, must be tracked), and could put some employees into an estimated income tax situation in which, if they do not anticipate the options spreads they will receive, could end up forcing them to pay tax penalties. Note, however, that ISOs could, under some circumstances, trigger the application of the alternative minimum tax for some highly paid employees.

Labor markets and the company's stage of development also are factors in choosing an ISO or NSO. A startup company, for instance, may not be able to hire the talent it needs without offering an ISO, especially if its cash flow makes higher salaries impractical. At the same time, it might not be worried too much about not having a tax deduction, even some years from now, if it foresees plowing all its profits into growth strategies anyway. An established, large company with substantial tax costs and attentive public shareholders, by contrast, may see NSOs as more practical.

Who Is Eligible and Who Will Actually Get Options?

It is first important to distinguish between theoretical and actual eligibility. Many public companies draft their plans so that everyone or most people are eligible, but state that who actually will get options, or whether any options will be granted to certain employee groups at all, is up to management's discretion. In part, this is done to ease approval rules for New York Stock Exchange-listed companies, where such broad eligibility rules exempt a company from Exchange rules for shareholder approval of option plans. In part, companies draft plans this way to maximize their future flexibility. So a company might want to draft very broad eligibility rules into a plan even though it has no current plans to follow through on this approach. For the purposes of this paper, however, we are focusing on plans that are drafted with eligibility rules that are intended to be used in the near future.

In the past, the answer to the question of who is eligible for options was very simple for most companies: just the "key" people. In some ways, this is still how companies view options; it is just that their definition of "key" has changed. For many companies, everyone is a key person. When the reception-ist answers the phone, that person is "the company" to whomever is calling. When the warehouse people fail to ship the right software (designed by all those key technical people), they represent the company to the customers. Moreover, many companies are pushing down more decision making to all levels of the company, asking employees to make business decisions on a regular basis. Management at these companies reasons that if it wants people to think and act like owners, it should make them owners. At the same time, for some companies in some labor markets, it is necessary to provide options at all levels just to attract and retain people.

For companies in these situations, the answer to "who's eligible?" is simple—everyone is. Other companies choose a more complex approach, however. There are several criteria that can be considered in making this decision.

Tenure

At the simplest level, companies can require that people only can get options after they have worked a minimum amount of time, often one year. This assures at least some commitment on the part of the employee to the company.

Full-Time/Part-Time

In the past, it was unusual to provide options to part-time employees. Inno-vators like Starbucks, however, have provided options to everyone, arguing that many of their part-time people would (or if properly rewarded could) be long-term employees. Changes in both the workforce and the nature of some jobs, however, have made part-time workers more an integral and, in some cases, stable part of a company's total employment. Given the high cost of training and recruitment, providing an incentive for part-time people to stay makes sense for them. In making this decision, companies need to con-sider how important it is to retain part-time people, or whether these employ-ees are more seasonal and short-term and thus very unlikely to stay with the company more than a short time under any circumstances.

When Options Will Be Granted

Options can be granted either according to some kind of merit judgment or on the basis of a universal rule, such as allocating options annually; on the date of hire or promotion; or upon the achievement of an individual, group, or corporate objective. These methods are not mutually exclusive; most companies use a combination of these techniques.

A typical merit-based plan would provide work unit managers (or a single manager in a smaller company) with a number of options that can be granted to employees in the group based on a performance appraisal. That appraisal might come from the manager or from an employee peer group. This approach has the advantages of flexibility and providing employees an incentive to perform, but the discretionary and individually based nature of the plan could cause some employees to see it as unfair and arbitrary. Moreover, unless the performance appraisal standards are set very clearly at the outset, employees won't know exactly what they need to do in order to achieve an option award. To resolve this, companies might set individual performance goals for each option period (that could be a set amount of time such as one or two years, or it could be whatever time is needed to achieve the goals). Setting so many personal goals, however, would be a very time-consuming process, and it could end up making employees focus too much on their personal targets at the expense of working collaboratively.

An alternative to individual merit judgments is to provide that a pool of options will be given to a work team on the achievement of their own goals. If the goals are met, the pool could then be divided equally, by salary, by a consensus of the group, at the discretion of the group leader, or according to some other formula.

At the other end of the spectrum is an automatic formula based on compensation, seniority, promotion, or some other work-related, measurable construct. For instance, a number of larger companies, such as Wendy's, provide all employees meeting basic service requirements with 10% of pay every year in stock options. The argument behind these formulas is that compensation reflects management's judgment of an employee's contribution to the company, and options are simply another form of compensation. Employees are more likely to see these plans as at least being equitable, if not necessarily fair (they may think the underlying compensation distribution is unfair).

Providing options on hiring, with additional grants on promotion or periodic refresher grants (commonly called "reload options"), is another common allocation rule. Linking additional option grants to promotion gives employees an incentive to improve their skills and rewards those people the organization believes are making greater contributions. On the other hand, it can lose the attention of employees who may be very good performers but who are not in jobs that can easily lead to a promotion. It is particularly a problem in very flat organizations in which relatively few people get promoted.

Refresher grants give employees additional options when they exercise some of the options they were previously granted. For instance, if an employee has 1,000 options and exercises 200, then he or she would be given new options on another 200 shares at exercise. The objective here is to maintain a constant level of equity interest in the company. Similarly, refresher options might be granted when the company issues additional shares so that an employee maintains the same percentage of potential ownership as was held before the dilution (this feature would be more common for executive plans). While these automatic additional grants help to keep the employee's equity interest high, shareholders might object to the ongoing dilution.

Finally, some companies provide one-time grants, often with an indication that additional grants might be forthcoming. The NCEO's *Current Practices in Stock Option Plan Design* study found that 20% of the broad-based plans used a one-time approach. For instance, a company might announce that all employees were receiving options on 100 shares to celebrate a milestone, such as an anniversary or the achievement of a corporate objective; other companies might announce that employees will get options if a certain objective is met. In most of these cases, management announces that it might provide additional grants in the future, but makes no commitment to do so.

The advantage and the disadvantage of a one-time grant is precisely that it does not commit the company to an ongoing program. This provides more management flexibility and may be less objectionable to shareholders, but it also may be seen by employees more as a reward for past behavior or an idiosyncratic occurrence than an expression of a corporate philosophy that ongoing employee ownership is an important part of the corporate culture. A one-time grant also runs the risk that the options will either never have any value or that they will do exceptionally well. Either way can create distorted perceptions should the company provide additional grants in the future. By contrast, regular grants let employees go through a number of ups and downs and thus educate them to have more realistic expectations.

When Will Employees Be Able to Profit from the Options?

There are two issues in deciding when employees will be able to convert their options into cash: vesting and exercise periods. Vesting provides that an employee accrues an increasing right to the options granted based on the number of years worked. The exercise period allows the employee to exercise a stock option for a defined number of years into the future.

Vesting patterns are fairly consistent across companies, with three- to five-year graduated vesting being the most common schedule. A more difficult decision is whether to provide for immediate vesting upon an event, such as going public or sale. This clearly provides a good benefit for employees, but it may make it more difficult to sell a company or take one public, especially if potential buyers perceive that employees will now have fully vested options that, if they can also then be exercised, may be valuable enough so that some essential employees will just walk away.

In public companies, by far the most common exercise period is 10 years. Some exercise periods are shorter, but they are rarely longer. There is nothing magical about 10 for nonqualified options, but for incentive options, the exercise period cannot exceed 10 years. To simplify plan design, most companies coordinate the exercise periods of their ISOs and NSOs. The more volatile a company's stock, the more important a longer exercise period is so that employees can weather the downturns. Some public companies, however, do not allow employees to exercise their options until a defined event occurs, such as the achievement of a certain stock price or earnings goal. This accomplishes two things. First, it provides an incentive to meet the goal, and second, it reassures investors that option dilution will occur only if the company meets certain targets. Once these targets are met, employees would normally be given a certain amount of time after the event to exercise the options, anywhere from a few months to several years. Alternatively, a company could provide that options can be exercised upon the occurrence of an event or after x number of years pass, whichever comes first, and could continue to be exercised for y number of years into the future after that.

In closely held companies, allowing exercise only upon sale or going public is a very common approach. If a company allows exercise before then, employees end up owning stock and having a tax obligation if their options are NSOs; if they are ISOs, employees have no tax, but are holding shares whose value could decline by the time they actually can sell them. Unless the company can provide a market for the shares (an issue discussed below), this combination may not seem like much of a reward. Consequently, many closely held companies restrict exercise until sale or an initial public offering. This can sound better than it is, however. Few companies actually go public (a few to several hundred per year in strong market years, many fewer in weak years). Finding a buyer is much more likely than doing an IPO, but most closely held companies will not be sold during anyone's foreseeable future. So providing for exercise only on these events should be carefully and realistically considered and other market-making alternatives weighed.

It is also important to consider, as with vesting, that if employees can exercise upon a sale or an IPO, buyers of the stock may not find the company so valuable. A minority of closely held companies are thus now restricting exercise to some time after a sale or an IPO (in a sale situation, this would require the acquiring company to provide options in the new employer).

Finally, the plan design should be specific in its compliance with applicable securities laws and stock exchange rules that can restrict the exercise of options and/or the sale of shares acquired through options by certain employees for a specified period after an IPO.

Providing a Market for the Shares

For publicly traded companies, providing a market for shares obtained through stock option exercises is not an issue, but for employees of closely held companies, it is one of the most important of all design issues. The majority of closely held companies solve the problem by limiting the exercise of options to when the company is sold or goes public. This makes sense for companies who realistically see these alternatives likely to happen in the foreseeable future. Some company leaders who call us, however, assume that they can *only* provide for marketability upon these events because a closely held company, for one reason or another, cannot provide a market itself. These companies at least should be aware of the other alternatives. Moreover, some companies prefer to stay closely held. There are a variety of ways these companies can provide a market.

Purchases by Other Employees

Other employees can purchase the shares directly, although this is not likely to provide enough of a market for all the shares. When an employee purchases shares, the purchase is normally done with after-tax dollars. It can also be subject to securities laws (see the section below for more details). Companies can help employees buy the shares by loaning them the money, although the interest subsidy on loans that are on less than arms-length terms could involve taxation to the employee. A few large closely held companies even provide their own internal stock markets, creating periodic trading days for the buying and selling of shares. This requires establishing in-house broker dealers and complying with complex securities rules in each state where the company does business.

One way employees can purchase shares with pretax dollars is through their 401(k) plans. Shares acquired through options could then be sold to employees in the 401(k) plan who wanted to purchase them. The plan would have to provide that employees can make this choice, which can add expense and complexity to the plan's administration. These purchases would also be subject to the same securities rules as any plan. (Note that employees cannot hold options themselves in the 401(k) plan; Travelers Corporation tried to do this but ultimately was prevented from doing so by government rulings.)

Company Redemption

For a closely held company, the most practical method in most cases is for the company to buy back the shares, either directly or through an ESOP or 401(k) plan. If the company redeems the shares, the redemption is not a tax-deductible expense. If the company sets up an ESOP, however, it can make tax-deductible cash contributions to the plan (within certain limits), which can then be used to buy back the shares. While sellers to an ESOP that owns 30% or more of a closely held company can normally defer taxation on the gain from the sale by reinvesting in qualified replacement securities, owners who hold their shares as a result of stock options cannot get this benefit. The sale of their shares to the ESOP would be treated in the same way as a sale to any other buyer.

Valuation of the Shares

Companies whose shares are "readily tradable on an established market" get off easy on this issue; the value of their shares is set every day by the market. Closely held companies, however, must determine how they will set a value for the shares subject to options. This applies both to the price at which options are granted and exercised. The technicalities of how shares are valued in closely held companies is beyond the scope of this chapter. Suffice it to say that a formal appraisal of a closely held company would first involve an estimate of what a willing buyer would pay a willing seller for the entire enterprise. These estimates are set primarily by looking at comparable companies, discounted earnings or cash flow, and book value. Discounts for the lack of marketability (shares of public companies are easier to sell and therefore worth more) and lack of control (the enterprise value assumes a buyer is purchasing control of a company, which is a valuable additional right not gained from holding shares that constitute a minority interest) are then applied to determine the value of an individual share.

If closely held companies do offer to buy the shares back from employees in a cashless exercise or equivalent program, they will have to account for the grant of the options on their income statement using variable accounting treatment. This means that when any restrictions lapse on the options (the shares are fully vested, typically), then the value of the option shows up as a compensation cost. Prior to that, an estimate of the future value would have to be made using an acceptable formula, such as Black-Scholes. The accounting treatment would parallel that for a stock appreciation right. Only if the plan requires that the shares be sold to a third party (an ESOP, other employees, outside buyers, or another company, for instance) can this kind of accounting be avoided.

Having a formal appraisal performed is clearly the best way to set a value. Nonetheless, most closely held companies choose to set a value internally, usually by having the board rely on a formula, such as a multiple of earnings, book value, or some other rule of thumb. At the very least, this should be done with the advice of an appraiser. Companies value stock in-house mostly to avoid the costs of an appraiser (typically $5,000 to $10,000 for this kind of assessment), but if their rule-of-thumb appraisal is off by just a small percentage, they could create at least two problems. If the appraisal is too high, then when employees exercise the options, they will be getting more value than the shares are really worth. If the shares are valued too low, then in order to deliver an acceptable level of value at the time options are granted, they will have to dilute the ownership of other owners more than would otherwise be the case. While some might shrug off these problems saying that one will offset the other, formula-based values can produce a value both too low at grant and too high at exercise if the essentials of the industry move in the right way for this to happen over time. As any appraiser would note, a formula that is appropriate in 1999 is probably not appropriate a few years later. Moreover, appraisals that are off substantially could lead to tax problems or lawsuits by employees or other shareholders.

Finally, companies need to be careful that they do not grant options at too low a price and then go public. The closer to an IPO underpriced options are issued, the more of a potential problem they become. Because this so-called "cheap stock" can raise tax and securities law issues upon an IPO, companies at the very least should get an independent appraisal about 18 months before an IPO.

How Often Should Options Be Granted?

The recent turmoil in the stock market has brought into focus the importance of designing broad-based stock option plans in ways that work under the normal conditions of stock markets, rather than the extraordinary year-after-year growth of the last several years. Stock options inherently involve risk, but the design of plans can accentuate that risk. Companies that provide one-time grants or grants on the occurrence of an event, such as hiring, promotion, or meeting some corporate target, base most or all of an employee's ownership interest in the company on the price of stock at a single point in time.

This practice accelerates the risk of options both for the employee and the company. Options granted at a high price may never be "in the money" (i.e., at a point where the market value exceeds the option price so that the employee can make a profit); those given at a low price may cost the company more than it ever intended when they are redeemed. Employees who happen to get their chunk of options at a good time end up doing very well, while those who have gotten their grants when the price was not so favorable don't do well at all. Creating an ownership culture of "we're all in this together" can be very difficult in these circumstances.

For many companies, the best way to deal with these potential problems is to provide option grants in smaller amounts but more frequently. This works best for companies using stock options as a compensation strategy. Start-ups whose stock value is close to zero anyway or who use large initial grants to attract people away from other opportunities may find this less appropriate. It also won't work for companies that want simply to make grants of options at the occasional discretion of the company, often on the attainment of some corporate milestone. These companies see options more as a symbolic reward than as ongoing ownership strategy.

Assume a company wants to give an employee options on 600 shares over the next few years of their employment. Rather than provide all 600 at once, the company could make grants in 100-share increments over a period of two or three years. Some companies are now even making grants monthly.

This is easiest to do in public companies where the share price is readily ascertainable and where share prices change continually. In a closely held company, there would be no point in granting options more frequently than the stock is valued. Giving an employee an option grant three times a year when the price per share is determined annually, for example, would give the employee three sets of options all at the same price.

This periodic allocation of options accomplishes a number of goals. First, it "dollar-cost averages" the options. Investors have long used dollar-cost averaging (periodically investing a set amount of money in the market so that fewer shares are bought when a stock price is higher and more shares are bought when it is lower) to smooth out the bumps in investing. If a small percentage of a portfolio is used to buy stock at a price that turns out to be near the investment's peak, not that much will be lost when it falls. Conversely, if shares are sold at what turns out to be a low point, many other shares will remain to take advantage of the higher prices later. The potential for outsized gains is diminished, but so is the possibility of large losses.

In the options context, this strategy works even better because employees usually have several years over which they can exercise their options. If they have been given their options in periodic grants, rather than all at once, the period of time during which they can exercise at least some of their options "in the money" is extended. Unless a company issues options at an historically high price over a long period of time, and they then fall and stay down for a long time, employees will find that (1) they are less likely to have most of their options underwater and (2) they are more likely to be able to sell options when their share price is favorable.

Finally, this approach gives employees more of a long-term, ongoing stake in the company. If a large grant of options is substantially in the money, employees may be more tempted to cash in and leave than if they have continuing blocks of options remaining to be exercised at any time. They also have a continuing equity interest in the company as long as they work there. With the vesting schedules attached to the repeated grants of options, employees are provided an even longer-term interest in the company's performance. Finally, there will be fewer big winners and losers among employees with otherwise similar jobs.

Frequent grants are not all good news, of course. The more often options are granted, the more complex their administration becomes. Even with the best software, there will be much more data entry, many more forms to file and disseminate, and many more errors that can be made.

Securities Law Issues

The granting of options does not in itself raise federal securities law considerations (although it may raise securities law issues at the state level, as in California, for example), but when employees exercise their options, that is considered an offer to sell and hence is subject to securities laws. This chapter is not intended to provide a primer on the complicated issues involved with state and federal securities laws, but rather to describe briefly the general issues so that plan designs can be created that will not lead to unexpected regulatory burdens.

The two key elements of securities laws are registration and disclosure. Registration means the filing of documents with the state and/or federal securities agencies concerning the employer whose stock is being sold. There are registration procedures for small offerings of stock (under $1 million or $5 million, depending on the procedure) that can be done for relatively small legal fees (as little as $10,000 in some cases), but larger offerings require a lot of complex paperwork and fees often exceed $100,000. Registration requires the filing of audited financial statements and continuing reporting obligations to the federal Securities and Exchange Commission (SEC) and appropriate state agencies.

Disclosure refers to providing information to buyers about what they are getting, similar to, but frequently less detailed than what would be in a prospectus. At times, there are specific state and federal rules about what needs to go in these documents, including objective discussions of risks, the financial condition of the firm, officers' and directors' salaries, and other information. In the absence of requirements for the registration of the securities, disclosure is intended to satisfy the anti-fraud requirements of federal and state laws.

Generally, offers to sell securities (stocks, bonds, etc.) require registration of those securities unless there is a specific exemption. In addition, companies with 500 or more shareholders are considered public firms under federal law and must comply with the reporting requirements of the Securities Exchange Act of 1934 even if they do not have to register under the Securities Act of 1933. There are various exemptions from registration for privately held companies, listed below. Whenever stock is offered for sale, however, the company may still need to provide appropriate financial disclosure to satisfy anti-fraud rules.

Under Rule 701 of the Securities Act of 1933, federal law, offers to a company's employees, directors, general partners, trustees, officers, or consultants can be made under a written compensation agreement. The maximum amount that can be sold under Section 701 in a 12-month period cannot exceed the greater of the following:

1. $1 million dollars (up from the current $500,000 figure);
2. 15% of the issuer's total assets; or
3. 15% of the outstanding securities of that class.

These rules, effective April 7, 1999, are considerably more flexible than prior rules. The offerings must be discrete (not included in any other offer, generally considered to be at least six months from the prior offer).

Another exemption is available under Section 4(2) of the Securities Act of 1933, which allows for exemptions from federal registrations in offerings of stock to a limited number of investors who have access to the same information normally provided in a public offering and who are accredited investors or sophisticated enough both to assess and bear the risks. This exemption has been interpreted in different ways by the courts. Whether it allows such approaches as offering stock to all of a company's "key employees" is unclear.

Another set of exemptions is available under Regulation D, issued by the Securities and Exchange Commission, which provides a number of exemptions for small offerings. The best known of these is Rule 505 and its related Rule 506, which provide an exemption to offerings of up to $5 million to as many as 35 non-accredited investors in any 12-month period. If every investor is sophisticated (Rule 505), however, there is no limit on the amount of the offering. Rule 504 allows offerings up to $500,000 (or $1 million if there is a registration for up to $500,000 with a state securities agency) to as many people as wanted, with no limits of their being sophisticated or accredited.

"Accredited investors" include directors, partners, or executives of the issuing company, anyone with a net worth (including that of their spouses) of over $1 million, and anyone with an income over $200,000 (or whose joint income with a spouse is $300,000) who has made that amount for the preceding two years and is likely to continue to make it. "Sophisticated investors" are people who, on their own or with the aid of a representative such as an accountant, are able to judge the risks, merits, and disadvantages of a particular investment.

Finally, offerings that are made only to residents of the state in which the offering is made are exempt if the offeror has its principal office in that state, gets 80% of its gross revenue from business conducted in the state, and has 80% of its assets in the state.

These exemptions from registration are available under federal law. Some states track federal exemptions; some do not. Thirty-nine states have "blue sky laws" (the general name for state securities laws) that comply with the Uniform Securities Act, which is partly based on federal law. Perhaps most important for offerings to employees, however, states that have a specific exemption parallel to the federal Rule 701 exemption (for offerings to employees) are the exception rather than the rule. State registration for such offerings may be needed, therefore, unless other exemptions are met. Some states have limited offering exemptions for sales up to 35 non-accredited investors and an unlimited number of accredited investors. Unless the buyers are sophisticated investors, issuers must believe the offering is suitable for the purchasers in terms of the purchasers' financial condition, including other securities holdings. Note, however, that even if all these exemption requirements are met, some states require companies to pay filing fees to operate their plan.

Public Company Issues

Public companies cannot use Rule 701 for an exemption from securities law filings. Instead, most rely on Form S-8, a simplified registration form that can be used to comply with securities laws in conjunction with an offering of options. Public companies do not have to offer a formal prospectus to potential buyers, as closely held companies would. They are, however, required to provide information to employee stock purchasers about the company and its option plan. The Form S-8 registration statement allows that to be done by reference to already available public documents or the dissemination of the required information.

Public companies must also make sure their plan design complies with trading restrictions that apply to corporate insiders. This requires the filing of various reports and the restriction of some trading activity, among other things. These issues are too technical for adequate discussion here. Public companies should consult with their legal counsel on these matters before designing their plan.

Design Issues Raised by Securities Laws

Because of the expense and complexity of dealing with securities laws, some closely held companies prohibit the exercise of options until the company is sold or goes public, when either the acquirer must deal with these issues or the public offering will make most of them go away. (Note that this discussion does not include, however, a description of special rules that public companies must meet for the exercise of options that are primarily focused on "insiders," a term whose definition would almost always exclude rank-and-file workers).

Most closely held companies, however, will be able to avoid securities registration requirements at the federal level even with a broad-based option plan; some will have to meet state requirements, but these are generally much less onerous. Anti-fraud disclosure statements will raise cost issues, however, and some companies may not want to divulge the required information. When designing a plan, therefore, these issues need to be considered carefully with qualified counsel to assure that the operation of the plan will not trigger requirements the company does not want to meet.

Methods of Exercising Options

There are a variety of ways employees can exercise their options. These must be specified in the plan's documents if employees are to be able to exercise their options. Some of these methods will work only for public companies, however.

Cash or Promissory Notes

The simplest approach is that the employee simply pays for the exercise of the option in cash. However, simplicity has its cost. If an employee is exercising a substantial amount of options, it could require a large amount of up-front cash that some people may not have. Companies can loan employees the funds for this purpose, but the plan document should spell out the terms under which such loans will occur.

Stock Swaps

If an employee already owns shares in the company, he or she can exchange those shares for the shares to be acquired by the exercise of the option. Because of potential unfavorable accounting treatment for the exchange of shares held for less than six months, the swaps should require that shares have been held at least this long. Some companies provide a "reload" option along with the stock swap. This approach provides that when an employee trades in stock to exercise an option, the employee gets an equivalent value in new options for the shares traded in. Stock swaps are generally useful only for more highly compensated employees who have significant amounts of company stock in their personal accounts; as a means to provide for exercise in a broad-based plan, they are not usually of much value. Another benefit of a stock swap is ability to purchase shares with pretax appreciation in already owned shares.

Same-Day Sale

This approach is intended for public companies. Its mechanics can be a bit complicated, but the concept is simple: an employee exercises options on a given number of shares, then has a broker (one working with the company) resell that number of shares the same day. The employee can pay with cash, but it is more common for the employee to exercise a "cashless" exercise. This approach involves a simultaneous option exercise and stock sale, with the sale proceeds used to cover the exercise costs of the option. The broker buys of the shares up front and the employee gets the spread between the exercise price, minus any applicable taxes, on the settlement of the trade. The spread could be delivered in shares or cash, although it normally would be cash.

Cashless Exercise in a Closely Held Company

A closely held company could arrange a transaction in which the employee only purchases the shares in the most technical sense. The employee buys the shares and the company immediately repurchases them, giving the employee the cash value of the difference, minus applicable taxes. A variation on this approach would give the employee shares equal to the value of the spread.

Note, however, that any form of exercise in which the employee sells shares sooner than one year after exercise will not qualify for incentive stock option treatment.

Accounting, Corporate, and Communications Issues

The discussion above focuses on matters that need to be addressed in a plan document. In designing a plan, however, it is important to consider a variety of other issues. For instance, the accounting treatment of stock options requires at least a footnote disclosure on a company's income statement. Will these disclosures cause adverse reactions from other owners? How will the present value of the options be determined for this disclosure? Are there corporate bylaws or other policies that need to be changed, aside from the mandatory shareholder approval requirements for ISOs? Finally, how will the company communicate how options work to employees, and, more importantly, what new roles will employees play as "owners-in-waiting?"

Conclusion

At the NCEO, we get a lot of calls from people seeking a template for a broad-based stock option plan. As this chapter shows, there isn't one. Designing a plan that works for a company requires a careful assessment of at least the company's goals, culture, finances, corporate structure, demographics, and labor market situation, as well as consultation with peers and experienced advisors.

CHAPTER 6

Establishing and Maintaining Employee Stock Benefit Programs

Emily W. Van Hoorickx
PaineWebber, San Jose Corporate Services Consulting Group

Stock benefit plans express a great deal about a company. How well a company uses this tool is a very visible indication to the employees, the shareholders, and the investing public of how well the company is managed. If the company is innovative in delivering benefits while carefully aligning employee goals with those of the shareholders, one would assume that the same creative culture extends to the rest of the business. A cumbersome program that is expensive to run and delivers little value to anyone also speaks volumes. On the other hand, even with a well-designed plan, sloppy day-to-day management of routine clerical tasks can result in oversights that require public disclosure. As you design a plan, you need to think about the practical aspects of ongoing plan maintenance. Consider how your plans will be perceived before putting into place a program that will run for the next decade. If you currently run plans, review them periodically to ensure that adequate controls are in place and that you are processing benefits in a way that integrates with other aspects of the business.

Set Plan Goals

First, you must articulate what you want to accomplish with the plans. Be honest and specific. If you simply want to say you have a plan for recruiting purposes, and you truly do not care how many employees participate, then adopt a typical plan and hire any competent administrator to implement it. Putting together an "off-the-shelf" employee stock benefit plan can be relatively simple, especially if your corporate counsel and other service providers have significant recent experience in the area. Conversely, if you really want an outstanding plan, you must put some thought into the process. Just as other areas of the business, your stock benefit plans must have measurable and definable goals. A successful plan is judged on how close you come to those benchmarks. Typically, stock benefit plan programs are developed because they can closely align the goals of the employees with the broader shareholder base. Stock option plans, with their vesting provisions, work well as a merit-based compensation and retention tool. Employee stock purchase plans under Internal Revenue Code section 423 are useful vehicles for helping employees accumulate stock through a systematic savings plan and for placing shares in "friendly hands." Both programs, working well in tandem, should improve the average employee's view of how he or she is valued by the company.

As you spell out goals for the plan, focus on the current culture of the company as well as your vision for the future. Stock plan benefits convey the company's statement of purpose to the shareholders, the public, and the employees. Plans can be marketed to potential employees and can become part of a company's public relations material if you are running an innovative or broad-based plan. As such, plans should reflect the broader values and personality of the company. Make sure you know what you are saying. If you want a plan that has the potential to be extremely successful, you do not want to copy someone else's plan document and implementation plan unless your situations are very similar. Since you are asking for approval of plans that will exist long after the individuals on this task force have moved on to other assignments, it is important to your successors that you document the decision process. Also, consider your company-wide compensation strategy, because stock benefit plans can be an important tool toward meeting those goals. You want your vision of the company to show in your dealings with your shareholders, the investment community, and your employees.

Plan Design and Administrative Structure

This means that you must make choices. Just as you must work with the statutory limits on how much stock you can allow your employees to purchase in a qualified plan, you must consider how much stock your institutional shareholders will allow you to grant under an option program before they start to express concerns. Consider adopting an "evergreen" plan rather than one where you must go back to the shareholders periodically to ask for x number of shares to replenish the plans. Using this format, you state your ongoing share needs as a percentage of the shares outstanding or another formula rather than numerically. This frees you from having to go back to the shareholders periodically to authorize additional shares to replenish the plan, possibly at the same time you have controversial issues in the proxy. A little foresight as you structure your plan with counsel can help you avoid potential proxy contests in the future.

To incorporate this ongoing efficiency, you must be able to articulate your goals for the plan. You should be prepared to discuss how your stock benefit plans are helping you reach definable shareholder goals. Your investor relations staff should know your goals and be able to discuss how your plans enhance earnings rather than just create further dilution. You must be able to convey the goals of the plan logically and succinctly. Every individual charged with administration must know what benchmarks are going to be used to evaluate the efficiency of the plans. If you went through the process to have your plans qualify for favorable tax treatment, you will want your employees to understand that the company is looking out for their personal financial situation so they appreciate your efforts. If you are reporting to the financial press that you established the plans to increase your employee and management shareholder base, you should know how to assess how much stock is remaining in these hands over a multi-year period. This means you must have the ability to quickly track who owns your stock. From a practical viewpoint, this dictates that you must be willing to devote resources to survey employees' stock sale activity or get one of your service providers to do it for you. This may not be as difficult as one might think, because if your transfer agent and/or "captive brokers" are doing a lot of this type of work, they will be processing your work on a database that typically collects this data anyway.

A "captive broker" program is one in which the company negotiates a very favorable commission rate for selling stock under the benefit plans for the employees, and the "captive" (i.e., preferred) corporate services broker agrees to provide significant plan facilitation services. This can be a symbiotic relationship that helps you reach your plan goals. Captive brokers can help create value for the shareholders if they provide additional plan services and make sure that the disqualifying dispositions are being tracked efficiently so the company captures all the tax benefits to which it is entitled. On the other hand, the company should chose the service provider(s) carefully so that nuances in the way the plan is run do not inadvertently encourage employees to sell their stock contrary to plan goals.

Plan Document Provisions and Policy Guidelines

Once the goals are clarified and you are in the process of drafting your formal plan document, you should continue the discussions on policy issues. For example, how flexible do you want to be to individual employee requests? To terminated employee requests? How much paperwork do you really need from the employee pertaining to the benefits?

This is an area where a "default" policy can help. For example, consider establishing a policy of "We will sell your shares on a FIFO basis [i.e., the first shares acquired will be the first shares sold], unless you specify a particular tax lot." Such a policy saves the administrator from starting a conversation that will lead to a request for specific tax advice, while still allowing the employee to choose. Personal financial planning issues can be presented more efficiently in seminars or printed materials. Service providers are typically willing to provide excellent materials on this topic at little or no cost.

These policies are not typically published, but they should be documented. It can be very difficult for people coming in several years later to figure out why a particular decision was made if the internal work papers are not easily accessible. For example, if the plan document states that a Notice of Exercise must be made by submission of an original signed document, it would be helpful to know if that was because someone insisted on that formality for a still-valid reason or if no one anticipated the prevalence of fax machines or company e-mail. If you have a policy that encourages the usage of new technologies, then your successors will have an easier time adapting new administration enhancements to increase employee satisfaction and possibly lower costs.

Do not be lulled by the thought that the more vaguely the plan is written the better. Without guidelines, it will be a struggle to determine what is allowed, and it is likely you will have to go back to the corporate counsel more often to have issues resolved than would be otherwise necessary. For example, if the plan is too vague and you have no documentation on the decisions that went into the plan, it may be difficult for the administrator to decide quickly whether certain special requests can be accommodated. The only given is that things will change: the tax laws, your employees' marital status, your company's employment levels, and the stock's performance. As best you can, decide initially if you want the plans to accommodate special requests such as stock swaps as consideration of the cost of exercise, the potential of transferable options, and early retirement. Don't create more work than is needed. For example, there is really no reason to put in a plan document the requirement that refunds be made on a employee stock purchase plan at the end of a purchase period for the small amount of funds collected that is not enough to purchase a full share. Remember, you want the plan to be perceived as well-managed. This detail of small monetary value creates a lot of work for someone, and current employees don't perceive the value of having a very few dollars returned to them immediately as a significant benefit. Instead, they are likely to consider this reimbursement as a poor use of company time. However, the plan documents still do need to state that refunds need to be made to anyone withdrawing from the plan or terminating his or her employment.

Value Judgments

Keep in mind that allowing more flexibility typically means higher administration costs, even though the numbers may not be easily ascertainable in bundled programs. By the very nature of the plans, more choices means more work, either by the company or by a vendor. Those costs will be allocated somewhere. Because it is also easy for the company to lose control of the plan and have a trading violation or some other problem when the plan is very free in form, it may be more prudent to start with a very structured program and add services and additional choices for your employees as they become more familiar with plan. You also must decide whether you want the program to be as self-supporting as possible or whether the company is willing to incur some expenses often borne by the employee-shareholder. If you do not have in-house expertise and are considering a total outsource for your plans, you may want to analyze what more your existing service providers can do for you first. You may decide that just sharing more files with your vendors and streamlining existing processes you can increase efficiency at a lower cost through a customized "mini-outsource." There really is no such thing as a perfect stock benefit plan. The closest you can hope to get is one that strives to meet your goals and fits the culture of the company.

This is the point where the goals and the policies you set for the plan weave themselves into the day-to-day operations of plan, if it is to be successful. Do you want employees to participate and accumulate stock? Then you want to make sure it is easy to exercise and hold option shares and easy to sign up for the employee stock purchase plan. Follow through to be sure that your service providers work together and can help you create individualized forms, processing systems, and educational programs. It should be easy for an employee to sign up and understand how the benefits can be integrated into his or her family's financial planning process. Throughout your design process, you need to focus on your original goals. Do you want to facilitate sales or discourage them? Individuals charged with monitoring the plans should understand management's goals in this area. Since transfer agents and brokerage companies traditionally earn fees when shares are transferred, either by sale or individual share issuance, programs may be designed to encourage these activities. If you are being charged per stock issuance, make sure deliveries can be consolidated. If you really are looking to foster long-term employee ownership, then you do not want to encourage an "autosale" program in which employees can quickly and cheaply sell immediately after purchase. On the other hand, if you view the stock plan as simply compensation, it would make sense to automate peak sales periods. The logic is to choose a "look-up only" Interactive Voice Response or intranet Web-based solution if you want employees to hold their shares, and a similar program with on-line sales if you don't mind them selling easily. If your company culture is more paternalistic and one of your goals is to help your employees accumulate wealth, you should encourage educational activities designed to explain to employees the benefits of holding shares until they qualify for the best possible tax treatment.

Including your administrator(s) in the discussions during the development and subsequent modifications of the plan will save you from needing to make routine decisions concerning the plan later. It is imperative that everyone know how the success of the plan will be evaluated. The reality of this specialty area is that it is changing very rapidly and there are many ways to provide this service.

Let your staff know how you view your plans. If you see the plans as an executive perk, they will know that given a value judgment, you want them to favor highly compensated employees over the rank and file. If they know you are worried about getting enough participation from the lower-paid employees, your staff will be sensitive to this and investigate how transactions can be simplified and consolidated to address the needs of this employee population. If your overseas operations are crucial, it would help if your staff knew that all other things being equal, preference should be given to service providers with considerable experience dealing with international plan issues and the ability to offer inexpensive currency transfers to your off-site employees. If your staff members think they are being judged on how little each employee must pay to sell, they will choose the solutions that are the least expensive for the employees, even if that increases your costs, either directly or indirectly.

If management is being judged by plan participation levels, the increase in employee share ownership, and a tight compliance program, then the individuals charged with running the plan should be judged in light of the same standards if you want the plan to be successful. Daily operations of the plan can affect greatly whether you reach your corporate goals.

If your administrators know what their time is worth, what it costs to use outside counsel, and what the value of capturing the disqualifying dispositions is, they will run the program differently than people who do not know. If the administrators determine the company just does not have the procedures in place to avoid restricted stock "mistakes" and rightly fears the possibility of an Item 405 violation under Reg. S-K requiring proxy disclosures, they should look for other alternatives. They will either send more work out to the outside corporate counsel or see whether they can leverage their relationships with other professionals.

By clarifying these issues, you will then have the framework for deciding whether you want to train someone internally to manage your plans or whether you want to outsource the duties. Innovations in technology and processing efficiencies are reducing the routine clerical aspects of stock administration, while changes in securities and accounting laws are increasing the risks associated with making a mistake. There are so many overlapping requirements of these plans that the need for the company to have a point person with specific training in the interrelated disciplines who can manage the interfaces between payroll, accounting, information services, human resources, finance, and the vendors has become more important.

Even if you choose to totally outsource the function, the company is still ultimately responsible for any problems, so you need a person with the specialized skills to review the service provider's work. If you choose to coordinate stock plan administration internally, you will want to make sure these individuals have access to educational programs and information on the rapidly evolving laws affecting plans. There are several industry groups and at least one university providing programs for stock plan administration staff. The need for skilled oversight has become critical. Running stock plans efficiently demands a far different skill set than it did even a few years ago. No longer can administrating stock benefits be assigned to just anyone. These individuals must be capable of interpreting plan documents. They must know what and when they must report to remain in compliance with Security and Exchange Commission regulations. They need to work with the captive broker to maintain an effective insider trading policy, understand corporate accounting issues, and learn how stock benefits affect earnings. They also must have a working knowledge of Internal Revenue Service (IRS) issues as they pertain to both the company and the individual participant.

Another important policy issue is the decision of what kind of vendors you want and whether you want to limit employees to certain vendors. This can be a sticky decision, but it is a policy issue, not something that should be in the plan document. This policy is likely to evolve over the life of the plans, and the logic you used in your decision should be included in the additional internal information on the history of the plan you are creating. With this market changing so fast, the rationale for the initial decision may not be valid in the future. At first impulse, most managers will decide to let the employees chose any way they want to sell their shares or they will use an existing relationship with their personal broker or someone the underwriters introduced to them. Going this route could have a significant effect on the success of the plans and could increase costs. Typically, bundled services are cheaper, and considerable routine processing can be offloaded to service providers who specialize in this area. If you have only a few participants and a simple plan, the resources you can garner from your software vendor may be enough that you can justify coordinating transactions through several vendors. As plans grow in size and complexity, there is a definite trend toward consolidating as many moving parts as possible.

Leveraging Outside Resources

As you consider how to leverage your staff time, you need to consider the risks and make a value judgment. Errors reflect on the company publicly, and the fact the mistakes were made by an outside service provider and not the company itself is no excuse. Too many companies have watched a simple clerical oversight snowball into a violation requiring publication of their officers' names in the proxy, only to see the media incorporate the information into a larger story. If you are not following your plan properly, the IRS can declare your plan disqualified, which can result in fines. Many companies believe it pays to use professionals, especially as they often cost little more than a "no frills" service. No system is foolproof, but significant control can be gained by encouraging transactions to go through a specialized administration service or by using a captive broker. If such a service or broker agrees to take on a watchdog role, it can ban all employee trading, both during regular blackout periods or in advance of a material announcement. It will "remind" officers of trading restrictions and possible short-swing trading violations. The firm will file the SEC Rule 144 forms for you and/or will assist you in your efforts to make sure SEC Form 4s and 5s are filed in a timely matter. It typically can track most, if not all, of your disqualifying dispositions for you, and will help you with financial data and other services as part of its bundled program.

Additional leverage can be obtained if you make sure whatever you put into your plan can be processed easily on a database. There are standardized software programs designed specifically for stock benefit plans. A practical consideration would be to get information from at least the two major stock benefit plan software vendors before you finalize your plan document. Make sure the program can easily accommodate your proposed plans without a lot of customization. I suggest you pick the same company for all your plans (employee stock purchase plan, stock options, restricted stock options, stock appreciation rights, and so on) because often the data files can be shared to increase accuracy and efficiency, and maintenance fees are lower.

Purchasing software when you may have in-house expertise may seem extravagant initially, but with the laws so fluid in this area, the challenge of keeping an in-house program in compliance is sure to take resources that the company could better deploy elsewhere. In addition to keeping your program current, most of the major vendors offer educational conferences and information that can be invaluable to your staff responsible for administering or auditing the function.

Along those same lines, make sure the rest of the team are professionals. Can your transfer agent accommodate electronic share transfers? Is your paying agent on-line with the Federal Reserve? Does your paying agent or broker handle the currency transfers in-house, or do your employees have to wait for the underlying currency exchange to settle before money is sent? Who will your designated representatives be? There is a wide range of capabilities of individuals even within the same company. The company may have an excellent program in place, but that is not the same as working with a group that can help you enhance the plans. If needed, you may have to insist that you are assigned specialists who have a long history of servicing this market. You should ensure that you are working with someone whose files are full of sample forms and brochures and timesaving tips that can enhance your plan. It is imperative that you are using the best service providers possible. A competent transfer agent, a good software package, a brokerage group, and attorneys working together can help you avoid mistakes and save you more time and money than you could ever hope to save by trying to do the tasks yourself.

From a practical standpoint, make your plan documents as "administration-friendly" as possible. For example, if you are planning to put in an employee stock purchase plan, consider moving the purchase periods away from quarter-ends or other company-wide peak periods. There is no legal reason why a purchase has to be made on December 31, and there is no reason why someone should have to try to make the purchase before attending New Year's festivities. Along the same line, do not set the end of your purchase period just as the employees are going into a blackout period unless you have set a policy that you want them to hold their shares long-term. Make sure that when the compensation committee is discussing changes to the plan, you invite the individuals involved in processing the work to the meeting if at all possible. Their practical insight can be invaluable.

With employee stock option plans, consider carefully what you allow as payment for the option under the plan. Give your internal administration some latitude so processing time can be minimized. A little flexibility here can save you considerable administration effort on the bulk of the routine transactions, freeing staff time to focus on exercises that have a greater possibility to go wrong, such as those involving officers and terminated employees. Rather than demanding payment up front, before shares can be ordered from the transfer agent, determine what your definition of "consideration" is. Is a form or e-mail message enough? Can you put provisions in the grant agreement itself to protect the company? Can you control your broker enough to have the broker withhold payment to the employee it he or she neglects to complete your procedures? That may allow you to let employees exercise in a number of approved manners, which can make the plan much more "employee-friendly." There is always a need to strike a balance between the need for control and the fact that this is an employee benefit. You want employees to have a good experience every time they exercise their benefits.

Conclusion

Remember that there is no such thing as a perfect stock benefit plan. At best it is a work in progress. As an employer and a shareholder, you want to strive towards the best possible mix of processing efficiency, control, and flexibility to allow enhancements in the future. The process of developing a plan can be something of an art form—a dance between the interests of the shareholder, the employee, and the practical considerations of complying with the structure of statutory requirements.

CHAPTER 7

Equity Compensation in Closely Held Companies

Brian B. Snarr
Morrison Cohen Singer & Weinstein LLP

This chapter addresses the issues that arise when the board of directors or controlling stockholders of a closely held corporation decide to provide for employee stock ownership through means such as stock options but not through an employee stock ownership plan (ESOP).[1] Broad-based employee ownership can provide a corporation's employees with a proprietary stake in the company's operations and success. However, most closely held corporations do not choose to distribute their shares widely to employees. Broad-based employee stock ownership takes more planning and operational involvement than restricted ownership, especially where the structure for orderly stock transactions associated with an ESOP is lacking. In addition, other factors discussed below, such as retaining key employees, providing for business succession, and maintaining corporate control, often persuade the existing stockholders to keep ownership concentrated in a few hands. Further, broad-based employee ownership does not happen on its own. It requires a conscious decision. If stock ownership decisions are left until they arise in the ordinary course of events, inertia tends to keep stock ownership concentrated in the hands of the relatively few individuals who are sufficiently motivated and financially capable to acquire stock and join with or succeed the current generation of stockholders.

Historically, closely held corporations tended to be sole proprietorships or family-owned enterprises in which all the interests were held by a limited number of stockholders who were active in the business. With the growth of the U.S. economy since the Second World War, many closely held corporations such as M&M Mars and Cargill, Inc., have become national and even international operations. A defining characteristic of the closely held corporation, however, remains the high degree of identity between the owners and the managers of the business. A number of states have created a special category of "close corporations" that permits eligible and electing corporations to be governed more like partnerships, where the members must reach a consensus on important decisions.[2] This method of governance stands in contrast to the usual principles of stockholder democracy, under which corporate action is determined by majority rule on the board of directors, notwithstanding dissent among the stockholders.

Providing for broad-based employee ownership in the context of a closely held corporation thus runs counter to the trend in closely held corporations, since the very object of such broad-based ownership is to expand employee stockholdings beyond the ranks of management and family. Nonetheless, many of the issues that must be faced in extending stock ownership to employees are the same that any closely held corporation faces in dealing with ownership of its shares.

Reasons for Providing Stock to Employees

There are a number of reasons for providing stock to employees. More than one may apply to any particular decision to sell or grant shares to employees.

Performance-Based Incentive

Stock ownership can be used to tie the economic fortunes of the employees to the performance of the employer corporation. The stock can be purchased by the employees or awarded without payment. If the stock is purchased, the employees incur both the risk of economic loss if the corporation performs poorly and the benefits of an increase in value or dividends if the corporation performs well. If the stock is awarded without payment, the employees receive the "upside" benefits of stock ownership, but lack one element of an owner's risk: the possibility of a loss of capital.[3]

Key-Employee Retention

Many employers have found that they can increase the likelihood of retaining the services of key employees (for example, those who have cultivated important customer relationships or who have special knowledge or abilities that are critical to a company's success) if these employees become stockholders in the business. This may be initiated by the key employees themselves, who may want a "piece of the action" if they are to continue in employment without looking elsewhere or who simply want their positions of importance in the company to be recognized. Alternatively, controlling stockholders or management may wish to preempt employment offers from competitors, either known or unknown.

Business Succession

If a corporation lacks a management group to take control of the business after the death or retirement of the founding stockholders, it may survive its founding stockholders only briefly before succumbing to a lack of direction and continuity. Frequently, the best candidates to continue the business of a corporation are found among the existing employees. Other than the current managers and stockholders, these are usually the individuals most familiar with the business and who are therefore in the most favorable position to continue its operations.

By providing stock to promising employees in the years before a business succession takes place, a company can evaluate the employees' aptitude and commitment as owners. The issue of succession is often of particular importance where a successful business owner has built a corporation up over a lifetime's work but has no family members in the business who would be able to ensure the survival or prosperity of the corporation.

Management Buyout

As in the case of many publicly traded corporations, the management employees of a closely held corporation may seek to acquire a control block of employer stock from the existing stockholders. This sort of initiative may also raise issues of business succession and the retention of key employees. It typically presents additional, unrelated issues as well. Where management employees introduce the subject of stock ownership as part of an overall plan for acquiring control of the corporation, they generally come prepared with a financing plan, of greater or lesser sophistication, that assumes gaining control over the corporation's cash flow and borrowing capacity. In this case, the existing owners may find themselves more in the position of selling investors rather than co-owners; unless they receive the buyout price in cash, they will often want the financial protections and covenants that are customary in a stock purchase agreement with a third-party buyer.

Raising Capital

A less common reason for issuing stock to employees is a corporation's need for equity capital.[4] Very few corporations will look to employees who are not already owners as a source of funds needed to expand the business or retire debt capital. Securities law issues are also implicated when a corporation issues its stock purely as an investment, even to its own employees. If raising capital is a reason for issuing stock to employees, it is usually only one of several motives for the transaction, along with management incentives and succession planning.

Some businesses, particularly closely held investment firms or incorporated professional practices, raise working capital from "within the ranks" to augment or replace working capital withdrawn when a stockholder or group of stockholders retires or moves on.

Additional Compensation

Where a corporation regularly pays dividends, the existing owners can provide additional compensation to select employees by issuing them employer stock. Because dividends are generally only declared if the corporation has profits, such compensation has an inherent tie to corporate performance. However, because a corporation's compensation payments to employees are deductible for tax purposes but payments of dividends to stockholders are not, paying compensation is a much more tax-efficient way to put money in the hands of employees than paying dividends. Accordingly, the approach of providing dividend-paying stock for compensation purposes is usually seen only with S corporations.[5] For an S corporation, deductibility of dividends is not an issue because the corporation itself is not a taxpaying entity. S corporation income is attributed to the stockholders, who are taxed on their respective shares of the corporation's income as if they earned it directly. Most S corporations routinely pay dividends to stockholders because: (1) the stockholders usually need funds to pay tax on the S corporation income attributed to them; and (2) the distribution itself is tax-free to the stockholders and, if paid in cash, is generally without tax consequences to the corporation.[6]

Industry Practice

There are some businesses, particularly in "high-tech" industries such as software design and biotechnology, in which it has become a regular practice to grant shares (or options to purchase shares) to attract employees or consultants who have a particular expertise required by the company. If this is a routine industry practice, an employer may be required, as a practical matter, to offer shares to attract targeted employees or consultants. Often, only senior employees are offered stock, although many corporations, particularly startups, will offer shares to all employees. The ability of the employer to offer shares to employees often depends on its other financing. If venture capital is supporting the company, there may only be a limited block of shares available for grant or sale to employees.

Methods of Acquiring Stock and Their Tax Consequences

Compensatory Grant

An employer may choose to simply grant or give shares outright to employees. This method of acquiring shares is generally fully and immediately taxable to the employee based on the current fair market value of the shares (subject to the vesting rules discussed below.) The employer corporation will have a compensation deduction that matches the employees' income as to timing and amount. As noted above, if the stock is awarded without payment, the employee receives the benefits of stock ownership but lacks an owner's risk of the loss of capital.

Cash Purchase

An employer can offer to sell employer stock to employees at any price it wishes. If an employee pays the full value of the purchased shares with the employee's own money or with borrowed money, he or she does not have to recognize taxable income upon the purchase. If the purchase price is *less than* the current value of the shares, the employee will have W-2 income, and the employer a compensation deduction, to the extent of the discount (subject to the vesting rules discussed below).[7]

Financed Shares

Employer Financing Where an employee does not have sufficient funds to pay the purchase price for employer stock, or where the employee cannot afford the tax consequences of an outright grant, the employer can finance the purchase. The employee signs a promissory note, which the employer generally holds until the note is repaid or the employee's employment terminates, at which time the shares may be reacquired in satisfaction of the note. The employee may also sign a pledge agreement under which the employer will hold the shares to collateralize the loan until it is paid off. If the shares are subject to a stockholders' agreement that prohibits a pledge of shares, a waiver of this provision might have to be obtained.

Employee Financing An employee can, of course, secure credit from sources other than the employer corporation to buy shares. Because of the lack of marketability of shares in a closely held corporation, most commercial lenders do not favor loans secured only by such shares. Typical sources of funds to buy shares are an unsecured bank loan, a home equity loan, a loan against the cash value of an insurance policy, or a loan from family members. Also, the employer corporation or an existing stockholder can provide a guarantee to a commercial lender who wants credit enhancement but does not want a pledge of closely held shares.

Deductibility of Interest The interest on a home equity loan is generally deductible (up to a limit of $100,000 of debt).[8] Interest on other loans is deductible under the investment interest rule,[9] but only to the extent of the borrower's net investment income (from all sources).[10] Interest is allocated for deduction purposes under a "tracing rule,"[11] so that the loan is traced to the disbursements made with the borrowed funds, and interest deductibility is determined accordingly.[12] Consequently, where money is borrowed to buy employer stock, interest on the loan will only be deductible to the extent of the borrower's "net investment interest." If the stock does not pay dividends and the borrower has no other investment income, such as interest income, dividends, annuities etc., the interest paid will not be deductible (unless the loan is a qualified home equity loan of $100,000 or less).

Stock Options

A stock option, in the employer-employee context, is a contract giving an employee the right to buy stock from the employer at a stated price for a stated period of time. The two principal features of an option are: (1) the price is fixed, regardless of what happens to the stock's market price; and (2) it is enforceable only by the option holder. An agreement to *buy* shares is different from an option, since the agreement may be enforced by either side, the seller (the employer) as well as the buyer (the employee). Under an option, only the employee can enforce the contract and only the employer (option grantor) has a risk of loss. If the stock price rises, the employer forgoes receiving the full value of the shares upon exercise of the option and the employee obtains the shares for less than their current value.

The holder of an option thus receives the principal economic benefit of being an owner. If the stock value goes up, the holder's wealth increases; he or she has only to exercise the option to realize the benefit of the increase in value. However, the option holder avoids the risk borne by a stock owner. If the value of the stock falls below the exercise price of the option, the holder will simply not exercise the option. Unlike a stockholder who has paid for his stock, the optionee never incurs the loss if there is a downturn in value. To this extent, an option is a "free look" at stock ownership without the risk or economic commitment of becoming a stockholder.

Options come in two varieties: those that are "qualified" under the tax law and therefore enjoy special tax benefits, and those that are not. Employment-related options that are not qualified options are classified and taxed as nonqualified options.

Qualified Options   Qualified options or "incentive stock options" (ISOs) are defined in the Internal Revenue Code (the "Code").[13] The options provided under an ISO plan are restricted in the cumulative amount that may be exercised in any year ($100,000 per year); the period over which they may be exercised (10 years from the date of grant); the price at which they may be exercised (the fair market value of the stock on the date of grant); and the period of time after exercise during which the stock must be held (one year from exercise, two years from grant). Also, ISOs must be granted under a written plan approved by the stockholders of the employer corporation. If these conditions (plus several others) are met, the employee will not have taxable income when the option is granted nor when he or she exercises the option and acquires the shares. The employee is not taxed on an ISO until the option stock is sold, and even then, the gain on the sale is taxed at the long-term capital gains rate. However, the employer corporation gets no compensation deduction when an ISO option is granted to an employee or when it is exercised. To assist employees in funding the purchase of option shares, public companies sometimes grant stock appreciation rights in connection with the grant of options. A stock appreciation right is a contract that gives the employee a cash amount equal to the increase in stock value over the period of the right.

Employee Stock Purchase Plans An employee stock purchase plan, as defined in section 423 of the Code, permits an employer to grant a form of qualified options to a broad spectrum of employees. It is different from an ISO in a number of respects, principally that it cannot be limited to highly compensated or management employees. Because of its broad participation requirements and the tax advantages (discussed below), an employee stock purchase plan would appear to be the most favorable method of creating broad-based employee ownership. However, employee stock purchase plans are not widely employed by closely held corporations. This is probably due to the securities law problems for employers who do not already have publicly traded stock. Where an exemption from registration is not available, as it would not be for a general issuance of shares to rank and file employees not involved in the management of the corporation, an employer would have to comply with all the trouble, expense, and disclosure required by a full SEC registration of its shares and the option transaction, or risk serious securities law violations.

The options issued under an employer stock purchase plan must meet the following requirements (among others): they can only be issued to employees; the plan must be approved by the stockholders; no option can be granted to an employee who would thereupon own, directly or indirectly, 5% of the stock of the employer corporation (counting options as exercised); options must be granted on a nondiscriminatory basis, with almost all employees being eligible; the option price must be at least 85% of the stock value, either at the time of grant or the time of exercise; the maximum option period (between grant and exercise) is 27 months (60 months where the option price is at least 85% of market value on the date of exercise); there is a cumulative $25,000-per-year limit on the value of the stock that any employee may purchase under the plan; and the options are not transferable, except on death. To receive the favorable tax consequences discussed below, an employee must remain continuously in the employ of the issuing corporation until three months before the option is exercised and cannot dispose of the shares within two years of the option grant or one year of the exercise date. Many employee stock purchase plans employ payroll withholding to permit employees to accumulate the funds necessary to exercise the options issued under the plan.

As with ISOs, the recipient of an option under an employee stock purchase plan does not have taxable income when the option is granted nor when the option is exercised and the shares are acquired. The employee only realizes taxable income when the stock is sold. Generally, this income is taxable as capital gain. However, if the employee's option price was less than the fair market value of the stock on the date of grant (which is not possible with an ISO) this bargain element is taxable as ordinary income upon the sale of the shares or death of the employee. If the employee disposes of the shares within two years of the grant or one year of acquiring the shares, all gain must be reported as ordinary income.

Nonqualified Options   Any employee option that is not an ISO is by definition a nonqualified option. Employers have much more flexibility in providing nonqualified options to employees than they have with ISOs. However, the tax consequences of nonqualified options are less favorable for employees than those of ISOs. As with ISOs, the employee does not recognize income when the option is granted.[14] Exercising the option, however, is taxable: The employee has income upon exercise equal to the "spread" between the fair market value of the shares and the strike price paid under the option.[15] Assuming the shares are fully vested when acquired (see the vesting rules discussed below), there will be no further tax consequences until the shares are sold. The corporation's tax treatment parallels that of the employee: upon exercise of the option, the corporation is entitled to a compensation deduction in the amount of the income included by the employee.[16] This deductibility feature generally makes nonqualified options more attractive to employer corporations than ISOs.

Vesting of Share Ownership (Section 83)

Section 83 of the Code governs the tax treatment of property (as opposed to cash) received from an employer. There is a basic rule and a significant exception to the rule.

The Basic Rule

The basic employee is taxable on the bargain element of any property received. So, for example, if the employee pays $700 and receives $1,000 worth of stock, he or she will have $300 of income. Similarly, the employee will have $1,000 of income if the stock is granted without payment.

Taxation under section 83 is not imposed until property is actually transferred to an employee. As discussed above, the transfer of a stock option on stock in a closely held company is not taxable to the employee.[17] Similarly, if the stock is subject to an arrangement such that the employee lacks either the economic benefits or risks of ownership, no transfer of the stock will be deemed to have occurred for tax purposes. For example, if the employee buys shares with a promissory note on which he or she has no personal liability, then, unless the employee is actually required to make substantial and regular payments on the note, the arrangement is like an option to buy the shares, with no risk of loss, and is not considered a transfer of the shares.[18] Likewise, if the property must be returned at the termination of employment in exchange for the original purchase price, no matter how much it has increased in value, the employee does not enjoy the economic benefits of real ownership and no transfer is considered to have taken place.[19]

The Exception: Vesting

Once property is transferred to an employee, the tax consequences of the transfer will nonetheless be deferred until it is "substantially vested." Property is not considered substantially vested until it is either transferable by the owner or not subject to being forfeited. For example, if an employee pays $500 for stock worth $1,000, but the stock must be returned to the employer unless the employee remains employed for four years, the stock will not be vested until the employee's four-year anniversary. At that point, if the stock is worth $1,750, the employee will have $1,250 of income (the $1,750 value of the property upon vesting, less the original purchase price of $500). Common vesting events, in addition to remaining in employment for a set period of time, are the employee's attainment of a personal performance goal or the corporation's attainment of certain earnings levels.

The Exception to the Exception: The Section 83(b) Election

An employee who has received property that is not vested can accelerate the tax consequences of the transfer, and be taxed *as if* the property were immediately vested, by making a special election under Code section 83(b). Why would an employee do this, especially when the property on which tax will be paid today might be forfeited and lost before it vests? The answer lies in avoiding tax on the increase in the value of the stock when it finally does vest. In the example above, the employee paid $500 for stock worth $1,000 at the time of transfer. If the employee had made the section 83(b) election at the time of the transfer, he or she would have had $500 of ordinary income. There would have been no further tax consequences upon vesting, and upon a later sale, proceeds in excess of $1,000 would be taxable as a capital gain. Without the election, the employee would recognize $1,250 upon vesting, all of it ordinary income.

Three things should be noted about the section 83(b) election. First, a transfer of property is required. This means that an employee cannot make the election upon receiving an option or a transfer that is regarded as an option (see above). Second, the timing for making the section 83(b) election is very short: the employee has only 30 days from the date of transfer to file the election with the Internal Revenue Service (IRS).[20] Third, an employee who purchases non-vested shares at fair market value should *always* make the section 83(b) election. When an employee pays the full value of the non-vested shares, there is no tax cost to making the section 83(b) election because there is no bargain element in the sale. Case law has confirmed that where an employee pays full value for stock that is not vested, the tax consequences of the transfer will still be deferred until vesting occurs, even if the stock is then worth substantially more.[21] So by not making the section 83(b) election, an employee who pays $1,000 for unvested shares worth $1,000 shares can needlessly incur $4,000 of taxable income if the shares are worth $5,000 at the time they vest.

Valuation

One of the difficulties encountered in dealing with section 83 issues is determining the "fair market value" of the stock. Where the value is determined by a formula based on book value or a reasonable multiple of earnings, consistently applied, the IRS will generally respect the value so determined.[22] In many corporations, a stockholders' agreement specifies a method or formula based on book value or earnings for determining stock price. Some formulas also require that an independent third party, such as a CPA firm, perform the required calculations. Professional valuation companies, such as those that value closely held corporations pursuant to the administration of an ESOP, have, in addition, the expertise to arrive at an appropriate valuation of a stock interest in a closely held corporation, even where no method or formula is provided.

Issuance of Shares

This section discusses the source of shares transferred to an employee and the collateral issues that arise for the corporation and its stockholders.

Original Issuance Versus Sale by Stockholder

There are several potential sources for the shares to be transferred to an employee: existing stockholders; shares newly issued by the corporation; and treasury shares that the corporation previously issued, but that have been retired and are not currently outstanding.

Where an existing stockholder (rather than the employer corporation) sells shares to an employee at a discount from the current market value, the employee still realizes income (subject to the vesting rules discussed below). The transaction is treated for tax purposes as though the existing stockholder made a (tax-free) contribution of the shares to the corporation, which then re-issued them to the employee at the same discounted price the employee actually paid.[23] Any amounts paid to the existing stockholder are treated as if paid to him or her by the corporation, and are subject to taxation under the redemption rules of Code section 302.[24]

From the standpoint of corporate finance, a sale of shares by an existing stockholder, unlike a sale of shares by the corporation, does not put any additional funds on the corporation's balance sheet.

Valid Issuance of Shares

Depending on state law, shares issued by a corporation to an employee may or may not be considered "validly issued." Some states—New York, for example—deem certain non-cash consideration, such as an obligation to make future payments (e.g., a promissory note) as insufficient to support the issuance of fully paid and non-assessable shares.[25] This means that neither shares issued as an inducement to a new employee who has performed no services yet nor shares financed by a loan from the corporation may be validly issued. Until full payment is made on the acquisition loan, the shares may not be entitled to vote, receive dividends, or participate in the proceeds of a corporate liquidation. Some states, such as Delaware, provide that a promissory note payable to the corporation is sufficient consideration for shares to be validly issued.[26] Many other states have not modernized their corporate laws to this extent[27] and may provide that shares issued for future services are not validly issued.[28] Shares purchased from an existing stockholder (to the extent they were validly issued in the hands of the prior stockholder) are not subject to this potential impediment. In any event, counsel should check the appropriate statutes of the state of incorporation to ensure that any shares issued to an employee for consideration other than cash will be considered validly issued.

Stockholder Dilution—Preemptive Rights

Where an existing stockholder transfers shares to an employee, the proportional interests of the other stockholders are unaffected: the total number of shares outstanding does not change. However, when a corporation issues new shares (or reissues treasury shares that had been retired), the existing stockholders have their proportionate shares of the corporation's voting rights, dividends, and liquidation proceeds diluted.

Because of the consequences of stockholder dilution, the corporate law of some states provides that unless the certificate of incorporation states otherwise, existing stockholders enjoy "preemptive rights" that give them priority over non-stockholders to subscribe for newly issued shares and maintain their relative positions without dilution.[29] There are usually a number of circumstances in which preemptive rights do not arise. For example, treasury shares, shares issued for consideration other than cash (such as shares issued in exchange for services), or preferred shares that do not dilute the common stockholders' rights to vote or receive unlimited dividends or liquidation proceeds may not trigger preemptive rights. Also, when shares are initially issued by a corporation, preemptive rights do not become an issue because there are no existing stockholders whose interest can be diluted.

If the corporation's state of incorporation provides for preemptive rights, counsel for the corporation should either secure a waiver of preemptive rights from existing stockholders (either by a one-time waiver or an amendment of the certificate of incorporation to permanently eliminate preemptive rights) or ensure that the shares issued to employees qualify for one of the applicable exemptions from preemptive rights.

Different Classes of Stock

Closely held corporations ordinarily do not have complicated capital structures with many classes of stock. Such complexity usually comes about from a corporation's efforts to raise capital from outside parties who require express terms for the conditions on which they will invest. Closely held corporations may nonetheless have classes of stock that are economically identical as to dividends and the distribution of assets on liquidation, but that vary as to voting rights. This is one way for a corporation, or its controlling stockholders, to provide employee ownership without giving up, or even affecting, control of the corporation. In certain situations, such as a merger, consolidation, or amendment of a corporation's certificate, all shares and classes of stock may be entitled to vote, provisions in the certificate to the contrary notwithstanding.

Minority Stockholder Suits

One issue that is often raised when a closely held corporation first contemplates issuing stock to employees is the specter of minority stockholder suits and other "stockholder rights" concerns. The general rule of corporate governance is strict majority rule. The party or parties who control 50% of the voting shares can elect themselves or their nominees as directors and virtually control the corporation. This does not mean the majority stockholders have an unfettered right to treat the corporation as their personal property to the detriment of the minority stockholders. It has become well established since the turn of the twentieth century that the majority stockholders owe a fiduciary duty of good faith and fair dealing to the other stockholders when engaging in corporate activity. However, under what is known as the "business judgment rule," courts ordinarily give great deference to directors' decisions. (If it were otherwise, corporate action could be paralyzed, since any act of the directors could be scrutinized in court, resulting in endless delays.)

A court will interfere in corporate affairs only where the minority stock-holders can plainly show that the actions of the majority are so far opposed to the legitimate interests of the corporation that they can have been motivated only by a desire to harm the minority or usurp corporate property or opportunity for themselves, at the expense of the corporation and minority stockholders. Some states have enacted statutory provisions for protecting minority stockholders from certain kinds of majority oppression. Stockholders owning a specified portion of the corporation's shares, 20% for example, may be able to petition a court to either dissolve the corporation or require the majority to buy out the minority stockholders interest at a "fair value."[30]

In the case of a corporation that is being managed by the majority stock-holders to promote employee stock ownership, the possibility of a successful minority stockholder suit must be considered remote, considering the sort of outrageous and oppressive conduct that is generally required to prevail in such a suit. A more likely source of trouble is the risk of a groundless suit by minority stockholders that can be expensive and time-consuming to defend. This should ordinarily not be considered a significant drawback to encouraging employee stock ownership. A litigation-prone employee will not want for opportunities to sue the employer, whether or not the employee becomes a stockholder. Further, a suit that is brought for strategic purposes, with little hope of prevailing on the merits, is typically a battle waged in a war of attrition, in which the objective is not victory but depleting the opponent's resources through attorney fees in the hope of obtaining a favorable settlement. When an employee sues an employer corporation, there is usually little incentive for the employee to wage a war of attrition, since the costs of a suit are likely to become oppressive for the employee long before the employer is driven to seek a settlement.

Stockholders' Agreements

The stockholders of closely held corporations frequently find it desirable to enter an agreement, to which the corporation is usually a party, setting forth certain relationships and obligations concerning the operation of the corporation. If employees are offered stock in a corporate employer, the offer is usually conditioned on becoming a party to the stockholders' agreement.

Voting Agreements

Stockholders' agreements can take a number of forms, depending on the objectives of the parties. If voting control is the only consideration, the stock-holders can form a voting trust or enter a proxy agreement or vote-pooling agreement. Each of these agreements permits a different degree of control and autonomy. A vote-pooling agreement may relate to only one matter, such as the election of directors, on which the parties agree to vote in a predetermined fashion. A proxy lets one person, who may or may not be a stockholder, act as an agent and vote the shares the stockholders who have granted the proxy. A proxy can be narrow or broad in scope and of long or short duration. A voting trust is similar to a joint irrevocable proxy, except the stockholders contribute their shares to the trust in return for "voting trust certificates," and the trustee becomes the owner of the shares being voted, rather than simply an agent. Voting trusts typically have a limited life, commonly 10 years, dictated by statute. Further, some state statutes deem any agreement affecting stockholder voting to be limited to the period applicable to voting trusts.

Voting provisions similar to those found in a voting trust, proxy agreement, or vote-pooling agreement can also be incorporated into a more comprehensive stockholders' agreement. Finally, where the number of shares transferred to employees will not affect voting control, either because of the limited number of shares issued or the issuance of non-voting shares, there is no need to add voting provisions to a stockholders' agreement that does not already have them.

Creation of a Market

From the standpoint of a stockholder in a closely held corporation, one of the primary benefits of a stockholders' agreement is the assurance of a market for the corporation's shares. Without agreed procedures for valuing and transferring a corporation's shares, a stockholder may be entirely unable to sell his or her shares. Particularly where the corporation does not pay dividends or where a transfer of shares will not affect voting control, existing stockholders may have no desire to purchase shares from a departing employee. Yet, unless an employee–stockholder has the potential to cash in on an increase in the corporation's value, one of the primary motives for providing stock to employees cannot be realized. Following are a number of considerations and techniques that are raised in the drafting of a stockholders' agreement. Many existing stockholders' agreements employ one or more of these in combination, so they should not be viewed as mutually exclusive provisions.

Legal Purchase   In each of the situations below in which a corporation buys or proposes to buy shares, the corporation's financial books and records must be consulted to be sure the purchase is legal under the laws of the state where it is incorporated. If the corporation does not have sufficient earnings or capital surplus to repurchase the shares, it must either take steps to ensure that its capital will not be impaired, for example by transferring capital to surplus or reclassifying its shares, or it must refuse to make the purchase. A common provision to deal with this situation is for the stockholders' agreement first to provide that the stockholders will take all reasonable steps to create a surplus sufficient to permit the purchase, and if this is inadequate, then to provide that the stockholders will step in to buy their proportionate share of the stock agreed to be purchased.

Required Buyback by Corporation Some closely held corporations limit the universe of potential stockholders to current or former employees. This can be accomplished through restrictions in the certificate of incorporation. More often, however, it is provided in a stockholders' agreement. Typically, the termination of a stockholder's employment with the corporation, whether because of taking a different job, retirement, disability, or death, will trigger a buyback event. The value of the shares will be determined under the agreement's valuation formula and the price set. There is then a relatively short period for the transfer to take place, say 30 to 365 days. (Where shares must be purchased from an estate, sufficient time must be allowed for the executor named in the stockholder's will to be appointed and qualify.) The agreement may give the corporation the option to pay for the shares partly with a promissory note, especially if the corporation's cash resources would be strained by an all-cash buyback.

Buyout Option A corporation that is a party to an agreement requiring it to buy shares from a former employee faces the possibility of a liquidity short-fall. The corporation may not have the cash or borrowing capacity to fund a required buy back at the time one is required, especially if more than one stockholder terminates employment at or near the same time. This can be particularly painful for a corporation if there is a de facto spinoff in which a whole group of stockholder–employees leaves, and continues in business in competition with the former employer corporation.

One strategy for dealing with this problem is to give the corporation or the non-selling stockholders a right, but not an obligation, to buy the shares of a stockholder who terminates employment. Usually, the corporation is first given the right to purchase some or all of the available shares, with the stockholders having the right to maintain their pro rata stockholdings to the extent the corporation does not exercise its option. The difficulty with this approach, from an employee's standpoint, is that it does not guarantee an ability to sell shares. This can sometimes be handled to an employee's satis-faction by pointing out the fact that the corporation has a history or policy of buying shares from former employees, even where it only has a right and not an obligation to do so. If this approach is used, the corporation should take pains to make clear that it is not *obliged* to follow such a policy, so as not to inadvertently create a buyback agreement where none is intended.

Right of First Refusal Another approach that can be taken is for a stockhold-ers' agreement to grant the corporation a right of first refusal to meet the terms of any offer received by a stockholder from a third party to buy shares. The non-selling stockholders are usually given a right of first refusal if the corporation declines to redeem any portion of the shares subject to the third-party offer. This sort of right of first refusal is used principally to protect the closely held corporation and its stockholders from unwanted outside shareholders. Because it relies on the fortuitous occurrence of an offer from a third party to trigger a stock purchase, it is not particularly conducive to creating a market for the shares of departing employee–stockholders.

Non-Compete Provisions

A stockholders' agreement can provide that any note payments or other deferred payments to a former employee will be forfeited if the employee goes to work for a competitor. (Whether this will be considered a forfeiture provision that defers vesting for tax purposes depends on all the circumstances applicable at the time of grant.)[31] If competition from former employee-stockholders is a significant concern, a corporation may require such employees to execute employment agreements containing a non-compete clause.

If an employer corporation believes a non-compete clause in an employment contract has been breached, compliance can be difficult and expensive to enforce, involving the considerable expense of obtaining temporary restraining orders and preliminary and final injunctions. With this in mind, a stockholders' agreement can provide an additional disincentive to compete. The relevant buyout provisions can defer a significant portion of the payments during the non-compete period, subject to forfeiture if there is a breach of the non-compete agreement. One mechanism for achieving this disincentive is to recalculate the buyout price if the non-compete provisions are breached, using on the par value of the stock or some other nominal consideration instead of its full value.

Courts are more inclined to enforce a non-compete clause tied to the sale of an interest in a business than a bare non-compete agreement. The idea behind this principle is that while a non-compete agreement should not prevent an employee from making a living in his or her chosen field, a person who sells a business interest is usually getting paid for part of the "goodwill" or future earning capacity of the business and can fairly be prevented from trying to take with him assets, such as customer relationships, that he has purported to sell with the business.

Non-compete provisions can be a thorny issue in employer-employee relations. Unless it is an acknowledged industry practice, asking employee–stockholders to sign a non-compete agreement can be perceived as an overreaching demand. Although the blow can be softened by limiting non-compete consequences to a price reduction under the buyback provisions of a stockholders' agreement (rather than attempting to flatly prohibit working for competitors), this sort of limitation on the potential benefits of employee stock ownership tends to diminish some of the motivations that promote stock ownership in the first place.

Legending Shares

If a stockholders' agreement to which the corporation is a party restricts the transferability of a corporation's shares, both the Uniform Commercial Code and the corporate laws of a number of states require this to be "conspicuously noted" on the face of the stock certificates.[32] Otherwise, a good-faith buyer without actual knowledge of the restrictions will generally be unaffected by them. An example of a standard form of such a legend is as follows:

> Transfer of these securities is restricted pursuant to an agreement dated _____, a copy of which may be examined at the offices of the Corporation.

Conclusion

There can be many reasons to provide stock to employees, including performance-based incentives, retaining key employees, planning for business succession, and providing additional compensation to select employees. Employers can grant shares without payment, sell them to employees, or provide various kinds of options to purchase the shares, each with differing tax consequences for the employer and the corporation. Where employees buy all or a portion of the shares, there are a number of ways to finance the purchase in which the employer can be more or less involved. The form of financing affects the tax deductibility of interest paid by the employee on a loan to acquire shares. In providing stock to employees, the usual issues confronted by a corporation in issuing its shares must be addressed, such as the valid issuance of shares, stockholder dilution, and voting rights. Finally, a closely held corporation will ordinarily require an employee to become a party to a stockholders' agreement that may provide for voting arrangements, a market for the corporation's shares, and non-competition provisions.

Notes

1. Issues applicable solely to publicly traded companies are not covered here. "Publicly traded" for this purpose means employers with a class of stock required to be registered under the Securities Exchange Act of 1934 (the "1934 Act"), i.e., a class of stock: (1) listed on a national securities exchange or (2) with more than 500 stockholders where the corporation has more than $1 million of assets. It is also assumed that, because of the non-public nature of any stock offering solely to employees, the registration requirements of the Securities Act of 1933 (the "1933 Act") would be inapplicable to the transactions discussed in this chapter, because of § 4(2) of the 1933 Act. Topics not addressed include Code § 280G, applicable to "golden parachute" payments by public companies; stock registration requirements and Form S-8; the short-swing profit rule of § 16 of the 1934 Act; the executive compensation disclosure rules imposed by SEC Regulation S-K; and the $1 million deductibility cap on executive compensation paid by public companies imposed by Code § 162(m).

2. See, for example, Ariz. Rev. Stat. Ann. §§ 10-201 to 110-218; Cal. Corp. Code § 158; Del. Code Ann. tit. 8, § 342; Ill. Ann. Stat. ch. 32, paras. 1201-16; Kan. Stat. Ann. §§ 17-7201 to -7216; Me. Rev. Stat. Ann. tit. 13-A, §§ 102(5), 701; Md. Code Ann., Corps. & Ass'ns §§ 4-101 to -603; N.C. Gen. Stat. § 55-73(b) to (c); Ohio Rev. Code Ann. § 1701.591; Pa. Stat. Ann. tit. 15, §§ 1371-86; R.I. Gen. Laws §§ 7-1.1 to 51.

3. If stock is awarded without payment, the employee's resulting tax liability may create a de facto risk of loss: the employee has made an investment, albeit through the payment of taxes rather than to the corporation, which will be lost if the stock become worthless.

4. Stock, as equity capital, does not have a fixed repayment term, does not pay interest, and is subordinate in repayment to the corporation's creditors.

5. Code § 1361 et seq.

6. An S corporation that was previously a C corporation and has not distributed all of its C corporation earnings may have its distributions treated as taxable dividends to stockholders. Code § 1368(c). Also, even a regular S corporation will trigger a gain (the tax on which is payable by its stockholders) if it distributes appreciated property. Code §§ 1371(a)(1) and 311(b).

7. If the shares are not fully vested, taxable income on account of the purchase may be merely deferred until the time the shares vest, rather than being avoided altogether. See the section in this chapter titled "Vesting."

8. Code § 163(h).

9. Code § 163(d).

10. The recent Tax Court case *Commissioner v. Russon*, 107 T.C. 15 (1996), confirmed that interest on a loan to buy stock in a family C corporation is investment interest and only deductible to the extent of net investment income. Under the tracing rules, the unrestricted deductibility of interest on loans incurred for "trade or business" expenditures does not apply to the trade or business of performing services as an employee. Treas. Reg. § 1.163-8T(b)(7).

11. Treas. Reg. § 1.163-8T.

12. Ibid.

13. Code § 422.

14. If the option has a readily ascertainable fair market value, i.e., it is both freely transferable and publicly traded, it *will* be taxable when it is granted. Treas. Reg. § 1.83-7(a). Under the "readily ascertainable fair market value" test, an option on the shares of a closely held company will virtually never be taxable at grant.

15. Code § 83.

16. The employer's deduction is conditioned on required information reporting to the Internal Revenue Service. Treas. Reg. § 1.83-6(a).

17. See note 14.

18. Treas. Reg. § 1.83-3(a)(2).

19. Treas. Reg. § 1.83-3(a)(3) to (5).

20. Treas. Reg. § 1.83-2(b).

21. *Commissioner v. Alvez*, 734 F.2d 478 (9th Cir. 1984), *aff'g* 79 T.C. 864 (1982).

22. Treas. Reg. § 1.83-5(a).

23. Treas. Reg. § 1.83-6(d).

24. Ibid.

25. N.Y. Bus. Corp. Law § 504(b).

26. Del. Code Ann. tit. 8, § 152.

27. See N.Y. Bus. Corp. Law § 504(b).

28. Ibid.

29. Del. Code Ann. tit. 8, § 102(b)(3).

30. See N.Y. Bus. Corp. Law § 1104-a and 1118.

31. Treas. Reg. § 1.83-3(c)(1) to (2).

32. U.C.C. § 8-204(a).

CHAPTER 8

Employee Ownership and Initial Public Offerings

Fred E. Whittlesey
Compensation and Performance Management, Inc.

Jill Zidaritz
Sybase, Inc.

After the peak year for initial public offerings (IPOs) in 1997, initial public offering activity is still occurring at a brisk rate, particularly in the technology sector. The media and various data services typically report IPO activity in terms of the market value of offerings, the number of offerings, and, anecdotally, the millions of dollars earned by entrepreneurs who were major shareholders in those companies. In the past five years, thousands of companies have raised billions of dollars in capital through such offerings; many individuals in their 20s and 30s now own stock worth millions of dollars due to IPOs.

While these data and stories make for interesting reading, they overlook another aspect of IPOs: the significant transfer of equity value to a broad population of employees. In fact, most companies in the technology sector completing public offerings in the past few years have stock-based compensation programs in which all employees are participants.

Yet employee ownership is rarely, if ever, a primary objective of an IPO and at best is a side effect, not a cause. Technology companies in California's Silicon Valley have long used stock options as a "second currency," not to create employee ownership but to conserve cash and transfer employee compensation costs to the external market. The uproar over the Financial Accounting Standards Board (FASB) Statement 123 issue (FASB proposed that companies account for the fair value of stock options on their income statements) underscored these companies' reliance on stock options to attract and reward employees. Many of these companies' option plans feature monthly vesting schedules and cashless exercise programs, turning stock options into shorter-term cash delivery vehicles rather than long-term stock ownership tools.

At the other end of the spectrum, mature public companies such as Bank of America, Merck, DuPont, and EDS have adopted broad-based stock option plans to provide all employees with stock-based compensation opportunities, in part to realize the financial accounting and cash flow advantages. The key difference between the broad-based plans in mature companies and those of IPO companies is the tremendous difference in potential value transfer to employees holding options in IPOs.

For example, Bank of America's all-employee stock option plan introduced in 1997, the Take Ownership program, offered a minimum of 50 stock options every six months to its employees. In the first quarter of 1997, initial grants were made at a price of approximately $95. At an annual stock price growth rate of 18% (its trailing five-year average) over the next five years (the term of the options), 100 stock options with a grant value of $9,500 would provide a gain of approximately $9,600 (present value based on a five-year risk-free rate of 5%).

Contrast this to the employees of one technology company who received option awards before its IPO in May 1996 at an average option price of $3.50, with some as low as 25 cents. The company's initial offering price was $8.50 and in the following year was trading near $20. A comparable grant value of $9,500 at an exercise price of $3.50 provided gains in the first year of over $40,000 (using the same present value method). If those options were granted at 25 cents, the employee was not quite yet a millionaire, though at the stock's recent price of $27, he or she enjoyed that status.

The potential or actual economic value transfer of stock options is fairly simple to establish. More difficult is determining the answer to the question of employee ownership. Will Bank of America employees take ownership of the stock? Or will they, through a cashless exercise program, liquidate their position on the vesting date? And will they take ownership attitudes with respect to their jobs, their organization, and their customers? We will explore how these questions will be answered for the technology company's employees, several of whom are, at today's stock price, paper millionaires and many more who are at the top of the wealth distribution for their age.

Public Offerings

Before discussing the issues, it is important to recognize that much of the purported IPO activity includes spinoffs—divestitures of a segment of existing public companies. In the past two years, these have included AT&T's offering of Lucent and NCR, Sears' spinoff of Allstate, RJR's offering of Nabisco, and Ford's pending divestiture of Hertz. These transactions rarely provide the upside potential of a true initial offering, and present additional complexities of managing the change from a mature subsidiary or divisional culture to a new and growth-oriented freestanding culture. For our purposes here, an IPO refers to the very first public offering of shares of a company since its founding—a private company turning to the public equity markets to raise capital.

The Purpose of Initial Public Offerings

Understanding employee ownership issues in IPO companies requires understanding the reason for IPOs. While the monetary incentives to sell one's company to public investors is substantial in a stock market like the one we have experienced for the past 15 years, many founders struggle with the decision to give up privacy and control for millions of dollars that continue to be at risk and, in most cases, tied up in illiquid shares for years to come. An IPO is only one potential "exit strategy" for the founder(s) of a company. The outright sale to a competitor; a "synergistic sale" to a company in similar lines of business; a merger; a sale to employees through an employee stock ownership plan (ESOP); a sale to the current management team through a management buyout; or the liquidation of assets—all of these offer advantages and disadvantages, and each is appropriate for some situations.

As the founders contemplate growth and exit strategies—where to obtain the capital needed to grow the business and how to ultimately get their money out of the business—a public offering is an attractive alternative. IPOs typically become the preferred strategy when a founder's desire for liquidity is accompanied by other investors' desires for liquidity and/or the company's need for non-debt capital to grow and expand the business. While these issues are beyond the scope of this discussion, the IPO should not be seen as the cure-all solution, and many investors see it as a much lower-value alternative. The significant costs, restrictions, and continued risk of taking a private company public do not always satisfy investors' value objectives. Once the decision to pursue an IPO is made, however, a new set of issues immediately emerges.

Public Offerings and Employee Ownership

An IPO presents an immediate challenge to whatever degree of employee ownership may already exist in an organization. At the founding of a company, it is likely that all owners are employees, which may be only one or a handful of founders. These shareholders are typically hesitant to distribute equity too widely until the prospect for a liquidity transaction, such as a sale, a merger, or an IPO, arises. But many of these companies have a strong ownership culture exhibiting all of the ownership ideals: employee understanding of business priorities and performance measures, a team-oriented culture, participative decision-making, performance-based reward systems, and a true investment in the workplace. Most of these companies have no equity-based plans, or even phantom plans, during the private ownership phase, and the public offering provides the first opportunity for employees to get a "piece of the action."

When implemented properly, equity compensation can provide a winning situation for all stakeholders. But beyond the market risk, disappointments often stem from plan design and implementation that does not consider the multifaceted regulatory complexities unique to IPO situations.

The Financial Dynamics

An IPO is first and foremost a financial event, and the analysis that drives the offering is primarily financial in nature. The choice to use equity compensation

is strongly supported by financial factors, but plans must be carefully designed to optimize the benefits and avoid the pitfalls.

Accounting

Current financial accounting standards, even with the recent addition of the
requirement for the FASB Statement 123 footnote (i.e., the requirement that a
company disclose in a footnote to its financial statement the present value of
options if it does not recognize that value in the financial statement itself), create
a strong incentive to use stock options over cash compensation. Cash shows up
as a cost on the financial statement; options do not when they are only disclosed
in a footnote. The opportunity to issue stock options at a relatively low price
before the IPO allows substantial amounts of compensation to be delivered at
"no cost" in terms of compensation expense on the income statement. The
dilution incurred from the issuance of options can be offset by many times the
amount in option gains when a company is successful in the public markets.

The early issuance of stock options—i.e., a year or more before the offering
date— provides an opportunity to issue options at a price far below the ultimate offering price while avoiding securities and accounting regulations requiring recognition of a compensation expense for options and shares issued
at a discount from fair market value. The "implicit discount" is achieved
because the value of the private company with distant hopes for an IPO is far
below the value of a company with publicly traded shares.

A company must be cautious in granting options at a price too far below
what may be determined to be "fair market value" at the date of grant. The
Securities and Exchange Commission (SEC) has indicated, more through a
pattern of actions than through documented regulations, that stock and options granted during the year before an offering must be granted at a price
within a certain range. The acceptable range is related to the amount of time
remaining before the offering, the estimated current fair market value, and the
planned offering price. In general, the option price may be as little as 75% of
the offering price within the three-month period before the offering and as little
as 25% of the offering price when granted more than nine months before.

Failure to recognize these guidelines can result in significant accounting
penalties. For example, documents filed in connection with a recent offering
show the potential magnitude of these effects. The company, whose offering
was completed in 1996, granted options during the eight months before the
offering at prices ranging from 50 cents to $6.50 per share compared to the
offering price of $8.50. While details of this decision are not required to be
disclosed, the company did disclose it recorded a deferred compensation liability for some of these option awards of approximately $1.2 million, to be
amortized over the vesting period of the options, indicated to be "generally
five years." This company had revenues of just over $8 million and net in-
come of $317,000 in the year before the offering.

Adhering to the guidelines and issuing options at fair market value can still provide substantial gains for employees while avoiding negative effects on the income statement. The entire "spread" on these options is an expense-free form of compensation with respect to the company's financial statements, with one exception: dilution.

Dilution

While avoiding accounting charges, the use of stock as compensation dilutes the holdings of shareholders. Yet the act of going public, by definition, is a choice to dilute ownership. At a private company, a small number of typically sophisticated shareholders could easily analyze the tradeoffs of cash versus stock. Now, with a diverse group of public shareholders, the proposal to offer additional options immediately creates discussion over "dilution" and "overhang."

While the issuance of additional stock options by a public company sometimes raises investor concerns, the options issued before or coincident with a public offering are "part of the deal" presented in the prospectus and have the explicit approval of both previous and new investors.

And while earnings dilution and ownership dilution are a concern, many investors prefer a share of dilution to a dollar of cash outflow, regardless of whether the dollar appears as a compensation expense on the company's income statement. "Dilution" must be viewed as a two-sided issue. Certainly, issuing more shares lowers each shareholder's proportional share. But the substitution of a share for cash may provide more than just cash-efficient compensation in its motivational effects and rewards for superior company performance. In other words, the piece of pie may be smaller, but the pie is bigger. And we hope that the performance-based nature of stock-based pay provides an incentive to grow the pie still bigger.

Cash Flow

An IPO provides capital for growth, repayment of debt, or general corporate purposes, often relieving some or all of the cash flow pressures that can be mitigated by compensating employees with stock rather than cash. Nevertheless, most business managers would agree that more cash in the business is better than less, and stock-based compensation continues to be an effective financial strategy. In fact, the use of stock options not only avoids an operational cash outflow but generates a financing cash inflow as employees exercise their options. At exercise, proceeds flow into the shareholder equity account on the balance sheet. In addition, any corporate tax deduction realized from the exercise of nonqualified stock options (NSOs) or from disqualifying dispositions of incentive stock options (ISOs) are credited to additional paid-in capital.

Taxes

Of course, from the employee's perspective, a stock option results in the same or less tax as cash compensation, with more control over the timing. And with the legends of Microsoft millionaires and thousands more in Silicon Valley, stock options are highly attractive. Whether nonqualified options or incentive stock options are issued, the employee will have the opportunity for compensation taxed at a rate less than or equal to cash, with the choice of choosing when to receive the income (before the end of the option term).

For the employer, the choice of options creates a tax and cash flow choice: nonqualified options will provide the company with a tax deduction for compensation expense upon the employee's exercise of the option. No such deduction is realized with an ISO unless a "disqualifying disposition" occurs and the employer reports the income on the employee's W-2 form.

Companies that anticipate large gains from options, or larger companies paying relatively higher cash compensation, must also be aware of the "million-dollar cap" rule. Amounts exceeding $1 million paid in a single year to any of the five highest-paid executives are a tax-deductible compensation expense only if the amounts come from "performance-based compensation." To simplify a complex subject, base salary is not considered performance-based; cash bonuses are considered performance-based only if they meet a fairly restrictive set of conditions that many companies find unacceptable; and stock option gains will be classified as performance-based only if certain conditions are met. While most would think a stock option is inherently performance-based, the Internal Revenue Code outlines specific rules that may not be intuitive to most executives. The requirements for a performance-based stock option plan are relatively easy to conform to, however, and a company should ensure they are met.

Securities Regulations

Beyond the impact on a company's financial statements and an employee's W-2 form, another concern among those considering an IPO is the reporting of executive compensation levels, compensation philosophy, and compensation plan descriptions in the prospectus and subsequent proxy statements. For the founders, the disclosure of previously "secret" information is one of the first experiences of the new "life in a fishbowl." For investors, this provides a substantially detailed insight into many aspects of business operations.

The other dynamic driven by SEC rules is insider reporting requirements accompanied by trading restrictions. While not typically considered a "financial issue," consider the message many founders receive when discussing the prospects of an IPO: "You must share your ownership with others, publicly disclose compensation programs and levels, and report to the SEC each time you complete a transaction in your company's stock; additionally, you may have little or no liquidity for the first six months to two years after the IPO." Because corporate and personal financial decisions are commingled in the private founder-managed firm, these often are the underpinnings of the decision to go public.

Stages in a Public Offering

The financial dynamics and behavioral consequences of using stock options compel virtually every company to issue options to its management team, if not all employees, before an IPO. These key design issues of "who" and then "how much" are accompanied by a host of strategic and technical issues.

The answers to these questions often change as a company moves from considering an IPO to planning for an IPO to executing the IPO to life as a public company. Many executives are surprised at the number of constraints and expectations imposed on public companies. Base salaries cannot be too high, but should not be too low. Cash bonuses should be clearly related to performance and in line with competitive practice. The amount of stock reserved for option plans, the distribution of stock and options to employees, and the provisions under which such distributions are made are subject not only to regulatory constraints but to investor expectations, competitive norms, and media commentary. Written employment agreements, severance policies, change-in-control agreements, and other structures for managing compensation form a new set of rules. The earlier that these decisions are made, the better, particularly regarding equity compensation.

The Pre-IPO Period

Using Equity Compensation for the First Time   As companies contemplate an IPO and begin discussions with their various professional advisors, stock-based compensation becomes a "given." Investors expect to see it in the prospectus, and it is one of the cornerstones of "normal" compensation practice.

Favorable accounting treatment, tax planning considerations, investor expectations, and competitive norms dictate almost universal adoption of option plans. Companies should not overlook, however, the role of an employee stock purchase plan (ESPP), permitted under section 423 of the Internal Revenue Code (thus commonly known as a "423 plan"). Considered by some as a "purchase plan" and others an "option plan" (although, once enrolled, the employee no longer has an option but rather a commitment to purchase stock), an ESPP allows employees the possibility of purchasing company stock through a payroll deduction program, commission-free. With a rising stock price, the purchase may be executed at the lower price established at the beginning of the period. The company benefits from a continuing demand for its stock, periodic contributions to capital, and increased employee ownership.

Most companies can realize their financial and compensation objectives through this combination of plans. The myriad financial and regulatory factors dictate an early adoption of stock options and a subsequent implementation of a stock purchase plan.

Early Issuance of Options   Once a company decides to issue options, the next question is when to issue them. The earlier the grants come before the IPO date, the lower the option price that can be used without incurring earnings charges for discounted options. While maximizing option gains should not necessarily be a driving factor in compensation strategy, a company soon realizes that as long as it has decided upon a certain amount of dilution from options, it may as well allow employees to realize as much compensation as possible from those options. This "shifting of compensation costs to the marketplace" may take much of the pressure off the other elements of the total compensation package: base salary, cash bonuses, and benefits.

One constraint may be the need to convert to a C corporation before issuing options. Many private companies are structured as S corporations, limited liability companies (LLCs), or partnerships. Personal tax considerations of the founders often drive the timing of this decision. Some companies wait until the day of the offering to convert, often delaying the option awards until the offering day—and granting at the offering price. Other companies may award options much earlier and provide options at a fraction of the IPO price.

Participation   Two clear models exist today for stock plan participation: (1) the top group and (2) everybody (currently characterized as a "broad-based" plan). Current compensation trends, continued financial incentives, and increased interest in employee ownership as a management strategy are compelling companies to answer "who?" with "everyone." The decision is complex, involving compensation philosophy, strategy, market norms, total compensation mix, and so on. Stock option participation philosophy is seemingly driven by what is known as catastrophe theory in the physical sciences. Once a certain line is crossed, things default to the other extreme: "If we're going down to the supervisory level, then we should give them to everyone."

Interestingly, companies that were at the forefront of the technology revolution and have since grown to be *Fortune*-ranked companies have come full circle. Intel Corp. recently announced the decision to grant stock options to all employees. At companies such as Intel, which was already a heavy user of options to attract and retain technical talent, the increasing use of "options for everyone" is another example of small companies changing the behavior of larger ones.

Awards   After the "who," the other key decision is "how much" or, with stock options, "how many." In the typical frenzy of a public offering process, little analysis of these issues occurs. The issue is typically framed in terms of "how much the market will bear"—what level of dilution will investors find acceptable. This only answers the question in aggregate. Most public companies will feel comfortable reserving a number of shares below the threshold of 10% of post-offering outstanding shares. The earlier the option plan is adopted before an offering, however, the more difficult this analysis becomes. Most options issued to public company employees are "protected" from dilution resulting from a recapitalization. But in the pre-IPO company, several rounds of recapitalization may be planned, and all investors expect proportional dilution.

Once the aggregate pool is determined, individual awards must still be addressed. There is an increasing amount of competitive data to help companies determine the appropriate answer to this. But, like any element of compensation, referencing the "typical" level of compensation on a single element can be very misleading. Like the man who drowned crossing a river that on average was two feet deep, a company must understand that the "average" stock option award represents a wide variety of companies who vary the mix between salary, bonus, and options.

In addition, most of the data focuses on ongoing situations, not IPOs. While some studies have been done on the use of stock in IPO companies, it is relatively general in nature and may not provide the needed guidance for most organizations.

Finally, a company must address whether a pre-IPO option grant is a one-time event or the first of a series of annual awards. To the extent that the company decides to do a larger one-time award, communications to employees must be clear to avoid establishing the expectation of similar future awards.

The Upside IPO and the Downside IPO

For all of the success stories and employee millionaires, there are many optionees with "underwater options"—options with an exercise price above the stock's current market value for some time after the offering. Many studies of the IPO aftermarket indicate only about one-half of companies completing an IPO have their shares trading above the offering price three months to two years later. Many companies reprice options to restore the value despite proxy disclosure requirements and negative investor sentiment. This is even more controversial in IPO situations when investors have high expectations for price appreciation—and may feel that they "got in late."

A company that issues stock-based compensation to a broad group of employees must be prepared to deal with the potential for both prosperity and disappointment of stock price movements and trends. Educating employees is a key strategy, one often given inadequate attention. Providing information on why the stock price increases and decreases, what individual employees can do in their job to affect stock price, and the intended long-term nature of stock plans can soften the disappointment of a poorly performing stock and temper excessive exuberance over the short-term performance of stock after an offering.

After the IPO (1): The Good News

Few could argue against providing some or all employees with compensation levels that were never imagined and yet are still affordable to the company. Legends of the current economy of California's Silicon Valley, where houses often sell one hour after listing, above the offering price, and there is a waiting list for new Porsches, lend anecdotal evidence to the potential value of stock options in a company going public. These compensation levels often dwarf cash compensation and other benefits, allowing the company to essentially freeze or even reduce direct costs of compensation and benefits. New millionaires sometimes seem less concerned about getting their 4% salary increase. In the extreme, a company's strategy for enhancing operating cash flow through compensation planning is optimized.

Until a market exists for the shares, there is no liquidity, absent company repurchase agreements. A private company cannot afford to fund marketplace multiples of earnings that drive public company stock prices. Public equity markets provide a previously unavailable source of liquidity and earnings leverage, allowing the company to use stock options as a "second currency." This allows companies to reevaluate their mix of cash compensation and equity compensation. The use of monthly vesting schedules by many growth companies indicates that ownership and retention are secondary to delivery of cash as an objective of the stock option plan.

For the employee, the ultimate value of stock or an option is its cash equivalent, realized with the establishment of a public market for the company's shares.

After the IPO (2): The Bad News

Many a founder and stockholder has been disappointed to learn that the transaction purported to provide liquidity comes with limitations on and even prohibitions against selling shares. Underwriters of the transaction often require management and major stockholders to agree to a "lockup period" after the offering during which they may not sell shares, ranging from three months to one year. To the extent shares were acquired through a private placement or other transaction in which shares were not registered, the shares will be restricted by securities laws from sale for a period of time after acquisition. Even without these restrictions, market realities may prevent stockholders from selling significant portions of their holdings if the potential supply of shares exceeds market demand.

The good news of large stock option gains is accompanied by the bad news of taxes. The tax due at exercise of a nonqualified option requires either a large cash payment by the employee or the withholding of cash or stock proceeds, thus reducing the net gain and the resulting stock ownership position. And while the exercise of an ISO can allow deferral of income tax until the sale of the shares, the gain at exercise is included in the calculation of the Alternative Minimum Tax (AMT). For this reason, some companies permit the early exercise of options, when the gains are little or none. Some companies even allow the exercise of unvested options, with the resulting shares subject to the original option vesting schedule. When employees create a disqualifying disposition with ISO or ESPP shares through the sale of shares before the end of the required holding period, the gain is converted to ordinary income and added to their W-2. If the required federal and state taxes are not submitted as required, a penalty may be charged.

More than a few companies have seen their initial offering price become their all-time high stock price. Employees who received option grants long before the offering may still have "in the money" options. However, employees who received option grants closer to, or on, the offering date may have underwater options from day one. While many companies suffer from stock price declines and resulting underwater options, the anticipation surrounding IPOs often leads to greater disappointment when these options continue to be, and later expire, worthless.

An issue rarely addressed until it occurs is the challenge of integrating "new" employees with "old" employees. Individuals who joined the company in its pre-IPO period and received low-price stock options may have realized significant compensation from the IPO. As the company continues to grow and add employees, this newer group will probably not have the opportunity for comparable gains. In the most extreme situations, a group of "paper millionaires" sitting in adjacent offices and cubicles provide a visible reminder of the "missed opportunity."

As employees in a successful IPO company begin to realize the economic benefits, some may feel they have no need to work, to work at that company, or to work as diligently for that company. Many stock option gains have provided "seed capital" for competing enterprises, while others have encouraged early retirement by employees still in their peak productive years. Compensation planning efforts must consider this possibility and include strategies for retaining and motivating those whose personal economic situation may have far exceeded their wildest expectations. This may require implementing provisions that are restrictive and potentially perceived as negative by employees—but quite positive by investors. When Dames & Moore completed its public offering in 1991, converting from a private partnership on the day of the offering, its partners' capital accounts roughly quintupled in value. To ensure continued interest, the company adopted stock retention guidelines and liquidity restrictions that essentially penalized those who sold too much stock too quickly, while still allowing some gradual liquidity over time.

When companies see their stock price languish, decline, or plummet, the options that attracted key talent may lose their retention value. A company should avoid "spending" all of its options before the offering to prepare for this possibility. A deterioration of stock price may provide an opportunity for additional grants of options and an incentive to "get the stock price back up." While this should be structured to avoid offending investors who have "underwater shares," it is more favorable than canceling and reissuing existing options at the new, lower price (known as a "repricing").

Opportunities for the New Public Company

The public offering of shares creates a new, more liquid currency as a basis for compensation programs. Beyond stock options are a plethora of opportunities to use stock as a performance-based and ownership-oriented pay tool. In recent years, thousands of companies have used stock in creative ways to compensate employees using stock options, stock awards, stock purchases, stock matching or investments in qualified retirement and savings plans, and so on.

Challenges for the New Public Company

Even the most successful post-IPO companies realized the tradeoffs of the public markets. While these are typically discussed during the process of evaluating an IPO as an alternative, the reality can be more difficult than anticipated.

After the IPO, the company no longer belongs to the original owners. The founders and early hires realize that people they don't know own "their" company and vote on key corporate governance issues.

The flip side of liquidity is ownership. Employee-shareholders want to sell shares, while investors want to see executives as owners. While it may seem unnecessary to continue to grant stock options to an individual with a significant ownership position, this may be a key strategy in countering a tendency to "bail out."

A new focus of communication is created after the offering. No longer does the "inside group" sit around a table to review information and make business decisions. Now there is a board of directors with "outside" directors, including a compensation committee, audit committee, and one or more other committees. Shareholders and the media scrutinize quarterly earnings reports, the annual report, and the proxy statement. New accounting rules, such as FASB Statement 123, require a great amount of detail regarding stock option plan operation and the purported "cost" of these options.

Planning for the Public Company

Despite current concerns regarding a market correction and a cooling of IPO activity, the public offering will continue to be a viable alternative for most companies. The consideration of an offering often begins up to five years before such an event. As an IPO becomes a realistic alternative or a plan of action, stock compensation planning should become an active effort parallel to other financial and legal activities.

- Ensure that all of your professional advisers—attorneys, accountants, investment bankers, and consultants—are involved in the appropriate points in the process. The multidisciplinary nature of equity compensation mandates the integration of strategic, financial, behavioral, legal, and investor relations considerations.

- Review all compensation and benefits programs for opportunities to use stock rather than cash. Incentive awards, recognition awards, and retirement and savings plans can all use soon-to-be or newly tradable shares as a payment and funding vehicle.

- Implement a stock option plan as soon as possible before the IPO. For a given level of dilution, earlier grants will allow delivery of greater option gains to employees. Even if the IPO is delayed, vesting schedules and repurchase provisions can prevent expansion of the shareholder group in the absence of a public market for the company's shares.

- Consider the administrative requirements of stock options and learn about available software and outsourcing alternatives. Adopting an option plan and granting employee options requires minimal resources compared to the administrative needs that arise once options become vested and employees begin exercising. As a company grows and expands its optionee population, tracking option activity on a spreadsheet will become an impossible task.

- Ensure there is a process in place for proper documentation of plan adoption and operation decisions, including board resolutions and minutes as well as participant agreements.

- Define guidelines for option awards—by salary level, salary grade, job title, or other criteria—to ensure external competitiveness and internal consistency.

- Prepare an ESPP plan for adoption just before the IPO to provide a favorable purchase price point.

- Begin the process of considering a cashless exercise program and selecting one or more brokers. The firm with the greatest expertise in underwriting the company's offering is not necessarily the best qualified for administering the cashless exercise program.

- Implement a system for tracking stock sales resulting from disqualifying dispositions under both ISOs and ESPPs. The corporate tax deductions realized from capturing these data can be substantial.

These implementation and administrative considerations are critical in realizing the full financial benefit and employee impact of equity-based compensation programs.

Regardless of the past, present, or potential future structure of an organization, creating an ownership culture requires more than transferring equity to employees. An IPO presents a one-time opportunity to provide compensation and ownership levels that are difficult to replicate in private and mature public companies. But equity transfer and compensation delivery, while meeting many business objectives, may do little to create true employee ownership.

Because the focus of planning and executing an IPO is driven by financial and legal considerations, the strategic and behavioral aspects of stock-based compensation should be considered. It is ultimately the development of stock plan provisions, not just the plan, that supports ownership initiatives. More importantly, additional investment in employee training and communication can turn a lucrative economic opportunity for employees into an additional opportunity to be participants in the business.

CHAPTER 9

Creating an Ownership Culture: Tapping into the Real Potential of Broad Stock Options

Ed Carberry
The National Center for Employee Ownership

One of the most common reasons companies cite for setting up a broad-based stock option plan is to enhance business performance by linking the interests of employees to those of the company and its other shareholders. In fact, research indicates that broad employee ownership can have significant effects on a company's bottom line, but only if ownership is accompanied by a committed effort to create a culture in which employees are trained and encouraged to think and act like owners. Creating this kind of culture, even if it is backed by genuine commitment, is often a long and challenging process. This chapter discusses why employee participation can be so significant, reviews some of the necessary elements in creating an ownership culture, and examines what five companies with broad-based stock option plans have done in this area.

The Research on Employee Ownership and Corporate Performance

Research consistently shows that employee stock ownership has a significant impact on corporate performance only when ownership is combined with broad employee participation. "Participation" means creating opportunities for employees to have meaningful input into decisions in areas where they have, or could develop, expertise. Participative management typically involves work teams, enlarged job responsibilities, cross-functional teams, and informal opportunities for employees to contribute input, among other changes. Most companies also provide employees with information on company and work-level financial goals and performance.

A 1987 NCEO study looked at the performance of 45 companies with employee stock ownership plans (ESOPs) and 225 non-ESOP companies and found that companies that combined employee ownership with a participative management style grew 8% to 11% per year faster than they would have been expected to grow based on how they had performed before setting up these plans. Subsequent studies by academics in New York and Washington states and by the U.S. General Accounting Office used the same research design with different samples and found very similar results. Studies of companies that use participative management without employee ownership have found that participation does have a small positive impact on performance, but not enough to explain the synergy between ownership and participation that other studies have found.[1]

Why is this combination of employee ownership and participation so potent? There seem to be many reasons. First, employee ownership alone does not necessarily lead to significant gains. Stock ownership will motivate some employees to work harder and more carefully, but the effects of this on a company's bottom line are usually minimal. These efforts essentially reduce labor costs, often only a minority of total costs, and usually only by a few percent. Most employees already work as hard as any incentive system is likely to get them to work. The net impact of employee ownership is generally under a 1% annual improvement in sales or employment growth.

By contrast, new ideas and better information can have a dramatic impact on performance. Consider, for instance, a highly motivated employee who works an extra two hours a day to get a job done, but knows there is a way to change procedures so it could be done in half the time. If the company allows that employee input into how that job is done, her work and other people's work becomes much more effective. Otherwise, the company just has one hard-working, but inefficient (and probably frustrated) employee.

Employees are closest to their work and have the most intimate knowledge of daily work processes, technology, and customers, and companies can benefit significantly from tapping into the knowledge and skills employees bring to their jobs. Furthermore, as markets change and diversify at a bewildering pace and new technologies allow us to access more and more information at the touch of keyboard, the ability to process and use this information has become essential to staying competitive. A small group of managers can no longer process and use all of this information effectively. Companies need more people trained to make more decisions more quickly, and they need people to have a reason to do this right.

Stock Options and Employee Participation

It is important to note that most of the research noted above has focused on companies with employee stock ownership plans (ESOPs). ESOPs do have characteristics that make them very different from stock option plans. For one, ESOPs are set up as retirement plans, with employees receiving stock only when they retire or leave the company. Some experts believe that this is more conducive to fostering long-term ownership attitudes and behaviors than a stock option plan, in which employees can "cash out" much sooner.

Others argue that the more immediate, tangible return from stock ownership that stock options provide is a powerful incentive. Also, since employees actually purchase shares themselves through an option plan, this more closely resembles true ownership than an ESOP, in which employees do not purchase stock themselves.

There are no clear answers here. There is little reason to believe, however, that employee ownership granted through broad stock options cannot have the same synergistic effect when combined with employee participation as it does in ESOP companies. There is also little reason to believe that the participation structures that have worked well in ESOP companies cannot also work in companies with broad stock options. Indeed, while many ESOP companies have had great success in creating ownership cultures that have contributed significantly to improving corporate performance, many companies with broad-based stock options have also had similar successes.

What is clear is that in companies that demonstrate a true commitment to creating an ownership culture, stock options can be a significant motivator. Success depends on the company's goals for the plan, its commitment to creating an ownership culture, the amount of training and education it puts into explaining the plan, and the goals of individual employees (whether they want cash sooner rather than later).

Toward an Ownership Style of Management[2]

In some companies, stock options alone are a significant motivator, especially in companies that have a sophisticated workforce that understands how stock price is effected by different factors. In many high-technology startups, for example, employees arrive with entrepreneurial attitudes and know that if the company gets off the ground and has a public offering, options will provide a healthy payoff. Many of these companies also have informal and formal ways for employees to make decisions and contribute input. These companies often do not have to put great effort into creating an ownership culture.

For companies in which employees have little experience with and knowledge of owning stock or in companies where informal participation is not effective (and it rarely is in all but the smallest companies), more formal steps are necessary to communicate and educate employees about the plan and to get them involved as owners. While the concept of creating an ownership culture is relatively simple, many companies have a difficult time actually doing it successfully. First, there are no set rules, and the process is different for every company. Also, employees do not just jump into these new roles as owners, and there is likely to be resistance from employees at all levels of the company. Furthermore, all-encompassing structures like TQM can be very intimidating and can start off with great fanfare and high expectations, but become difficult to sustain after the initial enthusiasm wanes. There are, however, some key components to creating an ownership culture:

- View participation not as a "program" but as an ongoing process.

- Commitment from the top is essential.

- For employees to act like owners, they need education and training regarding the company, the stock plan, business basics and terminology, and so on.

- For employees to make informed decisions, they must have access to information.

- Participation means driving decision-making down to the level at which employees have the most knowledge on the issue being decided.

- Participation does not mean that everyone is involved in every decision.

These are only general guidelines, and the eventual form participation takes at a company depends on its size, industry, staff, and commitment to creating an ownership culture. Ultimately, each company needs to develop its own way to get employees to think and act like owners. Fortunately, there are many successful examples. Below are four case studies of companies with broad-based stock option plans that have developed innovative ownership cultures. Although the following examples are all very different from each other, they do illustrate the common themes sketched above. They are also all continually changing their participation efforts, but their commitment to creating a culture in which employees truly feel like owners and are trained to act like them remains constant.

Starbucks Coffee Company

In 1971, Jerry Baldwin, Zev Siegl, and Gordon Bowler founded the Starbucks Coffee Company. The original store sold whole coffee beans in Seattle's Pike Place Market. In 1982, Howard Schultz joined the company as head of marketing. On a trip to Italy, he noticed the central role of the coffee shop in Italian culture and social life. Schultz wanted to import this idea back to the United States, where he felt there was a vast, untapped market not only for gourmet coffee but also for coffee shops like the ones in Italy. Schultz left to form his own company in 1985 and returned in 1987 to purchase Starbucks for $3.8 million. At this point, Starbucks had 11 stores in the Pacific Northwest and about 100 employees.

Schultz' vision was to open up coffee shops and retail stores all over the country, and in less than 10 years this vision has become a reality. Starbucks has played, and continues to play, a dominant role in the creation and development of the gourmet coffee industry. It has grown exponentially since 1991. By the end of 1996, Starbucks was operating over 1,000 stores throughout North America and two in Japan, with a staff of over 20,000. The company's goal is for 2,000 stores to be in operation by the year 2000. Sales for fiscal 1995 were $465.2 million, a 63% increase from 1994, and the share price of Starbucks stock has more than doubled since its initial public offering in 1992.

From the beginning, Schultz believed that the most essential element to realizing his vision would be superior customer service, which he felt would only come from a motivated, educated, and committed staff, which Schultz referred to in *Inc.* magazine as "our only sustainable competitive advantage." To create a staff of this caliber, he knew that employees would have to be treated like business partners. Schultz' working-class roots reinforced this commitment to treating employees well. The company has taken direct and unique steps to translate this commitment and vision into action.

All employees are called "partners," and all (including part-timers) receive a significant benefits package. In addition to stock ownership, this package includes health, dental, and vision insurance as well as career counseling, paid vacation, and product discounts. While many similar companies do not want to pay the extra costs to provide benefits to part-time employees, Starbucks sees these costs as a worthwhile investment since over two-thirds of its partners work part-time. Most customers, therefore, interact with part-time partners on a regular basis. The investment has also paid off in turnover rates that are fraction of the industry average, which are chronically high.

Starbucks was the first privately held company to offer stock options to part-time employees. The company established a stock option plan in 1991 and a stock purchase plan in 1995. Approximately half of the employees participate in one or both of these programs. Stock options are available to any partner who is employed from April 1 to the end of the fiscal year, works at least 500 hours in this period (20 hours per week average), and is still employed when options are distributed in January. Partners receive options based on a percentage of annual wages. The target percentage is 10%, but the actual percentage has been consistently more in recent years, owing to the company's profitability. The grant price is that of the stock on the first day of the fiscal year. There is a five-year vesting schedule for stock options. Any partner can participate in the stock purchase plan after working at least 20 hours per week for 90 days. Partners can purchase stock at a 15% discount through a payroll deduction.

The commitment Starbucks has to its partners is one of the foundations of the company's cohesive culture, which is transmitted at all levels through extensive education, an open organizational structure, and refined channels of communication. The culture's cohesion, as well as its fluidity, allows the company to constantly redefine all of its participation efforts to adapt to industry and corporate changes.

Training and Education

Starbucks has created an extensive training program that aims to cultivate the skills and knowledge of partners. This program is constantly evaluated and modified to meet the changing needs of the company. Everyone hired to work in a retail capacity receives a minimum of 25 hours of training during his or her first two to four weeks with the company. These classes provide an orientation to the company and its benefits plans, as well as a substantial foundation in customer service skills, coffee knowledge, and drink-making techniques. Partners who have been specially trained by the company teach the classes.

A management training program coaches partners on leadership skills, advanced customer service, and diversity awareness, as well as succession planning and career development. Although not all managers take these courses now, that is the goal for the future. This includes store managers and corporate managers.

Meetings

Many different meetings at all levels help Starbucks maintain its culture and allow all partners to provide input and exchange ideas. Quarterly open forums, conducted by members of the senior management team, are held throughout the company. The purpose of these meetings is to update partners on developments in the company, go through financial information, and provide a chance for partners to ask questions and contribute their input on any issues. All partners are invited to attend these meetings.

Retail meetings occur on an ad-hoc basis to discuss any concerns pertinent to all or some stores within a particular region. Again, all partners receive an open invitation to attend.

At the corporate offices, educational meetings allow "non-retail" partners to learn about developments within the company, and partner connection groups try to get people together with similar interests and hobbies outside of work. Non-retail partners are also actively encouraged to spend a few days each quarter working in either a store or roasting plant.

Other Efforts

"Mission review" is a formal process that allows partners and customers to voice their concerns to the company by filling out a standard card that can be found in any Starbucks location. A group of partners at the corporate offices, who are specially selected and trained for this role, responds to each issue, question, or problem. The company receives hundreds of responses. The top two or three are reviewed at the open forums, including a description of the issues, how the company responded, what action was taken, and the results.

A "partner opinion survey" was distributed to all partners in 1994. It contained over 100 questions about every aspect of the company to evaluate how partners felt about working at Starbucks and to identify areas for improvement. The company also surveyed partners when it was trying to develop its benefits and ownership programs. Starbucks plans on conducting these surveys on an ongoing basis.

An employee newsletter, *Siren's Tale*, goes out to all partners and discusses developments within the company, as well as issues relating to benefits and ownership programs. *Coffee Matters* is a customer-oriented newsletter that is distributed monthly to retail outlets. It contains information and articles about the industry, the company, and product lines.

Each Starbucks store donates any coffee beans that have not been used or sold in one week to charity. The company is the largest corporate sponsor of CARE, an organization that works on various humanitarian aid projects in developing countries, including many regions from which Starbucks purchases its coffee (Guatemala, Kenya, Ethiopia, and Indonesia).

Whole Foods Market

The founders of Whole Foods will be the first to point out that although they are not traditionally trained business people, this has not impeded their success. Whole Foods pioneered the concept of the natural foods supermarket and remains the fastest growing such supermarket in the United States. It has accomplished this by eschewing the traditional top-down management model in favor of a mission-driven, decentralized, open organizational structure that seeks to create an environment that is "productive and rewarding" for all of its employees. It accomplishes this through broad stock ownership opportunities, gainsharing bonuses, a decentralized management structure based on self-managing work teams, open-book financials, and extensive communications within the company.

The company was founded n 1978 when John Mackey started Safer Way Natural Foods in Austin, Texas. In 1980, Safer Way merged with another Austin natural foods store, Clarksville Natural Grocery (owned by Craig Weller and Mark Skiles) to form Whole Foods. The concept behind the new company was to bring natural foods retailing to the supermarket format. Whole Foods opened its first store on September 20, 1980, with 19 employees and was an immediate success.

Whole Foods currently has 94 natural food retail groceries in 20 states and Washington, DC, with 14,000 employees. Whole Foods has grown through a public offering (NASDAQ) in 1992 and many acquisitions. In 1991, the company had 10 stores in two regions, with sales of $92.5 million. In 1996, it had 41 stores in five regions. It now has 94 from coast to coast. Sales for 1998 were $1.39 billion. Whole Foods plans to have 200 stores by 2003.

Stock Options

Whole Foods Market has offered stock options to employees since 1987. Over the years, the eligibility guidelines have changed. Currently, Whole

Foods grants stock options to all employees who have worked 6,000 hours as well as special grants for certain promotions, such as to team leader and store leader. Approximately 3,250 employees hold stock options. In 1993, Whole Foods established a section 423 stock purchase plan to enable any employee who has worked 400 hours to purchase stock at a discount through payroll deductions. Employees also receive gainsharing bonuses based on team and store performance.

Self-Managing Work Teams

The decentralized organizational structure of Whole Foods is based on self-managing, autonomous work teams. These teams are *the* organizational unit at Whole Foods: every employee is on a team (e.g., a store's produce department), and employees are accountable primarily to their team. This includes part-timers, which make up between 25% to 30% of the workforce. In fact, employees are not even called "employees" at Whole Foods, but "team members."

The team structure was created when Whole Foods opened its second store. At this point, the founders asked themselves whether or not they wanted to have central control over everything that was happening in all of their stores. They decided it would be much better to let individual stores function autonomously and let employee teams function autonomously within the stores. They believed this would encourage widespread innovation at all levels and that these innovations and new ideas could be shared among all teams and stores.

The team structure allows decisions to be made at the most relevant level and aims to create a workplace environment in which all team members feel more connected to the company and directly responsible for its performance. The teams are responsible for their own hiring, firing, training, setting performance targets (on which bonuses are based), purchasing, and scheduling. All teams are required to meet once a month and can meet more often if they choose. In addition to reviewing performance and goals, these meetings serve as a forum for problem-solving and informal sharing of information and ideas. The team structure operates the same way in non-retail settings throughout the company.

Widely distributed financial numbers track the performance of teams, and gainsharing bonuses are based on team performance. New hires work for a three-day trial period, and before they can become regular, full-time employees, they must be voted in by two-thirds of the team. Teams also compete against each other and against other teams in other stores. The company facilitates information sharing and "cross-pollination" of ideas between teams all over the country.

The team unit radiates out through the whole organization. Each team has a leader, and all of the team leaders form a team within that store, known as the Team Member Advisory Group. This team provides a forum to discuss broader issues relating to the store and the company in general. These teams meet once a month. Each of these teams has a leader, and each of these leaders within the seven geographic regions make up a team. The leaders of these seven regional teams make up another team.

Sharing the Numbers

To enable team members to make informed decisions relating to their team's work, Whole Foods has been extensively sharing detailed financial information with all employees since 1987. Employees have access to sales figures (company, store, and teams), profit margins, labor statistics, balance sheets, and other financial statements.

Each day at every location, a sheet is posted next to the time clock that lists the previous day's sales for each team and sales for the same date last year. Weekly sales figures for all stores in the region are also posted, along with the figures from the same week the previous year and sales figures from every store in the company. Every store also receives monthly reports of sales, profitability, and expenses, as well as these figures from other stores.

Employees also have access to all salaries, including those of the executive team. While this can sometimes create tension, the company believes it is better to have all of this out in the open. If there are individual salaries that do not seem justified, this can be brought up and addressed. There is a salary cap that limits compensation (wages plus profit incentive bonuses) of any team member to 10 times the average total compensation of all full-time team members in the company.

Sharing the Rewards

Whole Foods not only shares the responsibility of running the company with employees but also allows them to share in the rewards. In addition to a stock purchase plan and stock options, Whole Foods has gainsharing programs that give team members bonuses based on team performance, which is measured in various ways.

For example, each team in every store negotiates a certain percentage of its total sales as labor costs (base salary only). If the team's labor costs are below this percentage, its gets the difference as a bonus. For example, if Team A negotiates that its labor costs will be 10% of sales and these costs end up being only 8% of sales (say through increased sales with the same labor costs or through reduced labor costs while generating the same sales), the members of Team A split the 2% difference.

Communications

Employees at Whole Foods are also kept up to date about many other issues relating to the company, products, and work life. A company newsletter

(*Innerviews*) contains articles and columns about working at Whole Foods. It also serves as forum for team members to express views and opinions about the company as well as other issues. The newsletter is distributed to all team members the first week of every month.

Electronic vehicles facilitate information sharing throughout the decentralized organization. Most regional office teams and store management teams have computers and access to company email. These team members also have access to the company intranet, *Team Member Network*. Through the intranet, team members have access to information about products, company history, store locations, and archives of the company newsletters.

Science Applications International (SAIC)

SAIC is a private, high-technology engineering, research, development, and manufacturing company based in San Diego, California, with over 350 locations and 22,000 employees worldwide. Its primary activities include technology development and analysis, systems development and integration, technical support services, and the design and manufacture of high-technology hardware and software products. The company works with federal, commercial, and international customers in many different industries, including energy, environment, government, health care technology, information technology, Internet, telecommunications, and transportation.

SAIC was founded in 1969 by Dr. Robert Beyster, a nuclear physicist, who left a large defense company out of frustration with its bureaucratic structure and the influence outside shareholders had over the company. SAIC has been deeply committed to employee ownership and participation from its inception. The guiding principle at SAIC is that "those who contribute to the company should own it, and the ownership should reflect an individual's contribution and performance as much as feasible." SAIC initially gave employees the opportunity to buy stock in the company as they brought in new contracts.

SAIC has recorded 27 years of continuous revenue and earnings growth, and its current annual revenues exceed $2 billion. The company attributes this remarkable performance to employee ownership and the entrepreneurial culture it has developed around its innovative ownership structure. Employees are encouraged, both financially and psychologically, to think and act like owners, and they know they will be rewarded appropriately for doing so.

Stock Ownership Plans

Over 75% of the staff is technical, including professional engineers, computer scientists, and physical scientists. Employees own approximately 90% of SAIC through a stock program that incorporates various employee ownership mechanisms. Ownership is largely dispersed: the single largest share-holder is Dr. Beyster, who owns only 2% of the stock. While SAIC's stock program provides at least a minimal amount of ownership to all employees, it gives employees the opportunity to acquire significant amounts of additional stock through powerful merit and performance-based incentives. SAIC's ownership structure can be broken down into three main parts:

- *Entitlement methods:* An ESOP allows all employees who have worked a minimum of 850 hours to receive stock. The board of directors sets the contribution level, which is usually around 3% of salary.

- *Employee discretionary methods:* Employees can buy stock through a stock purchase or 401(k) plan. Employees who wish to purchase stock must receive permission from management, which rarely turns down requests. Employees can use between 3% and 10% of their after-tax pay to buy stock through the purchase plans at a 10% discount. The company is also planning to begin matching all or part of these purchases with options. The 401(k) plan allows employees to use up to 10% of pretax earnings to invest in mutual funds or SAIC stock. The company matches 50% of the first $2,000 employees defer and 15% above $2,000.

- *Management discretionary methods:* Line managers in the company's 40 different operating groups receive an annual pool of performance-based stock options and stock for bonuses for their divisions. These managers decide how this stock will be allocated within their group to motivate staff and insure that employees are rewarded according to how much they contribute. Employees may, for example, receive options for outstanding performance, for reaching predetermined business goals, or when they join the company. All employees are eligible to receive these options, which vest over four years and can be exercised five years after they have been granted. Currently, about 40% of SAIC employees have received options through this process.

To provide liquidity for its stock while remaining privately held, SAIC has developed its own internal stock market, Bull, Inc., which is a wholly owned broker-dealer subsidiary approved by the SEC. Four times a year, Bull matches buyers and sellers of SAIC stock, enabling any shareholder to trade through this internal market. Anyone who wishes to purchase stock must receive approval from the company. Employees own the majority of stock, and all other shareholders have a direct and significant connection to the company: directors, key consultants, immediate family members of employees, the company's retirement plans, and some former employees. Employees must sell their stock back to the company when they leave (this applies to all stock acquired by employees after October 1, 1981).

The fair market value of the stock is set by the board of directors through a formula that takes into consideration net income, stockholder's equity, number of shares, and a market factor that reflects the stock of comparable publicly traded companies. This valuation is examined and judged for accuracy by an independent appraiser.

Employee Participation

SAIC encourages employees to become deeply involved in their jobs and the company: to seek information, provide and solicit input, and take responsibility and act ethically to make the company profitable. This philosophy has been firmly embedded in SAIC's culture from the very beginning. The company makes every effort to place decision-making and responsibility at the lowest possible level. It realizes, however, that all employees can not be involved in every decision. SAIC has developed a "loose/tight" management style to address this situation. The "tight" element allows upper management to make decisions on fundamental matters such as ethical behavior, accounting, purchasing policy, stock policy, and similar issues. The "loose" element encourages a broader cross-section of employees to become involved in consensus decision-making where it is feasible and practical on issues that directly effect all employees.

Formal participation occurs through approximately 20 different committees, which deal with a wide range of corporate issues. Committees with board members deal with issues such as company ethics, stock policy, and technological advances. Other committees are predominantly management-oriented and promote discussion, communication, and consensus on issues such as business development, the outcomes of particular projects, operational issues, financial incentives for employees, capital expenditures, technological issues, marketing strategies, and potential risk areas.

Of the committees open to a broad cross-section of employees, the most important is the Technical Environment Committee (TEC). The purpose of the TEC is to monitor issues relating to the work environment and employee morale and motivation. It fosters communication between staff, solicits employee input, and makes recommendations to the board. The committee's members are "advocates of a sound technical working environment." The chairperson of the TEC attends board meetings to offer input from the committee and reports back on what is discussed and decided at board meetings. Issues the TEC has been actively involved with in the past include career development, fringe benefits, dispute resolution procedures, and various others.

The TEC is comprised of 35 staff-level employees from a broad cross-section of the company. Line managers in different divisions nominate employees to serve on the committee. Division managers are given the freedom to develop their own ways to choose nominees. Some divisions go through a formal, democratic process of nominating people, while in other divisions, the process is more informal. The TEC itself decides which nominees will serve on the committee. While the committee bases these decisions on many factors, it generally seeks to have a TEC that is representative of the demographics of the company as a whole.

Employees at all levels also serve on various ad-hoc committees formed to deal with specific issues that are of concern to all employees.

Training and Education

At most SAIC locations, employees from SAIC's stock and retirement departments conduct on-site seminars about the stock system. They also create and distribute literature explaining technical issues relating to the plans, how employees can participate in and benefit from stock ownership, as well as the corporate philosophy behind employee ownership. Throughout the year, employees receive literature that keeps them abreast of new developments, accomplishments, financials, and the activities of the committees. SAIC's intranet is rapidly becoming a popular way for employees to access information about the company.

Gasper Corporation

The Gasper Corporation, headquartered in Dayton, Ohio, develops software to manage computer networks for automatic teller machines and financial institutions and to manage other online processes, systems, and devices. The company was founded in 1983 by David Gasper and has grown rapidly in recent years, from 28 employees in 1996, to it current 99 employees. Revenues for fiscal year 1998 were $8.9 million.

In 1998, Gasper first granted an equal number of stock options to all employees. The company now makes ongoing, annual grants on a discretionary basis, for which all employees are eligible. Gasper is one of the few high-growth, knowledge-based startups with a formal open-book management program as well as a broad-based stock option plan. Gasper believes that its growth and continued success is a direct result of employees being involved in the company as owners by giving them access to financial information and encouraging them to act on this information.

Key Success Factors

Gasper has been practicing formal open-book management since 1995. The company shares a wide range of financial information with all employees through its intranet site, scoreboards, and monthly all-employee meetings. It is constantly modifying what numbers it tracks and how it does it. These performance measures are also linked to a bonus program.

At the center of this information sharing are three critical numbers that drive the company's performance. The company tracks these numbers very closely. These three numbers include revenue (from new sales), backlog (revenue that is booked for the upcoming months, i.e., sales made on products yet to be fully installed and operating), and recurrent revenue the company receives on an ongoing, annual basis from the maintenance of systems already in place. Gasper also shares detailed financial statements with employees, as well as detailed information about expenses and potential customers.

Employees have access to the critical numbers in a variety of ways. The numbers are updated monthly and posted on the company intranet. Gasper also posts these numbers on bulletin boards and in conference rooms throughout the company. The company holds monthly all-employee meetings to review the numbers. At these meetings, Dave Gasper goes through the critical numbers as well as a detailed breakdown of the financial statements, sales forecasts, backlog reports, and potential clients. These meetings are held off-site once a month for an hour and half and are videotaped for employees who are not there.

Broad-Based Incentive Program

The key numbers are not just put out there for employees to see but are tied directly to an incentive compensation plan. The company establishes annual goals for revenue and profits. If these goals are achieved, employees receive a cash bonus equal to 5% of their eligible base wages. It evaluates its progress towards these goals throughout the year and pays out the bonus a little bit at a time: 10% in the first quarter, 20% in the next quarter, 30% in the third quarter, and 40% in the last quarter. If the company hits the target, Gasper also deposits 5% of an employees annual total compensation into the employee's 401(k) plan.

Gasper communicates the stock option plan to employees in a variety of ways. Employees receive a new hire orientation about stock options when they join the company and have access to detailed information about stock options through the company intranet. Stock options also are discussed in the monthly all-employee meetings.

Notes

1.   These studies are summarized in *Employee Ownership and Corporate Performance*, rev. ed. (Oakland, CA: National Center for Employee Ownership, 1996).

2.   For a more detailed explanation of this topic, see Karen M. Young, Corey Rosen, and Edward J. Carberry, *Theory O: Creating an Ownership Style of Management*, 2nd ed. (Oakland, CA: National Center for Employee Ownership, 1996).

CHAPTER 10

The 1998 NCEO Broad-Based Stock Option Plan Survey

Ryan Weeden
The National Center for Employee Ownership

The sudden growth and popularity of broad-based stock option plans has put companies in an awkward position. On the one hand, they want to keep up with competitors to attract and retain employees. Yet they do not want to create a plan that is unnecessarily generous. Until now, there has not been accurate information on how companies are designing and implementing their broad-based stock option plans. With explosive trends of any kind, there is often a lag between the growth in interest in the subject and the appearance of information available on the subject. Today, the existence of a sufficient number of companies using broad-based stock options enables us to take a closer look at the specific characteristics of these plans. We at the NCEO did so in early 1998 with the help of nine cosponsoring organizations. At that time, we collected the names of over 1,300 companies that were likely to have broad-based stock option plans. The companies were drawn from the databases of the nine cosponsoring organizations and included companies ranging in size from small, closely held start-up companies to very large publicly traded companies. We received responses from 140 companies, of which 96 had broad-based stock option plans, which we defined as plans that grant to over half of their workforce.

This is the first substantial study of its kind and identifies some important trends in the use and design of broad stock options. This study is the first to look at stock option practices by industrial, geographic, and size subsets. It is also the first to take an in-depth look at communication tools, educational mechanisms that target nonmanagement workers, and employee participation programs in companies with broad-based stock options. Furthermore, it shows the extent to which these plans have been successful in meeting their objectives, and it takes an in-depth look at option repricing. This study also examines the distribution of options between management and nonmanagement employees, the average size of option awards to various classes of employees, and the exercise practices of employees in these companies.

The results are intended for use both by companies with stock option plans and those without. For existing stock option companies, the results can be a useful guide to how their option plans compare to others in the field. For companies without option plans, this data provides a resource for choosing design features that can be included in an option plan. Plan administrators, human resources officials, CFOs, boards of directors, and option plan design practitioners are the primary intended audience for these data, but certainly CEOs, COOs, compensation specialists, academics, and shareholder rights organizations may also find them useful.

The complete results of the survey are laid out and analyzed at length in *Current Practices in Stock Option Plan Design* (Oakland, CA: NCEO, rev. ed. 1999), a 230-page spiral-bound 8½-by-11-inch book that includes an extensive breakdown of the survey results by industry, region, and company size, as well as detailed treatment of survey results on repricing, company objectives and communications, and employee participation programs. This chapter summarizes our main findings and profiles some of the companies that responded to the survey.

Survey Design

One of the most notable findings of this survey is how different types of broad-based stock option plans are being designed and operated. We examined how four different types of stock option plans were designed and operated in the surveyed companies. The four types of plans are as follows:

- *Management:* Option plans that target executives, directors, managers (of all levels), and supervisors. Management employees may or may not receive additional options under the nonmanagement plans described in the survey.

- *Nonmanagement ongoing/periodic:* Plans that grant options to nonmanagement employees on a regular basis. Some plans grant options every year, others every other year, and some at other intervals. Plans that grant options to all employees under a "special" one-time option grant are not included under this definition.

- *Nonmanagement one-time:* Option plans that grant to nonmanagement employees for a one-time event, such as an anniversary, a corporate milestone (e.g, an acquisition, a merger, or meeting a profitability target), or for other reasons that are unpredictable, with no planned future grants. Option plans described in this category do not offer regular grants but may have provided more than one grant to nonmanagers.

- *Nonmanagement new hire:* Plans that grant options to nonmanagement employees either as an incentive to join the company or to provide new hires with an equity stake in relation to other employees who received options under ongoing/periodic awards. Often, new hire option plans are incorporated into the plan documents for ongoing/periodic awards.

Although the media pays a lot of attention to the "one-time" option grants in large publicly traded companies like Bank of America, Merck Pharmaceuticals, and Wells Fargo, this type of grant is actually the least common. Only 19% of the companies responding to our survey use one-time option grants, whereas 82% of companies use "ongoing/periodic" option plans for a broad group of employees. (Some companies use more than one type of option plan; therefore, some results reported here total more than 100%.) Although management plans are by definition not broad-based, managers are employees, and how a management plan is designed versus how a non-management plan is designed is a relevant piece of information.

The results presented here should not be taken as indications of how all companies are designing and using their stock option plans. The companies surveyed were selectively chosen because they were likely to have a broad-based stock option plan. There are no comparisons made to companies whose stock option plans are not broad-based.

What Is a Broad-Based Stock Option Plan?

To understand the results of this survey, it is important first to understand who was surveyed. Our survey focused solely on companies that provide broad-based stock options. For purposes of this study, a broad-based stock option plan is defined as a plan in which over half of all employees receive stock options.

There has been much debate among stock option practitioners, academics, and others on what defines a broad-based stock option plan. No clear consensus has been reached, however. Some in the field, for example, have defined broad employee stock option plans as those that make everyone eligible; others define them as plans that grant to a small number of nonmanagement employees. Too often, the media compounds the problem by applying the terms "broad-based option plan" or "employee stock options" inconsistently. The sheer growth in the number of companies granting options further and further down their organizational ladders, however, demands a more precise definition of the term "broad-based stock option plan."

Some individuals consider plans that make all employees eligible to receive options broad-based. Stock options, unlike other qualified employee benefit plans that require broad participation, such as employee stock ownership plans (ESOPs), 401(k) plans, and defined benefit plans, can be structured to give benefits to all, some, or none of the workforce. The decision to grant options rests solely with the compensation decision-makers in a company, as governed by the plan documents. Many of these plans have been approved by shareholders, and any changes in those documents would require additional shareholder approval. Because many companies want to avoid seeking additional shareholder approval repeatedly and want the most flexibility with their compensation programs, companies often design their stock option plans to include all employees as *potential* recipients of options.

Many of these companies that make all employees eligible to receive options, however, have no intention of actually granting options to all or even most of their employees. They simply want the flexibility to grant options in the future to whomever they want. The practice of only making employees eligible to receive stock options, without actually granting options, is in fact quite prevalent. William Mercer reported in 1997 that nearly 30% of the largest 350 companies in the US had option plans that made employees eligible to receive options, but in only 10% of the companies did a majority of employees actually *receive* options. The NCEO does not automatically classify as broad-based those plans that make all employees eligible.

The NCEO believes that an appropriate definition of a broad-based option plan is one in which most employees actually receive options. If companies are going to claim they have a "broad" option plan, then it is reasonable to expect that this means they grant to at least a majority of employees. If they grant options more selectively, it realistically can not be considered "broad."

Our definition does not necessarily require that all employees receive options every year, nor does it require that a majority of nonmanagement employees receive options in a given year. Some companies give options to a minority of employees (e.g., one-third of all employees) annually, but they rotate who receives options. This accomplishes a broad distribution of options over a number of years. To put it another way, in order for a plan to fit our definition of a broad-based plan, the total sum of all optionees, over time, must represent a majority of employees at a company.

Why not limit the term "broad-based" to plans that grant options to all employees? In light of how companies are actually granting options, this seems unrealistically restrictive. Many companies use options to attract and retain employees and may not necessarily grant to everyone, but to most. Likewise, many companies use options to reward performance and may not grant to everyone. These companies may still consider broad-based employee ownership to be an important corporate objective, but they may have practical reasons why they do not grant to all employees. Even companies that are using options to increase employee ownership may not necessarily grant to all employees. Overall, our definition of "broad-based" means that about 60% to 70% of employees who work for these companies typically have stock allocated to them at any one time.

Survey Features

We conducted our survey between February and July 1998, with the financial and technical support of nine cosponsoring organizations:

- *Arthur Andersen*
- *Certified Equity Professional Institute*
- *Compensation and Performance Management, Inc.*
- *Corporate Management Solutions, Inc.*
- *Hewitt Associates*
- *ShareData, Inc.*
- *Towers Perrin*
- *Watson Wyatt Worldwide*
- *WestWard Pay Strategies*

The NCEO approached these organizations in late 1997 to support a survey that no one organization alone could accomplish. In conducting a study like this, two factors could limit its success: money and access to company names. Together, the nine cosponsors provided the financial support for the study as well as many company names. The NCEO carried out the research, and each cosponsor received the data to analyze as it sees fit.

We sent the survey to over 2,000 individuals at 1,360 companies. The names of the individuals at the various companies were compiled from client lists of the cosponsoring organizations, a database of broad-based options companies that the NCEO maintains, and consultants in the field. We sent a copy of the survey to each individual and gave him or her approximately one month to complete it. We then placed telephone calls to each individual who had not initially responded to see whether they were interested in completing the survey. In the end, we received 141 responses to the survey, 96 of which describe, by our definition, a broad-based stock option plan. Twenty-six respondents either granted options to only a small percentage of their nonmanagement workforce or had management-only stock option plans. The remainder were either companies that did not have option plans or informed us that they would not have the time to fill out the survey. A response rate of over 10% is average for surveys of this nature. Considering that this survey took from one to five hours to complete, we believe the 10.4% response rate to be substantial and sufficient. We have no reason to believe that the data collected are skewed in any particular manner.

The respondents to the survey included stock option administrators; investor relations staff; chief financial officers; human resource vice-presidents, directors, and supervisors; compensation directors; vice presidents of finance, operations, and administration; and controllers. Answering the questions in the survey usually necessitated the collaboration of multiple departments, including human resources, stock administration, finance, and compensation and benefits. The need for collaboration in answering the survey is a noteworthy finding in itself. A broad option plan is not a typical benefit, and companies implementing these plans have to create and support links between many different departments and employees for the plan to run efficiently and meet its corporate objectives.

The companies in this survey represent dozens of industries, including manufacturing, software, semiconductor production, telecommunication, retail, and biotechnology. The size of the companies ranged from start-up companies with no annual revenues to a company with annual revenues of $91 billion; the number of employees within the sample ranged from 4 to 276,000.

Prevalence of Plans and Public/Private Ratio

Because companies are not required to register their stock option plans with the federal government or the Securities and Exchange Commission (SEC) except in certain rare cases with privately held companies, developing accurate estimates of the actual number of companies that provide broad-based options is difficult. A number of recent surveys, as well as increased media coverage and attention from many segments within the corporate community, indicate that the number of plans in both public and private companies has grown rapidly in the past few years.

Several studies have estimated the number of companies with broad-based stock option plans. These studies found that between 10% and 30% of all surveyed companies have such plans. The studies, however, use samples drawn largely from publicly traded or high technology companies. The most significant studies and their findings on this topic are as follows (see appendix 2 to this chapter for a summary of these and other studies):

- *ShareData Inc. and the American Electronics Association (AEA) (1997):* Surveyed 1,000 public companies using stock option plans and found that 53% of respondents granted stock options to all employees, 31% granted to key employees and above, and 15% granted to managers and above. In information technology fields, 88% of companies granted options to all employees and in companies with fewer than 100 employees, 68% granted options to all of them. This survey was an update to a 1994 study and found that the prevalence of broad-based option plans was increasing.[1]

- *William M. Mercer (1997):* Of the largest 350 companies in the U.S., 30% made a broad base of employees eligible to receive stock option grants. Of those companies, however, only 11% had actually granted options in a broad-based manner. Nevertheless, the trend in granting options broadly had been growing over a five-year period.

- *Coopers & Lybrand (1996):* Of the fastest growing companies in the U.S., approximately 15% used broad-based stock options.[2]

- *Hewitt Associates (1996):* Twenty-seven percent of companies surveyed made all of their employees eligible for their stock option plans. The most common company type was manufacturing (high technology and non-high technology), followed by retail, banking/finance/insurance, and energy.[3]

- *The Association for Quality and Participation (1995):* Thirteen percent of Fortune 1000 companies offered stock options to 60% or more of their workforce.[4]

The disparity of these results indicates the difficulty in estimating the number of companies with broad-based plans. It is equally difficult to measure the number of employees affected by these programs. Although only 10% of companies may have broad-based stock option plans, a far greater percentage of employees may be affected by these programs because they frequently are found in large public companies. Companies such as PepsiCo (480,000 employees), Eastman Kodak (96,600 employees), and Bank of America (80,000 employees) are just a few of the large companies offering options to over 50% of their workforces.

The NCEO estimates that at least 7 million employees are eligible to receive stock options in the U.S. It is clear that stock options are predominantly used by public companies, but determining the distribution of public and private companies is not straightforward. Coopers & Lybrand (1996) estimated that of private companies that have some form of stock option program, those that are planning to go public (or have recently become public) are more than three times as likely to offer all of their employees stock options. The 1997 ShareData/American Electronics Association survey found that the smaller the company, the more likely that it will have a broad-based stock option plan. Unfortunately, neither of these surveys provides an estimate of the ratio of public to private companies.

The NCEO estimates the distribution of companies with broad-based stock options to be approximately 80% public and 20% private, a ratio derived from our surveys and inquiries from interested individuals. Ninety-one percent of the companies responding to the NCEO survey were publicly traded. Only nine of the private companies that responded have broad-based stock option plans.

Because of the small size and in-house administration and design of their stock option plans, private companies may be underreported in this survey. On the other hand, private companies that are not planning on going public must address SEC regulation requirements on whether or not they qualify for exemption from registration requirements as defined in the Securities Act of 1933. This additional requirement may dissuade some private companies from implementing stock option plans (although in reality the requirements for exemption are usually met by small to medium-sized companies without any modification to their plans). Given the difficulty in identifying private companies, we feel that the actual ratio of private companies with broad-based stock options is slightly greater than the ratio of companies that was surveyed.

Estimates of the number of plans, number of employees, and distribution among public and private companies are useful but not entirely relevant to a company considering whether it should use a broad-based stock option plan. For that purpose, it is much more useful to examine how these plans are designed. The remainder of this chapter concentrates on these more significant design characteristics.

Geographic and Industry Distribution

It is impossible from a survey of this nature to extrapolate how prevalent broad-based stock option plans are in different parts of the country. To gain a sense of the prevalence and characteristics of broad-based options within the U.S. economy in general, one would have to survey a representative sample of all companies in the United States, determine the incidence of stock option plans in those companies, and then extrapolate from that data to the entire universe of companies.

What we can do is determine where the respondents are located in the U.S. as well as use information from the NCEO to determine where individuals interested in these plans are located across the country. The geographic distribution of the companies responding to the survey was as follows: West Coast, 48%; Mountain, 12%; Midwest, 9%; South, 14%; and Northeast, 17%. Because the NCEO receives dozens of telephone calls per month from individuals interested in establishing stock option plans, we can use the geographic distribution of these callers to establish the regions in which future plans are likely to be implemented. From mid-1996 through early 1998, the inquiries to the NCEO regarding broad-based stock options were distributed as follows: West Coast, 25%; Mountain, 7%; Midwest, 14%; South, 26%; and Northeast, 29%. These two sets of figures show that although the highest concentration of companies using broad options is still on the West Coast, the appeal of broad-based stock options is spreading beyond the traditional Silicon Valley region.

Companies surveyed come from dozens of different industrial sectors. Survey respondents were asked to identify their primary Standard Industrial Classification (SIC) number, which describes the type of business that the company operates. We were able to create six groups of companies for comparison purposes: SIC codes 283x, biotechnology/pharmaceutical; SIC codes 354x-357x, general manufacturing; SIC codes 366x-367x, semiconductor industries; SIC codes 382x-386x, high technology and biotechnology manufacturing; SIC codes 481x-484x, communication services; and SIC codes 737x, computer programming and software.

There were many other companies that did not fall into these groupings, including companies in oil and gas extraction, long-distance trucking, commercial banking, insurance, and engineering. Although many claim that the high technology sector uses stock options more than others, these results indicate that companies in many industries are looking to use stock options to enhance employee ownership and provide a substantial and meaningful incentive to their employees.

Sales

The companies surveyed had annual sales figures ranging from zero to over $90 billion. From the findings of this survey as well as research by ShareData and Hewitt Associates, there does not seem to be a minimum revenue threshold that companies reach before they decide to implement broad-based stock option plans. In fact, the use of stock options as a major part of compensation for employees of many high technology startup companies is well known. One startup in Silicon Valley negotiated a compensation package with its first few employees in which cash compensation was $1 per year with hefty allocations of stock options. When the company went public, each of the original employees became millionaires.

Number of Employees

The average number of employees found in the companies surveyed was 7,955 for public companies and 3,749 for private companies. The presence among our survey respondents of many large, well-known public companies such as AT&T, Conoco, and Times Mirror may give the impression that companies with broad-based plans are generally large.

Other research, however, indicates that broad-based plans are more likely to be found in smaller companies. As mentioned earlier, the 1997 ShareData and American Electronics Association (AEA) survey found that 68% of companies with less than 100 employees and 74% of companies with less than $50 million in sales grant options to every employee. The ShareData/AEA survey may overstate the actual number of smaller companies using broad-based stock options because only high technology companies were surveyed. A 1991 ShareData study that surveyed companies from many different industries found that companies with 100 to 499 employees were most likely to grant options to all employees. Companies with under 100 employees were the next most likely to give all employees options.[5]

There are two reasons why companies with relatively small numbers of employees might be more likely to use broad-based stock options than larger companies. First, in a small organization, each employee has a more direct effect on the profitability of the company. Through stock options, employers can align the interests of their employees with those of the owners. Second, in small organizations that require specialized labor skills, employee compensation packages are often lower than those offered by larger companies. By broadly distributing options, small companies can improve employee compensation packages by giving employees a share of future corporate gains. There may also be more of a feeling of common purpose in small, high-growth companies that dissipates as they grow.

General Plan Design Characteristics

Type of Options

Two types of stock options are commonly awarded in broad-based plans. Nonqualified stock options have particular tax benefits to the company and are the most common type of option used in the companies surveyed. Forty-four percent of the respondents grant only nonqualified stock options to nonmanagement employees. Incentive stock options were the only type of option used in 28% of companies surveyed. The remaining 28% use a combination of both nonqualified and incentive stock options depending on who is receiving the option and the reason the option is being awarded. Respondents commented that ISOs were of little use as an additional incentive because employees often desired to cash out their options before completing the qualifying period for favorable capital gains tax treatment.

Companies grant nonqualified stock options and incentive stock options in approximately the same proportion for management and nonmanagement employees. Larger companies grant nonqualified stock options to nonmanagers more often than smaller companies.

Eligibility

In our survey, nearly all employees were eligible to receive option awards. This is because of the sample we chose to survey (companies likely to have broad-based stock option plans). In general we found that between 90% to 100% of employees in a given category are likely to be eligible to receive stock option awards. Our eight categories of employees were divided between management and nonmanagement employees. The management categories include senior executives, executives, senior managers, and supervisors. The nonmanagement categories include professionals, technical, administrative, and other. The only significant variation from this eligibility rule is among "other" employees in ongoing/periodic option plans. Only 18% of these employees were eligible to receive option awards.

Of the companies who have union employees (26% of respondents), 58% of them make union employees eligible to receive options. Forty-one percent of companies make part-time employees eligible to receive awards.

Allocation

The allocation of options is perhaps the most significant and most variable feature of stock option plans. Creativity abounds in this area of stock option design. As mentioned above, we examined three types of nonmanagement stock option programs (ongoing/periodic, one-time, and new hire grants), each of which has distinct design characteristics. The two main design variations include the size of the option award and method that is used to determine whether employees will receive option awards.

The average value of the most recent ongoing/periodic stock option grants to nonmanagement employees (defined as the number of options granted times the share value on the date of grant) was $37,000 and $41,000 for professional and technical employees respectively and $12,500 for administrative employees. These averages vary tremendously, ranging from $162 to $700,000. The range for the most recent management grants is $325 to $23 million.

Contrary to popular perception, over 80% of the companies provide ongoing awards to nonmanagers, not just one-time grants. Most grants are made on a discretionary or merit basis. Grants to nonmanagement employees on the date of hire are 10% to 40% larger than the grants made to nonmanagement employees on an annual basis. One-time stock option grants to nonmanagers are typically nominal awards, with values ranging from $875 to $23,370. Most companies make these grants to all employees. A number of companies combined more than one type of stock option plan, using either ongoing/periodic grants or one-time grants with new hire awards.

Although stock options do not represent a fixed value, if we consider the historical performance of the stock market, the typical frequency of option grants, and the typical terms of the options, in the average plan employees garner between 12% and 20% of annual pay in the form of exercisable stock option spreads, an amount in the same range as the benefits provided through ESOPs.

The determination of how options are awarded can be a central feature in the success of a broad-based stock option plan. Companies use four different means to determine whether an employee will receive an option award, including company/group performance, promotional grants, merit-based decisions, and discretionary grants. Except for new hire awards, the most common allocation method of these four types is merit-based. New hire awards are by definition not based on past individual performance in the company, so it makes sense that other methods are used to determine new hire awards.

Discretionary grantmaking is quite popular in the companies surveyed. Presumably, granting options on a discretionary basis gives them more flexibility and prevents them from being locked into annual awards of options.

The use of "reload" or "refresher" option programs was relatively uncommon among survey respondents. These types of programs replenish options as they vest or are exercised. Reload options were used by 9% of respondents for their management stock option plans and by only 7% for nonmanagement ongoing/periodic option plans. No respondent with a one-time option program used reload options.

Distribution of Options Between Management and Nonmanagement Employees

On average, management received 55% of the total options allocated under the most recent stock option grants. In companies with over 10,000 employees, this average was 71%. Biotechnology and software companies allocated the highest proportion of options to nonmanagers, with an average of 55%.

Exercise Period

A stock option's "exercise period" is the amount of time the employee has to act on the stock option grant. The exercise period can be modified in a number of ways to meet the objectives of the stock option plan, but most are not longer than 10 years. Many companies have both ISO and NSO plans in existence (although nonmanagement employees may receive one type of option and executives and management another type) and use the same exercise period out of convenience. Although 10 years is the most common exercise period, any type of option plan can have a shorter exercise period.

In our survey we found that approximately 90% of companies use 10-year exercise periods for their management, nonmanagement ongoing, and nonmanagement new hire grants. One-time nonmanagement stock option grants use expiration periods ranging from 1 year (11%) to 10 years (68%).

Exercise periods also can include restrictions and policies surrounding the retirement and termination of employees. There are two important considerations here. The first concerns the expiration of options. When an employee leaves due to death, disability, or retirement, most of the companies surveyed give employees, or their estate, three months to one year to exercise their options. With voluntary or involuntary termination, most companies give employees one to three months to exercise their options.

The second consideration regarding the retirement and termination of employees surrounds the vesting of shares in an individual's account. Depending on corporate goals, a plan can be designed that allows employees to continue vesting their shares in accordance with the original vesting schedule, allows them to have all their options immediately vest upon retirement, or gives them the right to exercise only those shares that are vested on the last day of employment. Of the companies surveyed, the continuation of vesting for termination of employment due to death, disability, or retirement is more common than when an employee leaves either voluntarily or involuntarily.

Most companies (55% to 92%, depending on the type of plan and the reason for termination) have policies that forfeit all unvested options upon voluntary or involuntary termination of employment.

Vesting

The vesting of a stock option refers to the amount of time it takes for an option to become exercisable. Companies typically determine vesting schedules for stock options according to two factors. First, vesting can be by one of four general methods:

- *Cliff vesting:* all of an employee's options become exercisable at one time on one date (e.g., 2 years from the date of grant).

- *Straight vesting:* an employee's options become exercisable at the same percentage each year (e.g., 4-year vesting in which 25% becoming vested each year at the anniversary date of the grant).

- *Step (variable) vesting:* the percentage of options exercisable each year (period) varies according to some individual formula (e.g., 4-year vesting in which 40% vests in year 1 and 20% vests in each of years 2, 3, and 4).

- *Performance vesting:* an employee's options become fully exercisable when the company achieves particular corporate goals (e.g., a share price target, a revenue goal, or another measurable determinant).

The second component of vesting is the length of time that employees must wait for their options to become exercisable. These two components are interrelated. Cliff vesting may be the best for employees if the length of time is relatively short, e.g., under two years. If a longer cliff vesting is used, however, an employee will not be able to exercise his or her options over time as the options move in and out "of the money." Vesting periods range from immediate to seven years. The most typical vesting design is three or four years, with a straight vesting schedule.

Employee Exercise Practices

Companies usually provide a few different mechanisms by which employees can actually exercise their stock options. A common way is for the employee to simply pay cash to exercise his or her options. Many nonmanagement employees, however, do not have the financial means to cover the cost of exercising their options. Therefore, many companies have established broker-assisted mechanisms in which employees do not have to come up with the cash. The most popular broker-assisted mechanism is the "cashless exercise" or "same-day sale," which allows a broker to briefly lend money to an employee to allow him or her to exercise the options and immediately sell the stock, paying back the broker and receiving the difference between the exercise price and the grant price in cash (minus any amounts for tax withholding). A "sell to cover" plan is identical except that the employee receives the difference between the exercise price and the grant price in the form of stock instead of cash.

The most common types of exercise methods are cashless exercise, cash or check, sell to cover, and stock swaps. Nearly all companies (98%) provide a cash or check alternative to allow employees to exercise options, and 86% provide for cashless exercise of the options.

The vast majority of employees (71%) were reported to use the same-day "cashless" mechanism to exercise their stock options. Although the 1998 NCEO survey did not analyze how long employees waited to exercise, previous studies by the NCEO and others have shown that employees typically exercise their options well before the end of the expiration periods due to personal financial needs. A 1996 study by two professors at Duke University and the University of North Carolina at Chapel Hill found that 90% of employees receiving stock options sold their stock immediately after they exercised their options. The researchers also found that two-thirds of the exercise activity of lower-level employees occurred within six months of the options being vested and "in the money." Senior executives were half as likely to exercise their options within six months.[6]

Repricing

Over one-third (36%) of respondents had repriced their stock options within the last three years. Repricing is a practice whereby companies "reset" the price of the issued stock options when the current market price drops below the original grant price of the options. The companies that repriced experienced an average drop in stock price of 45% before they repriced, and on average, the stock had been "underwater" for five months. The companies with the highest frequency of repricing were semiconductor companies, companies located on the West Coast, those with 16%–20% overhang, and those in which the distribution of allocated options between management and nonmanagement employees was approximately equal. Eighty-two percent of the semiconductor companies surveyed had repriced in the last three years. Larger companies and more established companies (those in operation for over 80 years and those that had been public for more than 19 years) did not reprice their options.

Overhang

The average overhang (total number of options granted and unexercised as a percentage of outstanding shares) was 12.6%. Almost two-thirds of the plans had overhang above 10%, with almost one-third above 15%. Semiconductor companies had the highest overhang, with an average of 16.6%, followed by companies on the West Coast, which had rates of 14.5%.

Objectives

Although the primary objectives for implementing a stock option plan vary considerably, we can make a few generalizations. The most commonly cited objective for implementing a broad-based stock option plan is "to attract and retain employees." "Linking employee and shareholder interests" and "increased employee ownership" were other commonly cited objectives for the plans implemented in the companies surveyed. An average of 90% of the respondents felt that the plan had "mostly met" or "fully met" its key objectives.

Communication Methods

One of the most important elements for the success of any option plan in meeting its objectives is an effective communication program. Although most companies communicate the plan in some way, only a small percentage of companies are creating comprehensive programs that incorporate multiple techniques. Seventy-five percent of the companies surveyed use a letter from senior management to communicate the option plan to employees, 60% hold some type of group meeting, and 60% conduct individual meetings between employees and supervisors. Electronic communication mechanisms were the least popular methods.

Employee Participation

Most companies believe that by giving employees stock options, employees will be more motivated and the company will do better. Previous research on the relationship between employee ownership and corporate performance indicates, however, that only when employee ownership is combined with a committed effort to create ways for employees to think and act like owners will improvements in corporate performance be seen. (However, this research mainly deals with ESOP companies.) The 1998 survey asked companies whether or not they use particular employee involvement practices that have been identified as key elements of ownership cultures in ESOP companies.

Over three-quarters of the survey respondents hold regular or periodic meetings to discuss company performance and developments. Just over half share financial information above and beyond what is required by law with employees. Although most companies have created some way to get employees involved as owners, only a small percentage are using multiple techniques to encourage employee involvement.

Other Equity Compensation Programs

Stock option plans are only one of the equity compensation programs offered by many of the companies surveyed. Stock purchase plans, 401(k) plans with company stock as the match to employee contributions, restricted stock, stock appreciation rights (SARs), ESOPs, and phantom stock arrangements were all present in the companies surveyed. Section 423 employee stock purchase plans and 401(k) plans that match in company stock were the most commonly used equity compensation strategies (respectively 49% and 41% of respondents). Twenty-one percent of the companies surveyed use stock options as their only form of equity compensation. In none of the companies surveyed was a stock option plan introduced to replace an existing equity compensation plan.

Summary

The findings from the 1998 NCEO survey indicate that broad-based stock option plans are being designed in dozens of unique ways to address a wide range of corporate objectives. From rewarding employees for past performance to creating an ownership culture, stock options are being used as a flexible employee compensation tool that any employer can use.

The survey found that stock options are rarely being used to replace existing employee benefits. Instead, they are being used in addition to other compensation programs to link pay to performance in an increasingly competitive market. In addition, stock options are filling a gap that other, more traditional compensation tools are not meeting. Stock options are not the exclusive domain of high technology companies. Companies ranging in size from small private service industries to public corporate giants in all industries are beginning to recognize the benefits of stock options.

This survey revealed great variations in exercise periods, vesting schedules, and allocation methods. Although it is difficult to generalize from such a small sample, we can develop a profile of a typical broad-based stock option plan. Such a plan would have the following characteristics:

- Option grants are made to over 50% of employees. Most plans make all employees or all full-time employees eligible to participate in the program. Eligibility, as noted earlier, does not mean that all employees receive options. Because of overlapping grants, approximately 60%–70% of all employees usually have outstanding options at any one time.
- Options are granted at fair market value on the date of grant.
- Options are granted on an ongoing/periodic basis, often with an initial option award at the date of hire.
- Vesting is for three to five years, with equal annual vesting over the term.

- The option life is 10 years, conditional on employment.

- Grants are allocated annually to employees depending on grade level and/or salary, or grants are allocated according to merit.

- There is no imposed holding period, even on the granting of ISOs.

- Employees are given a choice between a same-day "cashless" exercise and sale and purchasing options with cash.

The above description of a typical plan is not a cookie-cutter recipe for those interested in developing a broad-based stock option plan. Each of the characteristics of the typical plan works to address some of the underlying goals of a stock option plan. Each company should start by identifying the goals and purposes that they wish to accomplish through such a plan. Once these objectives are identified, creating the recipe will be a matter of weighing the pros and cons of various plan design features.

The 1999 TriNet/NCEO Survey

In 1999, TriNet VCO (a Bay Area-based human resources consulting firm) and the NCEO teamed up to conduct a survey of stock option plan design and grant practices in companies backed by venture capital. The survey was similar to the 1998 NCEO survey discussed in this chapter; however, it was shorter and included questions oriented to VCO companies. The survey takes an in-depth look at stock option granting practices within venture capital-backed startup companies. For a more complete description of the results, see appendix 1 at the end of this chapter.

Current Research

As of fall 1999, Douglas Kruse and Joseph Blasi, professors at the Institute of Management and Labor Relations at Rutgers University, have begun the first study to examine the corporate performance of companies using broad-based stock options. They will track the performance of companies before they implemented their broad-based stock option awards and compare this to the performance after the plan was put in place.

Additionally, the NCEO is currently conducting research on the prevalence of employee involvement efforts in companies with broad-based stock options.

Plan Descriptions

The following section contains descriptions of broad-based stock option plans in 20 U.S. companies. The information was collected through library research, phone interviews, and surveys. In some cases, written material was available on the company, but phone calls to the investor relations department, human resource department, or stock option administrators were not returned, leaving some gaps in information. Incomplete information is marked by "N/A."

Ninety-four companies with broad-based stock option plans returned surveys, but only 20 are listed here due to the similarity among some plans. Eleven companies are not identified at their request. These companies either did not want outsiders to know the specifics of their plan design or felt that divulging such information might be harmful in their bid to take their private company public. These eleven companies are identified as Companies A–L, and information that might identify them has been generalized (e.g., industry type, sales, and the number of employees). The information presented in each description includes the following:

- *General information:* Company, industry, public/private, number of employees, sales, start date of plan, and type of options granted.

- *Eligibility:* Who in the company is eligible to receive option grants.

- *Allocation:* Who in the company actually receives option grants and how options are distributed.

- *Vesting:* The period from the time of grant to the date when options can be exercised.

- *Option life:* The amount of time before the options expire (the time starts from either the date of grant or the last day of vesting).

- *Overhang:* The ratio of the amount of outstanding, unexercised options to the company's entire pool of stock.

- *Distribution of options between management and nonmanagement employees:* The allocation of the entire pool of options between management and nonmanagement employees.

- *Repricing:* Whether or not the company has repriced in the last three years. If it has repriced, information on the specific design attributes of repricing are provided.

- *Communication methods:* Methods that the company uses to communicate its stock option plan.

- *Employee participation techniques:* Tools and techniques that the company uses to share information with employees and to get employees involved in decision making at the job level.

- *Other plans:* Other retirement/profit sharing plans offered by the company. Nearly every company uses a 401(k) plan in addition to its stock option plan; however, such plans may or may not match in company stock. Such information was not collected.

AT&T

Industry
Telecommunication services

Public/Private
Public

Employees
115,000

Eligibility
All employees

Allocation
All employees received 100 options each in 1997.

Vesting
3-year cliff

Option Life
10 years from grant date. Upon death, disability, and retirement, original term of option is maintained. Upon termination, employee has three months to exercise vested options.

Overhang
6–10%

Distribution of Options Between Management and Nonmanagement Employees
Management 90%, nonmanagement 10%

Repricing
No

Communication Methods
Letter from senior management, brochures/flyers/newsletters, e-mail, and intranet/Internet.

Employee Participation Techniques
None stated

Other Plans
401(k) plan with match in company stock, section 423 stock purchase plan, nonqualified employee stock purchase plan, restricted stock, and performance-accelerated restricted stock.

Sales
$51 billion

Start Date of Plan
1997

Option Type
NSO

Conoco

Industry
Oil and gas—exploration, production, refining, and marketing.

Public/Private
Public (subsidiary of DuPont)

Employees
15,000

Sales
$21.4 billion

Start Date of Plan
1991

Option Type
NSO

Eligibility
All employees

Allocation
All employees received 100 options each in 1991.

Vesting
Performance vesting—all options vest when stock price hits $75 for five consecutive days.

Option Life
10 years from grant date. Upon death, employee has two years to exercise vested options. Upon disability and retirement, original term of option is maintained. Upon termination, employee forfeits all options.

Overhang
N/A—this is a subsidiary of DuPont.

Distribution of Options Between Management and Nonmanagement Employees
Management 75%, nonmanagement 25%

Repricing
No

Communication Methods
Letter from senior management, brochures/flyers/newsletters, and individual employee-supervisor meetings.

Employee Participation Techniques
Education or training program on general business concepts; sharing financial information (other than is required by law); self-managing/cross-functional work teams; regular or periodic meetings to discuss company performance, strategy, or future goals; and regular meetings and/or structured opportunities to contribute input about their jobs or work environment.

Other Plans
Stock appreciation rights and 401(k) plan with match in company stock.

Pioneer Natural Resources

Industry

Oil and gas—exploration, production, and refining

Public/Private

Public

Employees

1,000

Sales

$750 million

Start Date of Plan

1997

Option Type

NSO

Eligibility

All employees

Allocation

On an ongoing/periodic basis, all nonmanagement employees receive grants of between 180 and 510 options, and all management employees receive grants of between 1,000 and 59,000 options.

Vesting

3-year straight

Option Life

5 years after vesting. Upon death, disability, or involuntary termination (not for cause) employee has three to six months to exercise vested options. Upon retirement, original term of option is maintained. Upon voluntary termination, employee forfeits all options.

Overhang

1–5%

Distribution of Options Between Management and Nonmanagement Employees

Management 60%, nonmanagement 40%

Repricing

No

Communication Methods

Letter from senior management, brochures/flyers/newsletters, HR meeting/ group meeting, individual employee-supervisor meetings, and e-mail.

Employee Participation Techniques

Regular or periodic meetings to discuss company performance, strategy, or future goals.

Other Plans

Section 423 stock purchase plan and restricted stock.

Reynolds & Reynolds

Industry
Information management

Sales
$1.6 billion

Public/Private
Public

Start Date of Plan
1996

Employees
10,000

Option Type
NSO

Eligibility
All employees

Allocation
All nonmanagement employees receive 10% of their pay each year in options. Management employees receive between 10% and 90% of their pay in options.

Vesting
3-year cliff

Option Life
10 years after grant date. Upon death, employee has one year to exercise vested options. Upon disability or retirement, original term of option is maintained. Upon termination, employee has one to three months to exercise vested options

Overhang
11–15%

Distribution of Options Between Management and Nonmanagement Employees
Management 50%, nonmanagement 50%

Repricing
No

Communication Methods
Letter from senior management, brochures/flyers/newsletters, HR meeting/ group meeting, and individual employee-supervisor meetings.

Employee Participation Techniques
Self-managing/cross-functional work teams and regular or periodic meetings to discuss company performance, strategy, or future goals.

Other Plans
401(k) plan with match in company stock and employee stock purchase plan.

San Jose National Bank

Industry
  Banking

Sales
  $28 million

Public/Private
  Public

Start Date of Plan
  1996

Employees
  88

Option Type
  ISO & NSO

Eligibility
  All employees

Allocation
  All employees receive ongoing/periodic grants based on grade level within the company. The option grant sizes range from 500 for administrative nonmanagement employees to over 6,000 for executives.

Vesting
  4 years: 40% in year 1 and 20% in years 2, 3, and 4

Option Life
  10 years from grant date. Upon death or disability, employee has one year to exercise vested options. Upon retirement or termination, employee has one to three months to exercise vested options.

Overhang
  11–15%

Distribution of Options Between Management and Nonmanagement Employees
  Management 55%, nonmanagement 45%

Repricing
  No

Communication Methods
  Letter from senior management and HR meeting/group meeting.

Employee Participation Techniques
  Sharing financial information (other than is required by law); regular or periodic meetings to discuss company performance, strategy, or future goals; regular meetings and/or structured opportunities to contribute input about their jobs or work environment; and regular meetings and/or structured opportunities to contribute input about company policy or provide input to upper management or the board.

Other Plans
  401(k) plan with match in company stock.

The Gallery Group

Industry
N/A

Public/Private
Private

Employees
4

Sales
$600,000

Start Date of Plan
1997

Option Type
NSO

Eligibility
All employees

Allocation
All employees received options in April 1997. Nonmanagement employees received 10 options each and management employees 25 options each.

Vesting
1-year cliff

Option Life
N/A

Overhang
16–20%

Distribution of Options Between Management and Nonmanagement Employees
Management 80%, nonmanagement 20%

Repricing
No

Communication Methods
Individual employee-supervisor meetings.

Employee Participation Techniques
Education or training program on general business concepts; sharing financial information (other than is required by law); open-book management; total quality management; regular or periodic meetings to discuss company performance, strategy, or future goals; and regular meetings and/or structured opportunities to contribute input about company policy or provide input to upper management or the board.

Other Plans
Phantom stock

Times Mirror

Industry
Publishing

Sales
$3.4 billion

Public/Private
Public

Start Date of Plan
1996

Employees
22,000

Option Type
NSO

Eligibility
All employees

Allocation
All nonmanagement employees received 100 options in January 1996, and management employees receive option grants from 1,000 to 4,000 options on a regular basis.

Vesting
3-year cliff

Option Life
10 years from grant date

Overhang
N/A

Distribution of Options Between Management and Nonmanagement Employees
Management 80%, nonmanagement 20%

Repricing
No

Communication Methods
Letter from senior management, HR meeting/group meeting, and individual employee-supervisor meetings.

Employee Participation Techniques
Sharing financial information (other than is required by law) and self-managing/cross-functional work teams.

Other Plans
401(k) plan with match in company stock, restricted stock, ESOP, and phantom stock.

Union Pacific Resources

Industry
Oil and gas—exploration and production

Public/Private
Public

Employees
1,900

Sales
$1.93 billion

Start Date of Plan
1996

Option Type
NSO

Eligibility
Professional and technical nonmanagement employees and management employees.

Allocation
Professional and technical nonmanagement employees received 2,000 options in October 1996.

Vesting
3-year cliff

Option Life
10 years from grant date. Upon death, disability, and retirement, employee has five years to exercise vested options. Upon termination, employee has one to three months to exercise vested options.

Overhang
1–5%

Distribution of Options Between Management and Nonmanagement Employees
Management 95%, nonmanagement 5%

Repricing
No

Communication Methods
Letter from senior management, brochures/flyers/newsletters, HR meeting/group meeting, and intranet/Internet.

Employee Participation Techniques
Education or training program on general business concepts; sharing financial information (other than is required by law); open-book management; total quality management; regular or periodic meetings to discuss company performance, strategy, or future goals; regular meetings and/or structured opportunities to contribute input about their jobs or work environment; and regular meetings and/or structured opportunities to contribute input about company policy or provide input to upper management or the board.

Other Plans
Stock appreciation rights, 401(k) plan with match in company stock, and restricted stock.

Company A

Industry

Research, development, and production of advanced medical implants

Public/Private

Public

Employees

Fewer than 100

Eligibility

All employees

Sales

$10 million–$20 million

Start Date of Plan

1987

Option Type

ISO

Allocation

All nonmanagement employees receive between 1,000 and 3,000 options and management employees between 3,000 and 15,000 on an ongoing basis.

Vesting

4-year straight

Option Life

10 years after grant date. Upon death, disability, retirement or voluntary termination, employee has three to six months to exercise vested options. Upon involuntary termination, employee has one to three months to exercise vested options.

Overhang

6–10%

Distribution of Options Between Management and Nonmanagement Employees

Management 80%, nonmanagement 20%

Repricing

Yes. Options were underwater for six months before repricing. Company issued the same number of options as the initial grant.

Communication Methods

Letter from senior management and HR meeting/group meeting.

Employee Participation Techniques

Self-managing/cross-functional work teams and regular or periodic meetings to discuss company performance, strategy, or future goals.

Other Plans

Section 423 stock purchase plan

Company B

Industry
Biotechnology research and
development

Public/Private
Public

Employees
500–1000

Sales
$100 million to $250 million

Start Date of Plan
1990

Option Type
ISO

Eligibility
Most full-time employees.

Allocation
All eligible employees receive option grants based on salary. Nonmanagement
employees receive options worth 25% of their salary, and management employees receive options worth 25% to 1,000% of salary on an ongoing/periodic basis.

Vesting
4-year straight

Option Life
10 years from grant date. Upon death, disability, or retirement, employee has one
year to exercise vested options. Upon termination employee has one to three
months to exercise vested options.

Overhang
N/A

Distribution of Options Between Management and Nonmanagement Employees
Management 95%, nonmanagement 5%

Repricing
No

Communication Methods
Letter from senior management, brochures/flyers/newsletters, and individual
employee-supervisor meetings.

Employee Participation Techniques
None stated

Other Plans
Section 423 stock purchase plan

Company C

Industry

Biotechnology research and development

Public/Private

Public

Employees

Fewer than 100

Sales

Less than $1 million

Start Date of Plan

1991

Option Type

ISO

Eligibility

All employees

Allocation

All employees received a grant of 2,000 options in 1991.

Vesting

4-year straight

Option Life

10 years from grant date. Upon death, disability, or retirement, employee has one year to exercise vested options. Upon termination, employee has one to three months to exercise vested options.

Overhang

16–20%

Distribution of Options Between Management and Nonmanagement Employees

N/A

Repricing

No

Communication Methods

Letter from senior management and HR meeting/group meeting.

Employee Participation Techniques

Sharing financial information (other than is required by law) and regular or periodic meetings to discuss company performance, strategy, or future goals.

Other Plans

Section 423 stock purchase plan

Company D

Industry
Computer manufacturing and
assembly

Public/Private
Public

Employees
Fewer than 100

Sales
$20 million to $50 million

Start Date of Plan
1996

Option Type
NSO

Eligibility
All employees

Allocation
All employees receive ongoing grants, and new employees receive grants at start
date. Nonmanagement employees receive new hire grants ranging from 5,000 to
30,000 options. Nonmanagement employees receive ongoing annual grants of
between 2,000 and 3,000 options. Management employees receive ongoing
grants of between 3,000 to 50,000 options.

Vesting
2 years: 33% vest at grant date and 33% vest at year 1 and year 2 anniversaries.

Option Life
10 years from grant date. Upon death, disability, or retirement, employee has
three to six months to exercise vested options. Upon termination, employee has
one to three months to exercise vested options.

Overhang
11–15%

Distribution of Options Between Management and Nonmanagement Employees
Management 75%, nonmanagement 25%

Repricing
No

Communication Methods
HR meeting/group meeting and individual employee-supervisor meetings.

Employee Participation Techniques
Sharing financial information (other than is required by law); regular or periodic
meetings to discuss company performance, strategy, or future goals; and regular
meetings and/or structured opportunities to contribute input about company
policy or provide input to upper management or the board.

Other Plans
Stock appreciation rights, 401(k) plan with match in company stock, section 423
stock purchase plan, and restricted stock.

Company E

Industry
Software

Public/Private
Public

Employees
100 to 200 employees

Sales
$10 million to $20 million

Start Date of Plan
1993

Option Type
ISO

Eligibility
All employees

Allocation
All employees receive ongoing grants, and new employees receive grants at start date. Nonmanagement employees receive new hire grants ranging from 500 to 10,000 options. Nonmanagement employees receive ongoing annual grants between 1,000 and 2,000 options. Management employees receive grants (either at hire date or at plan start in 1993) of between 2,500 to 120,000 options.

Vesting
4 years straight

Option Life
10 years from grant date. Upon death or disability, employee has twelve months to exercise vested options. Upon retirement or termination, employee has three months to exercise vested options.

Overhang
16–20%

Distribution of Options Between Management and Nonmanagement Employees
Management 55%, nonmanagement 45%

Repricing
Yes. Options were underwater for six months before repricing. Company issued the same number of options as the initial grant.

Communication Methods
Letter from senior management, brochures/flyers/newsletters, individual employee-supervisor meeting, e-mail, and intranet/Internet.

Employee Participation Techniques
Sharing financial information (other than is required by law); regular or periodic meetings to discuss company performance, strategy, or future goals; and regular meetings and/or structured opportunities to contribute input about their jobs or work environment.

Other Plans
Section 423 stock purchase plan

Company F

Industry

Biotechnology research, development, and production

Public/Private

Public

Employees

Fewer than 100

Sales

Less than $1 million

Start Date of Plan

1992

Option Type

ISO and NSO

Eligibility

All employees

Allocation

All nonmanagement employees receive grants of between 750 and 2,500 options and management employees receive grants of between 1,750 and 20,000 options on an ongoing/periodic basis.

Vesting

5-year straight. If particular corporate objectives are met, the options vest immediately.

Option Life

10 years after grant date. Upon death, disability, retirement, or termination, employee has one to three months to exercise vested options.

Overhang

11–15%

Distribution of Options Between Management and Nonmanagement Employees

Management 65%, nonmanagement 35%

Repricing

No

Communication Methods

Letter from senior management, HR meeting/group meeting, and individual employee-supervisor meetings.

Employee Participation Techniques

Education or training program on general business concepts; sharing financial information (other than is required by law); open-book management; regular or periodic meetings to discuss company performance, strategy, or future goals; regular meetings and/or structured opportunities to contribute input about their jobs or work environment; and regular meetings and/or structured opportunities to contribute input about company policy or provide input to upper management or the board.

Other Plans

401(k) plan with match in company stock, section 423 stock purchase plan, and ESOP.

Company G

Industry
Medical device manufacturing

Sales
$1 million to $5 million

Public/Private
Public

Start Date of Plan
1996

Employees
Fewer than 100

Option Type
ISO

Eligibility
All employees

Allocation
All nonmanagement employees receive grants of between 1,100 to 11,000 options, and management employees receive grants of between 11,000 to 94,000 options on an ongoing/periodic basis.

Vesting
4-year straight

Option Life
10 years from grant date. Upon death, disability, or retirement, employee has twelve months to exercise vested options. Upon termination, employee has one to three months to exercise vested options.

Overhang
11–15%

Distribution of Options Between Management and Nonmanagement Employees
Management 30%, nonmanagement 70%

Repricing
No

Communication Methods
HR meeting/group meeting and individual employee-supervisor meetings.

Employee Participation Techniques
Education or training program on general business concepts; total quality management; regular or periodic meetings to discuss company performance, strategy, or future goals; and regular meetings and/or structured opportunities to contribute input about their jobs or work environment.

Other Plans
Section 423 stock purchase plan and restricted stock.

Company H

Industry
Telecommunications

Public/Private
Public

Employees
2,000 to 3,000

Sales
$100 million to $250 million

Start Date of Plan
1992 and 1997

Option Type
ISO

Eligibility
All employees

Allocation
All nonmanagement employees receive option grants between 250 to 1,000 at hire date. In 1997, all nonmanagement employees received an additional grant ranging from 250 and 1000 options. Management employees receive options ranging from 1,000 to 20,000 options on an ongoing/periodic basis.

Vesting
5-year straight

Option Life
10 years after grant date. Upon death, disability, or retirement, employee has twelve months to exercise all options (all unvested options vest immediately in these circumstances). Upon voluntary termination, employee has one to three months to exercise vested options. Upon involuntary termination, employee forfeits all options.

Overhang
Over 20%

Distribution of Options Between Management and Nonmanagement Employees
Management 40%, nonmanagement 60%

Repricing
No

Communication Methods
HR meeting/group meeting, individual employee-supervisor meeting, and e-mail.

Employee Participation Techniques
None stated

Other Plans
401(k) plan with match in company stock, section 423 stock purchase plan, and restricted stock.

Company I

Industry

Biotechnology research and development

Public/Private

Public

Employees

200 to 500

Sales

$20 million to $50 million

Start Date of Plan

1984

Option Type

ISO

Eligibility

All employees

Allocation

All employees receive option awards ranging from 500 to 10,000 options on an ongoing/periodic basis.

Vesting

4 years: 20% in years 1, 2, and 3, and 40% in year 4.

Option Life

10 years from grant date. Upon death, employee has twelve months to exercise vested options. Upon disability, retirement, or termination, employee has one to three months to exercise vested options.

Overhang

6–10%

Distribution of Options Between Management and Nonmanagement Employees

Management 80%, nonmanagement 20%

Repricing

No

Communication Methods

Letter from senior management and individual employee-supervisor meetings.

Employee Participation Techniques

None stated

Other Plans

Restricted stock and performance-accelerated restricted stock.

Company J

Industry
   Telecommunication software

Sales
   $50 million to $100 million

Public/Private
   Public

Start Date of Plan
   1997

Employees
   200 to 500

Option Type
   NSO

Eligibility
   All employees

Allocation
   In June 1997, all nonmanagement employees received awards of between 700 and 10,000 options and management employees received awards of between 32,000 and 1 million options. All employees hired after June 1997 receive option awards based on a schedule related to the 1997 grant.

Vesting
   4 years: 25% at year 1, then monthly vesting until year 4.

Option Life
   10 years from grant date. Upon death, disability, retirement, or termination, employee has one to three months to exercise vested options.

Overhang
   N/A

Distribution of Options Between Management and Nonmanagement Employees
   Management 55%, nonmanagement 45%

Repricing
   Yes. Options were underwater for two to three months before repricing. Company issued the same number of options as the initial grant.

Communication Methods
   Letter from senior management, brochures/flyers/newsletters, and intranet/Internet.

Employee Participation Techniques
   Regular or periodic meetings to discuss company performance, strategy, or future goals and regular meetings and/or structured opportunities to contribute input about company policy or provide input to upper management or the board.

Other Plans
   401(k) plan with match in company stock.

Company K

Industry
Computer hardware

Sales
$100 million to $250 million

Public/Private
Public

Start Date of Plan
1992

Employees
500 to 1,000

Option Type
NSO

Eligibility
All employees

Allocation
All employees receive ongoing grants and new employees receive grants at start date. Nonmanagement employees receive new hire grants ranging from 500 to 5,000 options. Nonmanagement employees receive ongoing annual grants between 250 and 2,000 options. Management employees receive grants up to 30,000 options annually.

Vesting
4 years: 25% at year 1, then monthly vesting until year 4.

Option Life
7 years after grant date. Upon death, employee has twelve months to exercise vested options. Upon disability, retirement, or involuntary termination (not for cause), employee has three to six months to exercise vested options. Upon voluntary termination, employee has one to three months to exercise vested options.

Overhang
6–10%

Distribution of Options Between Management and Nonmanagement Employees
Management 45%, nonmanagement 55%

Repricing
Yes. Options were underwater for eight to twelve months before repricing. Company issued the same number of options as the initial grant.

Communication Methods
Letter from senior management, HR meeting/group meeting, individual employee-supervisor meetings, and e-mail.

Employee Participation Techniques
Education or training program on general business concepts, sharing financial information (other than is required by law), total quality management, regular or periodic meetings to discuss company performance, strategy, or future goals, and regular meetings and/or structured opportunities to contribute input about their jobs or work environment.

Other Plans
Section 423 stock purchase plan

Company L

Industry
Software

Public/Private
Public

Employees
500 to 1,000

Sales
$250 million to $500 million

Start Date of Plan
1994

Option Type
NSO

Eligibility
All employees

Allocation
All employees receive new hire awards and annual grants under an "evergreen" plan. Nonmanagement employees receive new hire grants ranging from 250 to 4,000 options. Management employees receive new hire grants ranging from 4,000 to 75,000 options. Annual grants under "evergreen" plan are approximately 20% of the new hire grant.

Vesting
4 years: 25% at year 1, then monthly vesting until year 4.

Option Life
10 years from grant date. Upon death or disability, employee has three to six months to exercise vested options. Upon retirement or termination, employee has one to three months to exercise vested options.

Overhang
Over 20%

Distribution of Options Between Management and Nonmanagement Employees
Management 75%, nonmanagement 25%

Repricing
Yes. Options were underwater for three months before repricing. Company issued the same number of options as the initial grant.

Communication Methods
Letter from senior management, brochures/flyers/newsletters, HR meeting/group meeting, and intranet/Internet.

Employee Participation Techniques
Education or training program on general business concepts, total quality management, and regular or periodic meetings to discuss company performance, strategy, or future goals.

Other Plans
Section 423 stock purchase plan

Appendix 1: The 1999 TriNet/NCEO Stock Options Survey

In 1999, TriNet VCO (a Bay Area-based HR consulting firm) and the National Center for Employee Ownership teamed up to conduct a survey of stock option plan design and grant practices in companies backed by venture capital ("VCO companies"). The survey was jointly designed, conducted, and analyzed by TriNet VCO and the National Center for Employee Ownership (NCEO). The survey was similar to the 1998 NCEO survey discussed in the rest of this publication; however, it was shorter and included questions oriented toward VCO companies. All survey data was collected online at the NCEO's Web site from November 1998 to January 1999. TriNet then analyzed the data with the NCEO's assistance.

The survey takes an in-depth look at stock option granting practices within venture capital-backed startup companies. The results from this survey are intended for use both by companies with stock option plans and those without plans. For companies already granting stock options, the survey can be a useful guide to how their option plan compares to others in the VCO community. For companies without options, the survey provides a resource for creating a program that is consistent and competitive for their market and industry.

The survey focused primarily on the stock option granting practices of Voss. The intense competition for key employees at all levels and the scarcity of cash in VCOs has fueled the widespread popularity of stock options as a key part of compensation. For purposes of this survey, a VCO is defined as an emerging growth company (1) having an annual employment growth of approximately 30% or greater; (2) backed by private equity financing (equity capital invested from sources other than employees and management team); and (3) with a professional/technical workforce.

Results

The 1999 TriNet/NCEO survey followed the general structure of the larger 1998 NCEO survey, but focused exclusively on the stock option practices in VCO companies. This section summarizes some of the key findings of the survey, including: the frequency of options grants; the distribution of options between executives, managers, senior technical professionals, technical professionals, and administrative employees, type of options granted; vesting; exercise restrictions; overhang; plan objectives; as well as communication and employee participation programs. In general, the findings of the TriNet/NCEO survey indicate that VCO companies mirror larger, more established companies on many stock option practices, as represented in the 1998 NCEO survey discussed in the rest of this chapter. TriNet VCO will be publishing the full results of the survey.

Data Collection

A total of 187 companies from California, Massachusetts, Virginia, and Washington State were initially targeted, all TriNet clients. Additional publicity about the survey led to participation by several companies that were not TriNet clients. These companies are all equity-backed, emerging-growth, high-tech, or biotech companies. In total, 31 responses to the survey were received, a 16.6% response rate The respondents to the survey included chief financial officers, chief executive officers, vice presidents of finance, persons in operations and administration, and controllers. The companies that responded range in size from 10 employees to 200 employees. Companies are located in various regions throughout the United States, although the majority of respondents (69%) were from the San Francisco Bay area.

Frequency of Grants

The results reveal VCOs are using options most often as a recruitment tool. Eighty-three percent of companies reporting make new hire grants to *all* employees, with 68% making annual, ongoing awards with allocation determined by individual employee performance. Another 26% make ongoing awards on a discretionary schedule, depending upon company performance and other unnamed factors.

Allocation

The survey looked at allocation amount for employees at different levels in three different ways: percent of salary (as a target), number of options, and the "value" of the option.

   When reviewing the data on size of awards, it is important to remember VCO characteristics. Looking at the correlation between base pay and level in a VCO, the average pay for a senior technical employee is $93,000, while the average base pay for a Manager is $91,000. This compensation structure reflects the typical VCO in which the senior technical employee with the knowledge to get the product to market is more valuable than a manager. The average executive base pay, at $115,000, is not substantially higher than that of managers and senior technical employees, a differential that is probably much larger in more traditional and established companies.

   Stock options are targeted to be as high as 101% of total compensation for the top paid people, with the average executive targeted to receive up to 70% of total compensation in the form of options and the average manager and senior technical employee targeted to receive close to 40% of total compensation in options. These percentages decrease as we move down the salary scale. Employees making less than $30,000 per year are targeted to receive 6.2% of the their annual compensation in options.

We also looked at the "value" of these option awards. Our definition of the "value" of an option award is based on the method used in the rest of this publication and is defined as number of options multiplied by the strike or exercise price of the options. While this is not a scientific expression of actual value, it is a useful measure to make simple, quick comparisons. The "value" of these options often ends up being even higher than the targets, with the average executive receiving an award with a "value" of $110,433 and the average manager and senior technical employee getting an award with a "value" of $53,392 at the time of hire. Again, however, these numbers drop off significantly as we move down the salary scale. Employees in the $30,000-$50,000 annual salary range are receiving options worth over $5,000 at the time of hire, while those making less than $30,000 are receiving grants worth about $1,100.

The survey also reports on the number of options granted. While this is not a useful way to make comparisons between companies, since 100 options in one company is not the same as 100 options in another company, we can see that the averages for the different levels of employees follow the same pattern as the other measures, namely that the number of options decreases significantly as compensation and level in the company moves down.

This shows that the higher-paid people in VCO companies are receiving the largest option packages. This is consistent with trends in other companies, and VCOs are not necessarily breaking any new ground in terms of how options are distributed among employees. It is not surprising that VCO companies are rewarding the employees that they believe are the most "mission critical" with the most options.

Allocation Methods

To determine the size of new hire awards, most companies are using the historical size of previous grants. So, even though many of these companies do not have a long history, they are using the grant sizes of previous grants to determine subsequent ones.

Type of Option

Forty-two percent of the companies surveyed grant only incentive stock options (ISOs), as compared to 35% that granted both ISOs and nonqualified stock options (NSO). These percentages are higher than those found in the 1998 NCEO survey, which were 28% for both categories. The more common use of ISOs in venture companies is most likely due to the competitive pressures for recruiting top talent, since ISOs offer a potentially better tax treatment for employees.

Vesting

For vesting, the results are very similar to the findings from the 1998 NCEO survey. Most companies are using a 4 year, equal installment vesting schedule.

Valuation

Since all the companies in this sample were privately held, they all have to value their stock in some way in order to establish the grant price of the stock option. In 90% of the companies, the board establishes this price, with or without outside input.

Restrictions on Exercise Activity

In a private company, if an employee exercises stock options before a liquidity event (acquisition, merger, going public), this can trigger securities registration and disclosure requirements as well as raise corporate governance issues. Because of this, we expected that most companies would not allow their employees to exercise their options earlier and that many of the companies would have restrictions in place relating to employee exercise activity. Only 17% of the companies surveyed, however, included this provision.

Overhang

The survey also looked at overhang, defined as the number of current outstanding options and those reserved for future grants as a percentage of total outstanding shares. Overhang percentages ranged from 6% to over 26%, with the average overhang of the total pool 15.7%. The average overhang of allocated or issued options was 11.2%. This heavy usage of the option pool early on, however, is typical in a relatively early stage VCO that is working hard to recruit the talent needed for the growth and success of the company.

Plan Objectives

Not surprisingly, the most common objective for implementing a stock option plan among respondents was to retain key employees. The next two most common objectives were to create an ownership culture and to recruit top talent. These results are not dissimilar from the findings in the larger 1998 NCEO survey.

Communication Programs

The survey also looked at the prevalence of certain communication tools. The results show that over half of the companies are distributing a letter from senior management; three quarters hold individual meeting with employees; almost 30% hold an HR or group meeting; and 26% are using email. These results are very similar to the results from the 1998 NCEO survey, except there is a larger percentage of VCO companies using individual meetings to communicate stock options, 75%, as compared to 60% in the 1998 NCEO survey. In fact, that was the most popular technique among VCO companies.

Employee Participation

Finally, the survey looked at employee participation programs. When compared to the 1998 NCEO survey, the VCO companies had a higher prevalence of all but one type of employee participation. There is a slightly higher of percentage of VCOs using open-book management, self managing work teams, and regular meetings to discuss company performance. There are much higher percentages of companies using such techniques as regular opportunities to contribute input about jobs and work (65%, as compared to 38% in the 1998 survey) and regular opportunities to contribute input about compensation policy (45% as compared to 29%). Only one technique, business education and training, was less used by VCOs.

This may mean that VCO companies are taking more formal steps to create a participative environment than other types of companies, although it is difficult to draw a reliable conclusion from this data. This data definitely shows, however, that many VCO companies are using techniques to share information with employees and allow them to make decisions about their jobs and the company.

Conclusion

For those familiar with the use of stock options in the VCO setting, some of the results of the 1999 TriNet/NCEO survey may not be surprising. What is interesting is that a number of commonly held assumptions about stock options in VCOs, such as broad-based distribution and high levels of new hire awards, that have mostly come from anecdotal evidence have been confirmed by this study. Some of the trends reflected in the data, such as the lack of restrictions on exercise activity and the heavy use of ISOs may be surprising (particularly as they relate to trends uncovered in studies of non-VCO companies) when taken out of the context of the start-up world.

More specifically, the survey reveals that most employees in these companies are receiving stock options. It also shows that the distribution of options within VCO companies is similar to that of other types companies. i.e., those on the top of the pay scale are receiving many more options than those at the bottom of the pay scale. In terms of plan design characteristics, such as vesting schedules, types of options, and overhang, VCO companies are mostly in line with stock option plans in other sectors.

It may seem odd that VCO companies, commonly seen as the vanguard of stock options trends, do not seem to be doing anything dramatically different in terms of stock option plan design than other types of companies. Perhaps, however, these similarities are an indication that the stock option practices of small, knowledge-based startups have become the norm in companies in all sectors of the economy.

This appendix was written by Siobhan Hurley together with Ed Carberry, Ryan Weeden, and Scott Rodrick of the NCEO. At that time, Ms. Hurley was Manager of Equity and Executive Compensation at Venture Management Resources, a division of TriNet VCO. She is now with PricewaterhouseCoopers.

Appendix 2: Summary of Previous Research

***Stock Plan Design and Administration Survey* (National Association of Stock Plan Professionals (NASPP) and PricewaterhouseCoopers LLP, 1998):** The 1998 survey conducted by NASPP and PricewaterhouseCoopers provides information on a variety of different types of stock-based compensation in 395 public companies, including information on the prevalence of plans, plan design features, administration practices, as well as communication programs. The survey breaks down most of the results by high-technology and non high-technology companies. It also provides some detailed information on stock-based compensation to international employees, and this is one of the first surveys to do this. Broad-based stock option plans are not broken out in a distinct, consistent way, however. The results show that about one-third of the sample companies that grant stock options grant them to nonexempt employees, and that broad-based options are more common among high-technology companies. It notes that the median minimum salary for eligibility is around $70,000. Over half of the companies granting to nonexempt level employees do so every 12 months.

The survey confirms the trends of basic plan design observed in other surveys. Of the companies that grant stock options, 98% grant options with a grant price equal to fair market value on the date of grant. Ninety-two percent of the option companies have an option term of 10 years. Nonqualified stock options remain the most popular and are even becoming more popular in high-technology companies. Eighty-seven percent of the survey respondents are granting nonqualified stock options, while 47% are granting ISOs. Ten percent of the companies granting options had repriced at some point. Close to 90% provide for a cashless exericise. The survey also shows that companies are not putting great effort into their communication programs. Although 81% distribute material other than what is required, only 30% provide ongoing educational materials to employees.

For all types of equity compensation plans, the typical annual grant at high-technology companies was between 3–6% of total shares outstanding, as compared to 1–2% for non high-tech companies. In high-tech companies, the total overhang, including current grants and shares reserved for future grants, ranged for 16–23%, as compared to 8–14% for non high-tech companies. Seventeen percent of high-tech companies have an evergreen plan, as compared to 13% for non high-technology companies.

***Stock Option Overhang: Shareholder Boon or Shareholder Burden?* (Watson Wyatt Worldwide, 1998):** Watson Wyatt conducted this survey to take a closer look at the issues of potential dilution created by employee stock options and how this impacts total return to shareholders. The sample was 940 companies, all in the S&P 1,500. The primary source of data was a publication of the Investor Responsibility Research Center (IRRC), "Potential Dilution from Stock Plans at S&P 1,500 Companies-1997."

The survey found that overhang rates vary a great deal by industry. Overhang at large US companies increased from 5% in 1988 to 13% in 1997. The median overhang of the sample was 10.6%. The highest was 47%. High-technology companies (134 of 940) had higher median overhang levels (16%) than the rest of the sample (10%). The results also break the sample into thirds in terms of median overhang. Those companies in the middle third with a median overhang of 10.6% had the highest median total return to shareholders (TRS) of 16.9%. Those with the highest median overhang had a median TRS of 13.5%, and those with the lowest median overhang had a median TRS of 16.2%. Institutional investors have not decreased their ownership in companies with high overhang, although "no" votes on stock option plans have increased from 3.5% in 1996 to 15.8% in 1997.

***ShareData, Inc. 1997 Stock Option Survey* (Sunnyvale, CA: ShareData, Inc., 1997):** With the assistance of the American Electronics Association (AEA) and other organizations, ShareData conducted a survey of over 1,000 public companies that use stock option plans. The survey shows that broad-based stock options are a key component of compensation in small companies and are becoming more popular in medium and large companies. The survey found that 53% of the respondents grant stock options to all employees, 31% grant to key employees and above, 13.7% grant to managers and above, and 1% grant to only senior executives. In information technology fields, 88% grant options to all employees; in manufacturing, 41%; and in financial services, 24%. Sixty-eight percent of companies with fewer than 100 employees grant options to all employees, and 74% of companies with less than $50 million in revenue do so. Fifty-one percent of companies with 500–999 employees offer options to all employees, as compared to 30% in 1994; 43% of companies with 2000–4999 employees offer to all, as compared to 10% in 1994; and 45% of companies with 5,000 or more employees offer to all, as compared to 10% in 1994.

Edward Hansen, *Stock Options Move Beyond Companies' Executive Suites* (New York, NY: William M. Mercer, 1997): Examining proxy statements of the 350 largest U.S. companies, this study found that 30% of these companies had broad-based stock option programs that made 50% or more of employees eligible to receive option grants. However, only 11% of the companies had yet made these grants. The analysts charted the growth of option activity over a five-year period starting in 1993. In this study, 17.4%, 19.4%, 23.4%, 27.1%, and 29.7% of the companies during the years 1993, 1994, 1995, 1996, and 1997, respectively, had plan provisions for broad-based option grants. During the same years, only 5.7%, 6.9%, 8.6%, 10.3%, and 11.1%, respectively, of these companies made grants.

Watson Wyatt Data Services, *1997/98 Survey of Top Management Compensation* **(Bethesda, MD: Watson Wyatt, 1997):** Surveyed 1,406 companies and found that the number of employees eligible for stock options in these companies rose from 12% in 1995 to 15% in 1997. Employees in service businesses were most likely to be eligible to receive options (27%), while utilities and energy companies made only 3% of their employees eligible.

National Association of Stock Plan Professionals (NASPP), *Stock Plan Deign Survey Report* **(Concord, CA: NASPP, 1997):** NASPP conducted this survey to gain a better understanding of how companies are designing and administering stock plans. Its findings are based on 380 surveys received from stock plan professionals within US companies. The survey covered all types of stock plans: stock options, performance share plans, restricted stock, stock purchase plans, 401(k) plans, and ESOPs. It examined broad-based plans, as well as those with more exclusive grants that cover executives, management, and smaller groups of employees.

All the respondents were public companies, and the sample was diverse in terms of geography, industry, and size. NASPP found that 36% of the respondents grant to all employees. In presenting the results, NASPP did not separate out broad-based option grants, so the following results relate to all options granted. The survey found that 92% of respondents grant nonqualified options, 54% grant ISOs, and 16% grant ISOs exclusively. Only 3% of respondents offer options at a discount on the day of grant. The most typical vesting schedule was four years. Less than 2% have performance vesting. Seventy-six percent of the respondents with option plans have a same day cashless exercise mechanism. The report noted that fewer companies are repricing, with only 3% indicating they had repriced in the first six months of 1996, which was down from 10% the previous year.

WestWard Pay Strategies, *Stock Compensation in the High-Tech Sector* **(San Francisco, CA: WestWard Pay Strategies, 1997):** In 1997, WestWard conducted an analysis of compensation practices within three groups of high-tech companies at different stages in their development: companies that were already public (the "Tech 250"), companies that had recently completed an initial public offering (the "IPO 50"), as well as 20 companies that were closely held. The survey provides detailed information on overhang, run rates, the impact of options on earnings per share (EPS), the present value of options, evergreen pools, and repricing.

WestWard found a median overhang of 15% for the Tech 250, 17.3% for the IPO 50, and 10.7% for the closely held companies. The median run rate (annual dilution created by actual option grants) for the three years prior to the survey among the public companies was 2.2%; for the IPO 50, 6%. Only 6.8% of the public companies have evergreen share pools. If the Tech 250 had charged the present value of stock options to their earnings (as FASB had originally proposed in 1995), the median reduction in EPS would have been 6%, although it ranged widely from 1% to 78%. In 157 of the Tech 250 companies, stock options had a present value that was 50% or more of fair market value on the day the options were granted. The median for all of the Tech 250 was 56.7%, and the highest was 86%. Fifteen percent of the Tech 250 had repriced their stock options. Thirty-one percent of these excluded officers from the repricing.

Hewitt Associates, *Non-Executive Stock Option Survey Report* (Hewitt Associates, 1997): This survey examined the design features, communication programs, and the perceived effectiveness of "non-executive stock option plans" within 20 larger, publicly traded companies. The companies were widely distributed across many different industries. Thirteen of the 20 companies grant or have granted options to all employees. Seventeen of the 20 companies make all employees eligible to receive options. The Hewitt survey found that most stock options granted to a broad group of employees are nonqualified, granted at fair market value on the date of grant, come with a 10-year life, and vest over 3 years. Ninety percent of the companies provide a cashless exercise mechanism for employees.

Sixty-six percent outsource plan administration. Fifty-nine percent of the companies with nonexecutive options believe that the plan has helped improve business results. The top three reasons for implementing a nonexecutive stock option plan were to foster a feeling of ownership (87%), communicate business objectives (45%), and foster teamwork (39%). The survey found that overall, the more an employee is paid, the higher the real dollar value of the option awards. Grants based on individual employee performance are typically worth significantly more than one time grants. Hewitt notes that between 1991 and 1997, the percentage of companies using broad-based stock plans increased from 8% to 29%. The survey also found that in companies that offer broad-based stock options, employees receive more cash compensation.

Coopers & Lybrand, *Trendsetter Barometer* (New York City: Coopers & Lybrand, 1996): This survey interviewed 434 CEOs of the fastest-growing US product and service companies. These companies ranged in size from $1 million to $50 million in annual revenues. Twenty-nine percent had option plans that "included" all employees. Companies with "broader" stock option plans grew faster in the 12 months before the survey than companies that granted options only to management. The former grew 37%, the latter 25%. Projected revenue growth of the next 12 months in companies with broader options programs was 40%, versus 24% in firms that granted options to management only.

Jane Irwin and Meg Marchese, *On Employee Stock Ownership* **(Lincolnshire, IL: Hewitt Associates, 1996):** Examined employee stock ownership plans at 55 companies. Twenty-seven percent of companies gave all employees options. An average of 6.5% of all outstanding stock was held by employee stock option plans. Forty-three percent of companies used straight distribution of shares (an average of 185 per employee), 31% used merit-based grants, 17% used grants as a percentage of pay (an average of 20% of pay per employee), and 9% used salary grades in allocating options to employees.

Steve Huddart and Mark Lang, "Employee Stock Option Exercises: An Empirical Analysis" (*Journal of Accounting & Economics*** 21 (1996), pp. 5–23):** Huddart and Lang, professors at Duke University and University of North Carolina at Chapel Hill, respectively, looked at exercise activity among 50,000 employees at eight US companies. They found that 90% of employees receiving stock options sold their stock immediately after they exercised their options. They also found that two-thirds of the exercise activity of lower-level employees occurred within six months of the options being vested and "in-the-money." Senior executives were half as likely to exercise their options within six months. This study shows that many nonmanagement employees may not be capitalizing on the optimum value of their stock options.

Edward E. Lawler, III, Susan Albers Mohrman, and Gerald E. Ledford, Jr., *Creating High Performance Organizations: Practices and Results of Employee Involvement and Total Quality Management in Fortune 1000 Companies* **(San Francisco, CA: Jossey-Bass Publishers, 1995):** Examining Fortune 1000 companies, this study found that 13% of the companies surveyed gave stock options to more than 60% of their employees. When measuring the success of performance-based reward practices, stock option plans were rated the most successful, second only to profit sharing plans. Overall, 54% of companies offered some employee ownership program to their employees.

ShareData, Inc., *ShareData/AEA Update* **(Sunnyvale, CA: ShareData, 1994):** With 600 companies responding, this study surveyed members of the American Electronic Association (AEA) and users of ShareData stock option administration software. Results include: 54% of respondents gave options to all employees and 40% gave options to all management-level employees, 83% of companies with less than 100 employees granted options to all employees, and 79% of companies with less than $50 million in revenue granted options to all employees.

Janice Hand, *Company Experience with Broad-Based Employee Stock Option Programs, 1993* **(Lincolnshire, IL: Hewitt Associates, 1993):** This study describes 19 broad-based stock option plans ("broad-based" being defined as those plans that at least cover employees at the $40,000–$50,000 level) in mostly

Fortune 1000 companies. Information reported about the stock option plans include: background information (year started, additional compensation programs, etc.), program design (option price, vesting, term limits, etc.), and program experience (communication, employee reaction, staffing requirements, etc.).

Matt Ward, *Stock Option Expense Survey* (San Francisco, CA: Watson Wyatt Worldwide, 1993): Watson Wyatt surveyed 139 companies in 22 industries with stock option or stock purchase plans to analyze the impact of possible changes to option accounting rules that were being considered by the Financial Accounting Standards Board (FASB) at the time. In general, the survey found that many high-tech companies would have taken a big hit to earnings if they were required to expense their stock option grants. The median total number of options granted to all employees (including executives) was 1.75% of total shares outstanding. For high-tech companies, this percentage was 4.5%. The median aggregate charge to earnings that companies would recognize under the then-proposed FASB changes for all options was $4.4 million. For high-tech companies, this amount was $6.5 million. The median Black-Scholes value of all stock options granted was 39% of fair market value; within the high-tech sector, this percentage was close to 60%. The median reduction in earnings per share from all stock options that would result from the proposed FASB changes was 10.8%. For the high-tech sector, this was 50%; for the other companies, the median was approximately 6%.

ShareData, Inc., *Equity Compensation Trends in Corporate America* (Sunnyvale, CA: ShareData, 1991): This study surveyed equity compensation professionals (300-plus respondents) to ascertain trends and issues in the field and determine the results of using various forms of equity compensation. It examined different methods that motivate, recruit, and retain employees at all levels. Comparing stock options, stock purchase, and performance-based stock awards, the study found that stock options were the preferred vehicle for equity compensation and that nonqualified plans were becoming more popular than incentive stock options. Results of the study include: yearly vesting was the most popular vesting period, followed by monthly vesting; five-year vesting periods were most popular of option terms, and grants were made according to subjective analysis, grade level, formula, and performance, in that order.

For a more in-depth analysis of previous research, see "Part 6: Previous Research on Broad-Based Stock Option Programs" in Current Practices in Stock Option Plan Design, *rev. ed. (Oakland, CA: NCEO, 1999).*

Notes

1. *ShareData, Inc. 1997 Stock Option Survey* (Sunnyvale, CA: ShareData, Inc., 1997).

2. Coopers & Lybrand, *Trendsetter Barometer* (New York City: Coopers & Lybrand, 1996).

3. Jane Irwin and Meg Marchese, *On Employee Stock Ownership* (Lincolnshire, IL: Hewitt Associates, 1996).

4. Edward E. Lawler, III, Susan Albers Mohrman, and Gerald E. Ledford, Jr., *Creating High Performance Organizations: Practices and Results of Employee Involvement and Total Quality Management in Fortune 1000 Companies* (San Francisco: Jossey-Bass Publishers, 1995).

5. ShareData, Inc., *Equity Compensation Trends in Corporate America* (Sunnyvale, CA: ShareData, 1991).

6. Steve Huddart and Mark Lang, "Employee Stock Option Exercises: An Empirical Analysis," *Journal of Accounting and Economics* 21 (1996): 5–43.

CHAPTER 11

The Phantom Stock Alternative

Brian B. Snarr
Morrison Cohen Singer & Weinstein LLP

A phantom stock plan is a contract under which an employer provides an employee with one or more of the benefits of stock ownership without actually making the employee a stockholder. "Phantom stock" is not really stock. It is a form of deferred compensation whereby the employer promises to make payments in the nature of a bonus to an employee based on the value or dividend performance of the employer corporation's stock, or both. A "stock appreciation right" (SAR) is another name for a similar compensation technique, which in effect consists of phantom stock without phantom dividends. For purposes of this chapter, the term "phantom stock" should be understood to include both phantom stock denominated as such and stock appreciation rights.[1] Phantom stock could also be described as a financial derivative—a contract whose value varies in accordance with the value of an external financial product, index or commodity—in this case based on the performance of the employer's stock.

This chapter primarily addresses the issues that apply to employers doing business as closely held corporations. Concerns pertaining to other employers, such as publicly traded corporations,[2] partnerships, or limited liability companies are not specifically addressed, although many of the same concerns will be applicable.

Reasons for Providing Phantom Stock

Many of the reasons to create a phantom stock plan are similar to those for providing actual employer stock to employees:

- **Performance-Based Incentive** Particularly with senior employees, an employer may wish to link the economic fortunes of the employee to the performance of the employer corporation. A phantom stock plan gives the employee the benefits of an increase in value or dividends if the corporation performs well, the same as if the employee owned actual stock. Furthermore, an employee who has phantom stock can receive the "upside" benefits of stock ownership, but will not have an owner's risk of losing invested capital.

- **Key-Employee Retention**   Many employers have found that they can increase the likelihood of retaining the services of key employees—for example, those who have cultivated important customer relationships or who have otherwise become critical to a company's success—by sharing some of the benefits of ownership. Phantom stock can offer the same direct economic benefits (dividends and capital appreciation) as actual stock. This may come about at the instance of the key employees, who want a "piece of the action" if they are to continue their employment without looking elsewhere, or who simply want their positions of importance in the company to be recognized. Similarly, the company may wish to preempt employment offers from competitors, either known or unknown. In addition, phantom stock permits an employer to grant economic benefits without affecting voting control.

- **Additional Compensation**   Where a corporation regularly pays dividends, the existing owners can provide additional compensation to select employees by issuing them employer stock or providing phantom stock that mirrors the corporation's actual dividend performance. Since dividends are generally declared only if the corporation has profits, such compensation has an inherent tie to corporate economic results. Here, phantom stock is more tax-efficient than actual stock because payments under a phantom stock plan, unlike a payment of dividends, are deductible by the employer for tax purposes. (See "Tax Consequences" below.)

- **Industry Practice**   There are some businesses, particularly in high-technology industries such as software design and biotechnology, in which it has become a regular practice to provide an interest in the company to attract employees or consultants who have a particular expertise required by the company. If this is a routine industry practice, an employer may be required to offer shares to attract targeted employees or consultants. Phantom stock can be used instead of actual stock. If venture capital is supporting the company, there may only be a limited block of shares available for grant or sale to employees, and phantom stock may be the only way to give employees an "equity stake" in the employer corporation. Properly structured, phantom stock can permit non-stockholder employees to cash in if the employer's stock "goes public" in an initial public offering (IPO).

There are some respects in which the incentives and effects of a phantom stock plan are significantly different than providing actual employer stock to employees:

- **Business Succession**   A phantom stock plan, unlike a plan for providing actual stock to employees, would not ordinarily be helpful in establishing a path for business succession after the death or retirement of the founding stockholders. Phantom stock, because it is primarily a device for compensation, does not involve the same ownership issues for the recipient that outright stock ownership does. In particular, capital risk and voting control are not concerns in a phantom stock plan as they are where actual stock is provided to employees.

- *Raising Capital* Unlike sales of actual stock to employees, phantom stock does not put any funds in the corporation's coffers. The effect of a phantom stock plan is to pay funds out of the corporation. A phantom stock plan is therefore not suited to raising capital for the corporation.

- *Management Buyout* A management buyout cannot be accomplished with phantom stock because it represents only a right to be paid by the corporation, not an ownership interest in the corporation. However, an employee could exchange all or a portion of the right to be paid with respect to phantom stock in payment for receiving actual stock from the corporation. Such an exchange would be taxable to the employee as ordinary income at the time. (See "Tax Consequences" below.)

- *Option Exercise* Phantom stock, in the form of a cash payment, can be used by an employee to pay the exercise price of an option. For this reason, employers sometimes award phantom stock in connection with a grant of options to buy employer stock. The payout timing on the phantom stock can be tied to the dates for option exercise so that cash from the phantom stock can be used to pay the option price and any taxes incurred upon exercise of the option.

Advantages of Phantom Stock

Phantom stock may enjoy several advantages over actual shares from the standpoint of the employer corporation. Employers generally have more flexibility in structuring phantom stock plans than they do in providing actual stock to employees. Phantom stock can be designed to relate to only the portion of the corporation's business or assets affected by the participant's responsibilities at the employer, and not the performance of the corporation as a whole. Also, phantom stock can be made subject to an earn-out or vesting schedule based on an employee's period of service or attainment of goals. And since both the award and earn-out of phantom stock is without tax consequence to the employer or employee until actually paid, the tax complexities associated with Internal Revenue Code section 83 and an award of actual shares to employees are avoided. (See chapter 6, "Equity Compensation in Closely Held Companies," for a discussion of this issue.) Further, any dividend equivalents paid by the employer under a phantom stock plan are deductible as compensation, unlike payments of dividends on actual shares.

Under a phantom stock plan, a participant has only a right to the payment of compensation and no rights as an actual shareholder. This absence of statutory shareholder rights can also be a significant advantage from the employer's standpoint. Voting rights are virtually never included as part of a phantom stock plan. A phantom stock plan can thus be adopted without upsetting the control balance of a closely held corporation. Issues such as dissenters' or preemptive rights are also avoided. Further, a stockholders' agreement is not needed to control the distribution or recovery of actual shares— the phantom stock plan provides the mechanism for distributing and then "buying back" the phantom shares without any action on the part of the employee.

Disadvantage of Phantom Stock

The principal disadvantage of awarding phantom stock, as compared with having employees purchase actual stock, is the resulting absence of an owner's risk. As noted above, an employee who purchases stock with his or her own funds incurs the risk of economic loss if the corporation performs poorly. Particularly where an employee is a decision maker whose actions can harm as well as help the employer corporation, phantom stock does not penalize poor decisions affecting the company's stockholders in same way as being an owner of actual stock does. There are still risks associated with poor decisions, such as a loss of employment, but many stockholders and boards of directors feel that an actual equity stake is better at imparting the proper balance between risk aversion and risk taking than a purely compensation-related device such as phantom stock.

Mechanics of a Phantom Stock Plan

A phantom stock plan can take one of the following forms, or it can be a hybrid, combining one or more of them:

- A formal phantom stock plan applicable to all employees who meet the criteria established in the plan document.
- A formal plan limited to employees individually selected by the corporation's stockholders or management.
- A contract with a single employee covering only phantom stock.
- A provision in a broader contract, such as an employment contract or deferred compensation plan, that covers the phantom stock in addition to other matters.

ERISA Issues

One issue an employer must keep in mind in designing a phantom stock plan and deciding which employees to cover is the possibility of ERISA coverage (and, perhaps more importantly, avoiding it). ERISA (the Employee Retirement Income Security Act of 1974) imposes a number of rules and restrictions on plans that fall under its governance. These include minimum vesting periods, minimum coverage requirements, reporting and disclosure rules, a trust requirement, fiduciary obligations, minimum funding requirements, and others. Plans that defer compensation for employees, as phantom stock plans do, are automatically covered by ERISA unless an exemption is available. The most likely exemption is for "top hat" plans that cover a "select group of management or highly compensated employees." A phantom stock plan should always limit participation to such employees unless the corporation is willing to undertake all the administrative, compliance, and reporting burdens that are associated with qualified retirement plans.

Basic Plan Features

While the operative provisions of phantom stock plans can vary, all phantom stock plans have certain things in common. Essentially, they promise to pay money to an employee later, under certain conditions, based on the actual or theoretical performance of the employer's stock. Unless the plan is based on individual agreements, it will provide for selecting which employees will participate and the number of "phantom shares" that will be awarded to each.

The plan must provide a baseline from which any calculations involving the stock price will be calculated, such as an assumed price per share on the date of grant. This can be determined by simply declaring a price, or by reference to a pricing mechanism that will be used for other plan purposes, such as the corporation's book value for financial accounting purposes.

The phantom elements that will parallel actual stock ownership must be specified by the phantom stock plan. The most usual measure of value in a phantom stock plan is the increase in stock value (if any) between the time the phantom stock is awarded and the date that it is cashed in, such as retirement. An employer can also provide for distributing phantom dividends that parallel any actual dividends paid on the stock, or for crediting such dividends for later distribution, even if they are not paid out currently.

A phantom stock plan needs a way to measure the performance of the phantom stock over time. In a closely held corporation, the stock price must be calculated because, by definition, there is no public market. Accordingly, some form of objective measurement is generally used. (If a subjective standard for stock price were used, a phantom stock plan would be more like a purely discretionary bonus, payable only to the extent the person with discretion decides to pay it.) Book value, as calculated for financial accounting purposes, is probably the most common measure of stock value in phantom stock plans. Another possibility is the earning power of the stock, expressed as a multiple of the corporation's net income over the most recent fiscal periods. The value is usually set at least once a year, with phantom stock transactions occurring between valuation dates being based on the most recent established value. Often, the valuation figure is required to be calculated by the corporation's independent certified public accountants, and may be adjusted for non-cash or other items affecting the valuation formula. Professional valuation companies, such as those that value closely held corporations pursuant to the administration of an ESOP, will also have the expertise to arrive at an appropriate phantom stock valuation.

The timing of payout on the phantom stock account must also be decided. Often, plans provide for payment after a fixed period of time, sometimes on a rolling basis. For example, if a grant of phantom shares is made in each of five successive years, payment of the phantom stock account may be made all at once or in five succeeding years as each grant matures. Less frequently, the phantom stock account may be payable only upon an employee's retirement, disability or other departure from the company. An incentive in which the reward is too long deferred may not have its intended effect.

Optional Plan Features

If an employee's responsibilities in a corporation extend only to a particular branch or division of the business, or if the corporation holds investment assets in addition to running an active business, the corporation may want to calculate the value of phantom stock by reference to the relevant portion of the corporation's business or assets, not the corporation as a whole. This tends to increase the complexity of the valuation exercise, but can avoid rewarding or penalizing the holder of phantom stock because of events unrelated to his or her performance.

Some phantom stock plans provide that the phantom stock vests over a period of time. Vesting questions (as distinct from questions of when payments under the plan will be received in the ordinary course) relate to what happens if an employee leaves the employer after "earning" phantom stock but before payment under the plan would be due.

Many phantom stock plans do not have vesting provisions apart from the plan's usual payout rules: If an employee leaves before being paid for the phantom stock, no more payments will be received. There are two situations, however, in which vesting provisions are likely to be seen. The first is when a block of phantom stock is granted all at once, with the idea that it will be earned over a period of time. The second is when a phantom stock plan permits participants to defer receiving payments after the date they would otherwise be paid.

If a plan does contain an earn-out period, either in the form of vesting or pursuant to its usual payout rules, a time period must be selected. Among the concerns in deciding what time period to select are: (1) recognizing that an employee can make a valuable contribution without spending an entire career with one employer; (2) limiting phantom stock benefits where a person competes unfairly with the employer after leaving employment; and (3) setting an appropriate term for accomplishing the employer's goals for which the phantom stock is intended as an incentive. Three to five years is a common earn-out period, although there can be a fairly wide variance among phantom stock plans.

Vesting can take place gradually or all at once. Gradual vesting can be accomplished by making a single grant of phantom shares that vest on a percentage basis over a number of years, or by making a number of grants in different years, each of which vests after a set time period. The technique of making grants in different years has the additional advantage for the employer of permitting it to "fine tune" the overall number of phantom shares and the recipients of those shares based on the corporation's changing circumstances from year to year.

Tax Consequences

Because phantom stock only involves the payment of cash compensation by the employer to the plan participant, the tax issues arising from a phantom stock plan are not terribly complicated. Unless the doctrine of constructive receipt applies (discussed in the next paragraph), an employee has no income upon the receipt or vesting of phantom stock and is taxed only when payments under the plan are made by the corporation. All amounts received under a phantom stock plan will be fully taxable as ordinary income to the employee and deductible by the employer under its usual accounting rules. For the employer, the standard withholding and employment tax rules will apply to cash payments under a phantom stock plan, with one possible exception. Proposed Internal Revenue Service regulations would require FICA withholding on deferred compensation, including most phantom stock, at the time the phantom stock becomes vested, even though payment is deferred. These proposed regulations are not yet effective. However, this issue should be reviewed by employers when phantom stock is granted. Payments to an employee under a phantom stock plan will be W-2 income. Payments to an independent contractor will be 1099 income. Phantom stock payments to an employee, as W-2 income in the year received, may affect any benefits, such as pensions, that are based on the employee's W-2 income.

It is possible, generally through an oversight or lack of awareness of the applicable tax rules, for a participant in a phantom stock plan to be taxable *before* payment under the plan is received. This can happen: (1) if payments under the plan are "constructively received" by the participant before actual payment or (2) if the employer sets aside funds or property in which participants have a right (prior to actual payments under the plan), beyond simply the employer's unsecured promise to pay. "Constructive receipt" refers to the situation that arises when an employee is currently entitled to receive a payment but chooses to receive it later. At the point at which the employer would honor the employee's request to "Pay me now," the employee will be taxable on the amount that could have been received. He or she will be considered to have "constructively" received the payment. As a consequence, if a phantom stock plan permits participants to defer payments beyond any initial earn-out period stated in the plan, the deferral election must be made *before* the time the participant becomes entitled to receive the payment in question. An election to defer made when the payment is already owing will be ineffective for tax purposes because of the constructive receipt rule.

A compensation technique known as a "rabbi trust" can be designed into a phantom stock plan without running afoul of the constructive receipt rule to help guarantee the payment of deferred payments to an employee. A rabbi trust provides a greater measure of security than a simple promise to pay, because assets are put aside by the employer into an irrevocable trust that can be broken only if the employer becomes insolvent. Because a rabbi trust is irrevocable and because the value of phantom stock, like the value of actual stock, can decline as well as increase, an employer wishing to use this technique would need to provide that at the end of the trust, any funds exceeding the amount owed to the employee at the time would be returned to the employer.

Conclusion

There are a number of reasons an employer might adopt a phantom stock plan, including performance-based incentives, retaining key employees, and providing additional compensation to select employees. Compared to awarding actual shares to employees, a phantom stock has several advantages: phantom stock plans are more flexible and can be more carefully tailored to an employer's objectives, payments are all tax deductible, and the complexities of Internal Revenue Code section 83 are avoided. Further, certain issues that add complexity to awards of actual stock are absent, notably shareholder rights concerns, stockholders' agreements, and voting issues. A perceived drawback of phantom stock compared to actual stock is the lack of an owner's risk in participants' decision-making. Drafting a phantom stock plan requires addressing which employees the plan will cover, the number of phantom shares that will be awarded, a means of establishing phantom stock performance, and the circumstances and timing in which payments will and will not be made under the plan. Because the payments under a phantom stock plan are made solely in cash, the tax consequences of the plan are essentially identical to regular bonus payments.

Notes

1. Stock appreciation rights are sometimes paid in the form of additional employer stock rather than in cash, particularly where the employer has a class of publicly traded shares (see note 2) outstanding.

2. A "publicly traded" corporation for this purpose means an employer corporation with a class of stock required to be registered under the Securities Exchange Act of 1934—i.e., a class of stock: (1) listed on a national securities exchange or (2) held by more than 500 stockholders where the corporation has more than $1,000,000 of assets.

A Primer on Stock Options for Employees

Ed Carberry
Ryan Weeden
The National Center for Employee Ownership

The Basics

What is a stock option?

A stock option gives you the right to purchase a certain number of shares of your company's stock at a fixed price for a fixed period of time. It does not require that you buy stock, but gives you the opportunity to do so. When you purchase the stock, this is called "exercising" the option.

Why would I want stock options?

The primary benefit of stock options is that they give you the opportunity to purchase stock at a fixed price. If the stock price goes up, you can exercise your options and purchase the stock at the fixed price and then sell it at the higher price. The difference between these two prices is your gain. For example, say you are granted 100 options at $10 per share and the stock price increases to $20 per share. If you exercise your options and sell the shares, the gain is $10 per share. With 100 options, your gain would be $1,000.

Why do companies set up stock option plans?

There are many reasons. Some companies believe that it is simply a good idea to give employees an ownership stake in their companies. Other companies use stock options as a way to reward employee performance. Also, stock options are a good way for companies to attract and retain quality employees, especially in start-up situations.

How long do I have to exercise my options?

Usually the options expire after 10 years, but this period can be shorter. Also, you gradually receive the right to exercise your options, through a process known as vesting. For example, your company may have a vesting schedule that allows you to exercise 25% of your options each year. So if you were given 100 options on January 1 of Year 1, on January 1 of Year 2, you would be able to exercise 25 options; on January 1 of Year 3, 25 more; and so on.

How much will I pay for the stock if I exercise my options?

Most companies grant options to employees at the fair market value on the day of the grant. (The price can, however, be higher or lower, depending on the type of grant and your company's goals for the plan.) This price is called the "grant" price or the "strike" price. This price is set for the life of the option. If your company is public, the fair market value will be determined by your company's stock price on the stock market. If your company is private, the shares will be valued according to a method established by financial analysts.

How many options do companies give out to employees?

This depends on many things, including your company's particular situation, its particular goals for the plan, and the number of shares it is willing to authorize for the plan. Companies have a great deal of flexibility in deciding how many options to give to employees. Companies can base rewards on any criteria. Some companies may give out the same number of options to everyone, such as Bank of America, which grants 50 options to all employees every 6 months; others may base rewards on salary or grade level; others may base rewards on performance.

The Different Types of Stock Options

What are nonqualified stock options?

Nonqualified stock options are the simplest and most common type of stock options. There are no rules or regulations that govern how companies grant these. The duration of the option, the exercise period, as well as who can participate, are all very flexible. Additionally, the grant price can be set at, below, or above the fair market value. In other words, the company is free to grant these options to as many or as few employees as desired, on whatever basis desired, and at any price. Usually, companies grant these options at the fair market value on the day they are granted. Companies are often reluctant to grant options below 85% of the fair market value because of securities law issues.

With a nonqualified option, you will pay personal income tax on the difference between the price at which you are granted the options and the actual price of the stock on the day you exercise the option. If you hold onto the stock any longer, you will pay capital gains taxes on any additional gain, i.e., the difference between the actual price on the day of exercise and the price at which you eventually sell the stock. Quite often, however, employees exercise their options and sell the stock on the same day, and therefore, pay only personal income tax on the difference between the grant price and the sale price. Furthermore, your company will be able to deduct from its taxable income the spread between the grant price and the price on the day of exercise.

What are incentive stock options (ISOs)?

These are different from nonqualified options because restrictions apply regarding who can receive them, what the grant price can be, and the amount of time the employee must hold the stock after exercising the options. One of the requirements of an ISO is that the price at which the options are granted must be at least 100% of the fair market value on the date they are granted. This figure increases to 110% of the fair market value for owners of 10% or more of the company's stock. Also, the exercise period of an ISO may not exceed 10 years, and there is a $100,000 maximum on the amount of options that can be exercised in the first year.

Finally, to qualify as an incentive stock option, the employee must hold on to the stock for at least one year after the exercise date and two years after the grant date.

If all of these rules are not met, an incentive stock option automatically becomes a nonqualified stock option.

If these requirements are met, you will not have to pay personal income tax when you exercise the options. You will pay only capital gains taxes on the difference between the price at which you buy the stock and the price at which you sell the stock. If you sell the stock on the same date you exercise, the incentive stock option automatically becomes a nonqualified option and you pay income tax on the difference between the grant and selling prices. Also, the company does not receive a tax deduction for the spread with an incentive stock option.

Even when you and the company meet all of the appropriate requirements of an ISO, you still may have to pay additional taxes relating to the alternative minimum income tax (AMT). The AMT is a tax that the IRS uses to capture some of the taxes it would have received if you had not received tax-favored option grants. In general, however, AMT applies to highly compensated employees.

Which is better, an incentive or a nonqualified option?

The primary difference from the perspective of the employee is related to how much tax he or she pays. One distinct advantage of an ISO is that employees do not have to pay taxes on the gain until the stock is sold. This means that employees do not pay taxes when they exercise the option.

If you have nonqualified stock options, you will not have to be concerned with meeting any required holding periods. Once you vest, you can exercise anytime and then either sell or hold onto the stock. Since stock prices generally go up, you may want to hold onto the stock for as long as possible, but this should be balanced with your expectations of the future performance of the company as well as your personal goals.

If you receive incentive stock options, however, the situation gets more complicated. The primary advantage of an ISO is that it gives you the opportunity to pay capital gains tax, instead of regular income tax, on your gain. The capital gains tax is currently 20% if your regular tax rate is 28% or higher and 10% if your regular tax rate is 15%. It is up to you to decide whether you want to meet the ISO requirements and get the favorable tax treatment or if you want to treat it like a nonqualified option. The trade-off is that you have to hold onto the stock after you exercise for at least one year. This involves more risk, since the price could go down.

In some cases, however, the difference between your payroll taxes and capital gains taxes may not be that much. If this is the case, it may not be worth the risk of holding onto the shares for the required year to save only a minimal amount in taxes.

For example, say that your personal income tax rate is 28%, you have ISOs with a grant price of $20,000, and the stock is selling for $30,000. If you exercise the options and sell the stock immediately (the same tax consequence if you had a nonqualified stock option) the gain will be $10,000, so you will have $2,800 in taxes ($10,000 × 28% personal income tax rate). If you hold onto the stock for a year (or more) and sell, you will pay $2,000 in taxes ($10,000 × 20% capital gains tax rate). If your personal income tax rate is 39.6%, however, and you have the same $10,000 gain, you will pay $3,960 in taxes ($10,000 × 39.6% personal income tax rate). Depending on your personal tax situation, the differences can be significant between ISOs and nonqualified options. In the first scenario, an employee would net $800 more by keeping the stock for the one-year holding period. In the second scenario, the employee would net $1,960 more if the holding period were met. Note, however, the savings you receive on taxes must be balanced with your expectation of the stock's future growth.

What is a 423 stock purchase plan?

A section 423 stock purchase plan functions similarly to a stock option plan. In a 423 plan, employees are given the opportunity to purchase stock, usually at a discount, at various times during the year, generally paid for through payroll deductions. Basically, employees build up cash for a certain period of time through payroll deductions. On specified purchase dates (most commonly every six months), employees will take the money they saved and purchase stock at the discounted price.

A 423 plan requires that all employees who have been employed for at least two years and work for a minimum of 20 hours per week receive the right to purchase stock through the plan. Highly compensated employees can be excluded, and any employee who owns or will own 5% or more of the company's voting shares may not participate in these plans.

How much will I pay for my 423 stock?

The price an employee pays for stock through a 423 plan depends on several factors: the discount provided to employees, the length of the offering period, and the performance of the stock. With a 423 plan, stock can be purchased at the lesser of a 15% discount from the stock's price (1) at the beginning of the offering period (when you enroll and begin saving) or (2) the end of the offering period (when you purchase the stock).

If the offering period is short, the difference between the stock price at the start of the offering period and the end of the offering period will not be large. If the offering period is long, then the potential for stock price appreciation from the time you enroll and the time you purchase could be substantial.

The company's stock price volatility also will influence what the ultimate financial gain will be from the purchase of the stock. Stable stock prices will tend to not increase substantially or decrease substantially over time, whereas volatile stock prices will fluctuate sometimes 10% to 20% over the course of a few days or weeks. Volatile stock prices yield the highest returns and highest losses and often are associated with companies with higher risks rather than those with stable stock prices.

Looking at two scenarios of a company that has a 15% discount but different offering periods and volatility illustrates these issues. In a company with a short offering period and low stock price volatility, the stock price might be $10 per share at the beginning of an offering period and $11 per share at the end of that offering period. An employee who was able to purchase shares at a 15% discount from the lower of the offering price or the purchase price would be able to buy stock at $8.50 per share when the stock was worth $11 per share, a $2.50 per share gain. In a company with a long offering period and high stock price volatility, the stock price might be $10 per share at the beginning of the offering period and $23 per share at the end of the offering period. An employee who was able to purchase shares at a 15% discount from the lower of the offering price or the purchase price would be able to buy stock at $8.50 per share when the stock was worth $23 per share, a $14.50 per share gain.

What kind of taxes do I pay in a 423 plan?

If the employee holds onto the stock for at least two years after the start date of each offering period and one year after the purchase date, he or she pays capital gains tax (currently 20%, unless the employee is in the 15% tax bracket, in which case the capital gains rate is 10%) on the difference between the fair market value at the date of purchase and the sale price, and personal income tax on the difference between the purchase price and the fair market value on the date of purchase.

If the employee sells the stock earlier than two years after the beginning of the offering period or one year after the purchase date, he or she pays ordinary income tax on the difference between the purchase price and the fair market value when the stock is purchased, plus capital gains tax on any subsequent gains.

Exercising Your Options and Selling the Shares

When is the best time to exercise my stock options?

This depends on many things, but perhaps most importantly on the performance of the stock, since an option provides you with the opportunity to buy the stock at a fixed price. If the market value of the stock rises, you will be able to exercise your options and purchase the stock at a lower price. You can then either sell the stock for the higher price or hold onto it and hope for greater returns. If you plan to sell the stock immediately after you exercise the options, then you should establish a target price for the stock and exercise and sell when the stock reaches this target price. If you plan to hold onto the stock, either to meet your ISO requirements or to realize larger gains, you should carefully follow the stock and try to exercise and purchase your shares at a time when the stock is likely to subsequently increase in value.

With an option, you have the luxury to not exercise if the price falls. Once you exercise the option, however, you now own the stock and incur greater risk because if the stock falls, you may lose money. In general, academics and other professionals recommend that employees hold onto their options as long as possible because over time, stock values tend to increase even though their daily and yearly value may fluctuate. The longer the employee holds onto the option, the better the potential for a higher return.

Do I have to pay taxes when I exercise the options or sell the stock?

Yes, and this will also be a factor in your decision regarding when to exercise your options and when to sell the stock. There are two different taxes that effect stock options: capital gains and income tax. There are also two different types of stock option plans, nonqualified and incentive stock options, and depending on which type of plan your company has, this will determine how much tax you pay and when. (See "The Different Types of Stock Options" above.)

In general, you will pay tax on the spread between the price at which you buy the stock and the fair market value of the stock on the day you exercise the options. If you hold onto the stock after you exercise, you will also pay tax on the difference between the price on the date of exercise and the price at which you eventually sell the stock. If your options are highly valued or you make a high salary, additional taxes relating to the alternative minimum income tax may be due.

Do I have to exercise the options if the stock price does not go up?

No, and it would be unwise to do so. If the stock price does not go above the grant price, you can just let the options expire. Although you make no money in these situations, you also do not lose any.

How do I actually buy the stock when I exercise the option?

The most common way for you to purchase the shares is with cash via a check written out to your company. Another common way is through what is known as a "cashless" exercise. In this type of transaction, a broker will purchase the number of shares that you desire and sell them immediately. The proceeds will then be used to pay back the broker, pay broker's fees, and cover any appropriate taxes. You would receive the difference as either cash or stock. This mechanism allows employees to purchase stock who do not normally have the money up front to do so.

For example, say that you wanted to exercise 100 options with a grant price of $10, and the stock is selling for $20. The broker would pay $1,000 to purchase those 100 shares and could either sell them for $2,000 and give you the difference ($1,000) or sell 50 of them for $1,000 and give you the other 50 shares (also worth $1,000). Normally, if you wanted to receive shares instead of cash, you would also sell enough options to cover broker's fees and the appropriate taxes.

How do I sell the stock?

If your company is publicly traded or is planning on it in the near future, you can sell it on the stock market through a broker. Your company will either set up formal procedures for you to do this or will give you the names of the brokers who can do it for you. You could also sell it back to your company.

What if my company is not public?

If your company is not public and is not planning on going public, it should develop some way for you to sell your exercised options. Although the company is not required to do this legally, if they did not want employees to actually reap the rewards of the plan by selling the stock, it would not have gone through the trouble to set it up in the first place.

Usually, privately held companies use a buyback provision clause that is written into the plan. Although they are not obligated to do this, most companies will try to find ways for employee to sell back their stock to the company or to existing shareholders. If there is no such provision, employees can sell the shares to other willing buyers outside the company.

Your Rights As an Employee

What are my legal rights under a stock option plan?

You do not receive any specific rights as a plan participant, except as specified in the plan document. The plan document is a legal contract that basically gives you the opportunity to purchase stock at a fixed price and for a fixed period of time. The contract will also state the various parameters according to which you can exercise the options and sell the stock.

If you exercise the option and you hold onto the stock, however, you do receive the same rights as other shareholders, unless the plan states otherwise.

By having options, do I get voting rights to the stock?

When you exercise the option and actually own the stock, you will receive voting rights unless the plan document states that the stock purchased through the stock option plan can not have voting rights. It is rare, however, that you would hold onto this stock for a long enough time to actually exercise these voting rights and even more rare that enough employees would own enough stock through options to constitute any kind of voting block.

Who decides what kind of options I get?

In general, top management decides who receives options and how many options will be granted. Companies will establish plans to meet particular corporate objectives. In some companies, division heads choose which employees will receive options based on performance. ISO plans must specify the number of grants that will be available for distribution, and the plans must be approved by the board of directors.

What happens with my stock options if I leave or get fired?

Usually, you will have a certain period of time after you leave to exercise your options that have been vested. The specific terms depend on the company. Normally, if you are fired you will have to exercise these options immediately upon termination. If you are leaving the company because of retirement, disability, or on amicable terms, you will probably have longer to exercise your options, although usually not more than one year. Some companies even allow retiring employees to continue to vest after retirement. In the event of death, your estate will often have a certain period during which to exercise the options.

If you have received incentive stock options, to qualify for capital gains tax treatment you must maintain employment at the company during the qualification period (two years after grant and one year after exercise) or else their options will be treated as "disqualified dispositions" and gains on options will be taxed at ordinary income tax rates. Employment requirements state that an individual must be an employee at all times during the period beginning with the date of grant and ending three months before the option is exercised. Exceptions to this are if the employee requirement was suspended because of death or if the employee had left employment within the prior twelve months because of disability.

What kinds of information will I receive about the plan?

Usually you will receive a grant agreement that states the grant date of the options, type of stock option, the number of shares, the grant price, the vesting schedule, as well as the expiration date of the options. This document may also describe the procedures for exercising your options.

Additionally, you may receive a copy of the actual plan document or a plan prospectus, which contains details of the company and the plan. You may also receive more detailed information to help you understand the financial impact of your grant. There is no law that specifies that your company must give you information on when and how you should exercise your options, although many employers will provide this advice. Also, you will probably receive information regarding stockbrokers that you may use as well as information from these brokers.

Who should I talk to within my company about the plan?

Normally, companies operate these plans through the human resource or finance departments and, depending on the complexity of the plan, will have one or more persons in charge of the plan and fielding inquiries. A company may also have a help line or intranet system set up to answer questions.

Can I receive stock options if I am in a union?

Yes, and in fact in recent years, unions have been pushing for stock options as part of collective bargaining agreements.

ABOUT THE EDITOR AND CONTRIBUTORS

Editor and Book Designer   Scott Rodrick is the editor-in-chief of the *Journal of Employee Ownership Law and Finance*, published by the National Center for Employee Ownership (NCEO). He also created and maintains the NCEO's Web site at *http://www.nceo.org/*. Mr. Rodrick is the author of *An Introduction to ESOPs* (NCEO, rev. 3rd ed. 1999); a coauthor of *An Overview of How Companies Are Granting Stock Options* (NCEO, 1999) and *Current Practices in Stock Option Plan Design* (NCEO, 1998); the editor of *Selling to an ESOP* (NCEO, 5th ed. 1999), *Leveraged ESOPs and Employee Buyouts* (NCEO, 2nd ed. 1999), *Model Equity Compensation Plans* (NCEO, 1997), and other books; and the coeditor of *Employee Stock Ownership Plans* (Harcourt Brace, 1996, 1999). He served at the U.S. Department of Labor as an attorney-advisor before coming to the NCEO.

Introduction; Chapter 9, "Creating an Ownership Culture: Tapping into the Real Potential of Broad Stock Options"; Appendix   Ed Carberry is the director of communications at the NCEO. He is the author of *Corporate Governance in Employee Ownership Companies* (NCEO, 1996); a coauthor of *An Overview of How Companies Are Granting Stock Options* (NCEO, 1999), *Current Practices in Stock Option Plan Design* (NCEO, 1998), and *Theory O: Creating an Ownership Style of Management*, 3rd ed. (NCEO, 1996); and the author of numerous articles on employee ownership for trade and business publications.

Chapter 1, "Employee Stock Options and Related Equity Incentives"   David R. Johanson is a partner with the law firm of Johanson Berenson LLP, which has offices in California; Washington, D.C.; and Virginia. Mr. Johanson's office is located in Napa, California. Mr. Johanson is a member of the NCEO's board of directors and of the editorial board of the NCEO's *Journal of Employee Ownership Law and Finance*. His practice focuses on employee ownership, ESOPs, executive compensation (i.e., all types of non-ESOP equity incentive plans, including stock option plans), business succession planning, and mergers and acquisitions (and related tax planning).

Chapter 2, "Administering an Employee Stock Option Plan"   Mark A. Borges formerly was general counsel for E*TRADE Business Solutions Group, a subsidiary of E*TRADE Group, Inc., a provider of online investing services. He now is with the U.S. Securities and Exchange Commission.

Chapter 3, "Valuing Stock Options"   Susan E. Thompson is a consultant with Hewitt Associates LLC, a compensation and employee benefits consulting firm, in the firm's compensation practice. She designs and structures executive compensation and other plans, including long-term incentive programs. When she wrote this chapter she was a senior associate with Valuemetrics, Inc.

Chapter 4, "Accounting for Stock-Based Compensation"   Benjamin S. Neuhausen is a partner with the Professional Standards Group of Arthur Andersen LLP. He is a member of the Financial Accounting Standards Board (FASB) Task Force on Stock-Based Compensation. Alan A. Nadel is the managing director of Arthur Andersen's Human Capital Services Consulting Group in New York. A CPA, Mr. Nadel frequently writes and speaks on compensation, benefits, and retirement plans. Gregory M. Kopp is a senior consultant with Arthur Andersen's Human Capital Services Consulting Group in New York.

Chapter 5, "Designing a Broad-Based Stock Option Plan"   Corey Rosen is the NCEO's executive director and cofounder. He received his Ph.D. from Cornell University in political science in 1973, taught government at Ripon College until 1976, and then served as a Senate staff member until 1981, when he cofounded the NCEO. As a Senate staffer, he helped draft some of the current ESOP legislation. Mr. Rosen has coauthored four books and written over 100 articles on various aspects of employee ownership for a variety of professional, academic, and trade publications. He has lectured on the subject across the U.S. and abroad.

Chapter 6, "Establishing and Maintaining Employee Stock Benefit Programs"   Emily W. Van Hoorickx, a vice president—investments and principal with the PaineWebber San Jose Corporate Services Consulting Group, is a Certified Financial Planner, a Certified Equity Professional, and an investment advisor representative. Ms. Van Hoorickx is a founding member of the National Association of Stock Plan Professionals (NASPP) and is the current president of NASPP's Silicon Valley chapter. She also sits on the advisory boards of NASPP and the Certified Equity Professional Institute at Santa Clara University.

Chapter 7, "Equity Compensation in Closely Held Companies"; Chapter 10, "The Phantom Stock Alternative"   Brian B. Snarr is a partner in the New York office of Morrison Cohen Singer & Weinstein LLP. He has practiced in the area of federal taxation since 1982 and has concentrated in the areas of employee benefits (with an emphasis on ESOPs) and corporate, partnership, and international taxation.

Chapter 8, "Employee Ownership and Initial Public Offerings"   Fred E. Whittlesey is the founding principal of Compensation and Performance Management, Inc. (CPM), a management consulting firm based in Newport Beach, California. He has worked with companies on public offerings, mergers, acquisitions, privatizations, and other corporate transactions. Jill Zidaritz, CEP, is the director of employee shareholder services for Sybase, Inc., in Emeryville, California. Her experience with stock plans includes IPOs, stock splits, option repricings, nine mergers and acquisitions, and implementing a cashless exercise program and employee stock purchase plan.

Chapter 10, "The 1998 NCEO Broad-Based Stock Option Survey"; Appendix Ryan Weeden is a project director at the NCEO. Before coming to the NCEO, he completed his master's degree in public policy at the University of Wisconsin at Madison, writing his thesis on employee ownership and economic development. Mr. Weeden is the author of *The Employee Owner's Guide to Cyberspace* (NCEO, 1997) and the coauthor of *An Overview of How Companies Are Granting Stock Options* (NCEO, 1999), *Current Practices in Stock Option Plan Design* (NCEO, 1998), and *Open-Book Management and Corporate Performance* (NCEO, 1998).

The National Center for Employee Ownership (NCEO) is widely considered to be the leading authority in employee ownership in the U.S. and the world. Established in 1981 as a nonprofit information and membership organization, it now has over 2,800 members, including companies, professionals, unions, government officials, academics, and interested individuals. It is funded entirely through the work it does. The staff includes people with backgrounds in academia, law, and business.

The NCEO's mission is to provide the most objective, reliable information possible about employee ownership at the most affordable price possible. As part of the NCEO's commitment to providing objective information, it does not lobby or provide ongoing consulting services. The NCEO publishes a variety of materials—such as this book—explaining how employee ownership plans work, describing how companies get employee owners more involved in making decisions about their work, and reviewing the research on employee ownership. In addition, the NCEO holds approximately 50 workshops and conferences on employee ownership annually. These include "introduction to stock options" and "introduction to ESOPs" workshops, meetings on employee participation, international programs, and a large annual conference. The NCEO's work also includes extensive contacts with the media, both through articles written for trade and professional publications and through interviews with reporters. Finally, the NCEO has written or edited five books for outside publishers during the 1980s and 1990s: *The Equity Solution* (Lexington Books, 1986); *Taking Stock: Employee Ownership at Work* (Ballinger, 1986); *Employee Ownership in Public Companies* (Quantum, 1990); *Understanding Employee Ownership* (Cornell I&LR Press, 1991); and *Employee Stock Ownership Plans* (Harcourt Brace, 1996, 1999).

Membership Benefits

NCEO members receive the following benefits:

- The bimonthly newsletter, *Employee Ownership Report*, which covers ESOPs, stock options, and employee participation.

- The *Employee Ownership Resource Guide*, which lists over 150 members who are employee ownership consultants and describes other organizations and resources in the field.

- Substantial discounts on publications and events produced by the NCEO (such as this book).

- The right to telephone or e-mail the NCEO for answers to general or specific questions regarding employee ownership.

NCEO Annual Membership Fees

$70 *Associate* (non-employee ownership companies, organizations, and consultants not listed in the *Resource Guide*)

$240 *Consultants* (listed in the *Resource Guide*)

Employee Ownership Companies:
$70 1–50 employees
$125 51–100 employees
$240 101–500 employees
$350 Over 500 employees

Add $10 to any of the above amounts if your mailing address is outside North America.

Flat Rate for Introductory Membership Regardless of the above subcategories (such as the $350 rate for large employee-owned companies), an introductory one-year NCEO membership is simply $70 ($80 if outside North America), or $30 for full-time students or faculty members ($40 if outside North America). To join, see the order form on the last page of this book.

NCEO Publications

The NCEO offers a variety of publications on all aspects of employee ownership and participation, from employee stock ownership plans (ESOPs) to stock options to employee participation. Following are descriptions of some of our main publications in these areas.

We publish new books and revise old ones on a yearly basis. To obtain the most current information on what we have available, visit our extensive Web site at *www.nceo.org* or call us at 510-272-9461.

ESOPs

- *The ESOP Reader* is an overview of the issues involved in establishing and operating an ESOP. It covers the basics of ESOP rules, feasibility, valuation, and other matters, and then discusses managing an ESOP company, including brief case studies. The book is intended for publicly traded companies and anyone with a general interest in ESOPs and employee participation.

   Cost: $25 for NCEO members, $35 for nonmembers

- *Selling to an ESOP* is a guide for owners, managers, and advisors of closely held businesses. It explains how ESOPs work and then offers a comprehensive look at legal structures, feasibility, valuation, financing (including self-financing), and other matters, especially the tax-deferred section

1042 "rollover" that allows owners to indefinitely defer capital gains taxation on the proceeds of the sale to the ESOP.

Cost: $25 for NCEO members, $35 for nonmembers

- *Leveraged ESOPs and Employee Buyouts* discusses how ESOPs borrow money to buy out entire companies, purchase shares from a retiring owner, or finance new capital. Beginning with a primer on leveraged ESOPs and their uses, it then discusses contribution limits, valuation, multi-investor buyouts, legal due diligence, transaction structures, accounting, feasibility studies, financing sources, and more. It is applicable to both public and closely held companies.

Cost: $25 for NCEO members, $35 for nonmembers

- The *Employee Ownership Q&A Disk* gives Microsoft Windows users (any version from Windows 3.1 onward) point-and-click access to 500 questions and answers on all aspects of ESOPs in a fully searchable hypertext format. The keyword search allows users to search the entire file in seconds and see all the search "hits" in context. Distributed on a 1.44 MB 3.5-inch diskette with a printed manual.

Cost: $75 for NCEO members, $100 for nonmembers

Stock Options and Related Plans

- This book, *The Stock Options Book,* is a comprehensive resource covering the legal, tax, and design issues involved in implementing a broad-based stock option plan. It is our main book on the subject.

Cost: $25 for NCEO members, $35 for nonmembers

- *Model Equity Compensation Plans* provides examples of the plans discussed in the *Stock Options Book* (incentive stock option, nonqualified stock option, stock purchase, and phantom stock plans), together with brief explanations of the main documents. A disk is included with copies of the plan documents in formats any word processing program can open.

Cost: $50 for NCEO members, $75 for nonmembers

- *Stock Options: Beyond the Basics* begins with a detailed overview of the field, followed by chapters on specialized topics such as repricing and evergreen options, and ends with a lengthy glossary.

Cost: $25 for NCEO members, $35 for nonmembers

- *Current Practices in Stock Option Plan Design* is the full report on our 1998 survey of companies with broad-based stock option plans. It includes a detailed examination of plan design, use, and experience broken down by industry, size, and other categories. It has individual chapters on repricing; objectives, communications, and participation; and prior research in the field. An appendix discusses the results of the 1999 Trinet/NCEO survey.

Cost: $50 for NCEO members, $75 for nonmembers

- *Incentive Compensation and Employee Ownership* takes a broad look at how companies can use incentives, ranging from stock plans to cash bonuses to gainsharing, to motivate and reward employees. Includes both technical discussions and case studies.

Cost: $25 for NCEO members, $35 for nonmembers

- *Equity-Based Compensation for Multinational Corporations* describes how companies can use stock options and other equity-based programs across the world to reward a global work force.

Cost: $25 for NCEO members, $35 for nonmembers

Employee Communication and Participation

- *Theory O: Creating an Ownership Style of Management* discusses how a company with an employee ownership plan can develop a better, more productive workplace through employee participation programs. Includes both a practical discussion of critical issues and 20 detailed case studies. Most of the companies that are discussed are ESOP companies, but a few use stock options.

Cost: $20 for NCEO members, $30 for nonmembers

- The *ESOP Communications Sourcebook* is a looseleaf publication for ESOP companies. It includes ideas, reproducible forms, and examples on how to share financial information, explain ESOP features, and produce events to create an "ownership culture." It also addresses marketing employee ownership to customers.

Cost: $35 for NCEO members, $50 for nonmembers

- *Communicating Stock Options* offers practical ideas and information about how to explain stock options to a broad group of employees. It includes the views of experienced practitioners as well as detailed examples of how companies communicate tax consequences, financial information, and other matters to employees.

Cost: $35 for NCEO members, $50 for nonmembers

Other

- *Section 401(k) Plans and Employee Ownership* focuses on how company stock is used in 401(k) plans, both in stand-alone 401(k) plans and combination 401(k)–ESOP plans ("KSOPs"). It addresses a whole range of issues that arise, including plan design, KSOPs, special techniques such as the "switchback," employee participation, and so on.

    Cost: $25 for NCEO members, $35 for nonmembers

- *The Journal of Employee Ownership Law and Finance* is the only professional journal solely devoted to employee ownership. Articles are written by leading experts and cover ESOPs, stock options, and related subjects in depth. The *Journal* appears four times a year and usually is from 140 to 200 pages long.

    Cost for one-year subscription:
    $75 for NCEO members, $100 for nonmembers

To join the NCEO as a member or to order the above publications, mail or fax the order form on the following page, use the secure ordering system on our Web site at *www.nceo.org,* or telephone us at (510) 272-9461 with your credit card in hand. If you are not already a member but join at the same time you order publications, you will receive the members-only publication discounts.

Order Form from *The Stock Options Book,* Revised Third Edition

To order, fill out this form and mail it with your credit card information or check to the NCEO at 1736 Franklin Street, 8th Floor, Oakland, CA 94612; fax it with your credit card information to the NCEO at 510-272-9510; telephone us at 510-272-9461 with your credit card in hand; or order securely online at our Web site, *www.nceo.org.* If you are not already a member, you can join now to receive member discounts on the publications you order.

Name

Organization

Address

City, State, Zip (Country)

Telephone   Fax   E-mail

Method of Payment: ❑ Check (payable to "NCEO")   ❑ Visa   ❑ M/C   ❑ AMEX

Credit Card Number

Signature   Exp. Date

Title	Qty.	Price	Total

Subtotal	$
Sales Tax	$
Shipping	$
Membership	$
TOTAL DUE	$

Tax: California residents add 8.25% sales tax (on publications only, not membership)

Shipping: First publication $4, each additional $1 ($7 each outside North America)

Introductory NCEO Membership: $70 for one year ($80 outside North America)